*Twayne's United States Authors Series*

Sylvia E. Bowman, *Editor*

INDIANA UNIVERSITY

*Theodore Dreiser*

 52

# THEODORE DREISER

by PHILIP L. GERBER

California State Polytechnic College

TWAYNE PUBLISHERS

A DIVISION OF G. K. HALL & CO., BOSTON

To Gene

# Contents

# About the Author

Philip L. Gerber has taught American literature at universities in Texas, Utah, California, and South Dakota. He is currently Professor of English on the Brockport campus of the State University of New York, and also holds the rank of Faculty Exchange Professor within the SUNY system. He has published articles on a variety of modern figures including Theodore Dreiser, William Carlos Williams, Amy Lowell, Robert Frost, and Harriet Monroe; two of his books, *Theodore Dreiser* and *Robert Frost*, have appeared in Twayne's United States Authors Series.

# Preface

"WHAT MANNER OF MAN is Theodore Dreiser?" asked
Merton Lyon in 1916. His candid answer: "Simply a tall,
ungainly, unlovely man with something of the cast of Oliver
Goldsmith's features. Something lumpish, something rankly
vegetable is evoked. What? A huge rutabaga; a colossal, pith-
stricken radish. In this body dwells this interesting, this amazingly fascinating mind." Lyon could have been describing
either the man or his novels, for even as a personality Dreiser
evoked the same double response elicited by his writings: a
combination of attraction and revulsion, praise and condemna-
tion.

It is not uncommon for leaders of the vanguard to meet
resistance, but few American writers have found themselves so
constantly embroiled in the storm center of controversy. From
the day his first novel was published and suppressed in 1900,
Dreiser was rarely free from attack. Guardians of the social
welfare labeled his work obscene; literary critics judged his
style banal, crude, and amateurish; thinkers found his ideas
naïve, if not downright subversive. Yet the man plodded on,
writing exactly as Dreiser must; always saddened and often
roused to ire by his opposition, he never yielded to pressure
groups. And it is largely to this dogged battle that we owe
our present victory over prudishness in our national letters, a
battle sure to be fought on the defensive and likely as not
without allies.

Except for *An American Tragedy*, Dreiser's novels never sold
very well. Yet they have survived for over sixty years, their
own triumph of staying power and enduring significance over
the inexorable weeding-process of time—and time is, in the end,
the only and final arbiter of literature. Today we find his volumes everywhere that books are sold. They rest on shelves for
the general reader and are labeled "classics." Dreiser, I believe,
would not be surprised by this, though his personal life was
nearly always a tempest of frustrations, often provoked by
critics' refusal to understand or accept what he was doing.
Animosity toward the man, his ideas, his language, spilled over

into his critical reception; and, despite a band of loyal drum-beaters such as H. L. Mencken, the ferocity of his opposition deprived him of any Pulitzer Prize and thwarted his hopes for the Nobel award. During his lifetime the single official gesture toward recognition of his true stature—and this within a hairs-breadth of arriving too late—was the 1944 presentation by the Academy of Arts and Letters (to which he was never elected) of its gold medal for achievement in fiction.

What manner of man was Theodore Dreiser indeed? We are fortunate today in being able to answer Lyon's question in terms of man's writings rather than of his personal qualities. The shape of his nose, the size of his chin, even his disconcerting habit of twisting and untwisting his handkerchief, are no longer relevant. Time sweeps away such trivial considerations. We are left with the only thing that really matters in Dreiser's case, the upwards of a million printed words appearing under his signature. It is with these that the present study is primarily concerned.

Fred Lewis Pattee has said that "to weigh the man as a force in the period one must begin with his six novels, the rest of his output is but chips and explanations and excursions." Having designed my study of Dreiser as an introduction to the man and his work—a comprehensive study will require a work far more extensive than this—I have followed Pattee's advice. Except for the *Trilogy of Desire*, which is coherently treated only as a unit, I have arranged my chapters on the novels in chronological order of their publication.

This volume is not to be taken as a biography, although for the person who has newly discovered Dreiser it will probably furnish enough of the pertinent facts for understanding. I have taken the liberty of delving into Dreiser's life where this seemed germane to his fiction. We have two types of writers in America. One, like Henry James, prefers to begin with only the slimmest of external facts, embellishing them by his knowledge of man's life, enlarging them by imaginative resources, until he creates a story which may glow with the truth of reality even though its personages and events never existed in fact. The other—Thomas Wolfe is an example—creates images of recognizable reality by shaping, reorganizing, and generally fictionalizing his own personal experiences. Dreiser belongs with the latter. In each novel he is telling us something about his own life, his observations and ambitions and frustrations. Where the man's life impinges most directly upon his writing—he mined it well for his novels, after all—I have attempted to indicate the relevant circumstances.

Dreiser's avowed purpose in fiction was to render the broad, truthful outlines of life. In this introduction to his work, I have attempted to do the same for Dreiser.

PHILIP L. GERBER

*San Luis Obispo*
*December, 1963*

# Acknowledgments

It is impossible to acknowledge all of the influences which in one way or another affect such a study as this one of Dreiser, but I wish to recognize at least some of the individuals who, knowingly or not, played a part in its completion. At the University of Iowa, John C. Gerber's class in The Rise of Realism introduced me to Dreiser's works and kindled a lasting interest. This course was followed by Alexander Kern's seminar on Dreiser, which spurred me to my first serious research, in this case ferreting out of original sources for the *Trilogy of Desire*.

I feel indebted to my colleagues in the Department of English at the University of Utah as a group for supplying an atmosphere conducive to my labors. A number of them individually loaned me books otherwise difficult to obtain and volunteered the many suggestions which aid a writer in maintaining his direction. Lona Mosk Packer read a number of my chapters in manuscript and supplied discerning and forthright criticism. Dean Jack H. Adamson made possible a class schedule which provided time for research and writing. My chairman, Harold F. Folland, arranged for me to teach a class in Dreiser while I was writing my chapters on the novels. The members of this class made comments and raised questions, fresh because uncluttered by secondary readings, which helped me hew to the principal considerations in Dreiser's books. The University Research Committee, by providing two grants for additional research on Dreiser, inevitably contributed at the same time to the successful completion of the present study.

At the University of Pennsylvania, I received cordial and open advice from Mrs. Neda Westlake, curator of the Dreiser Collection. Both from her own substantial fund of information and from original documents in the collection, she aided me in locating answers to a number of nagging questions. The University of Pennsylvania Press has kindly furnished permission to quote from the extended letter in which Dreiser reveals the story of the suppression of *Sister Carrie*.

Finally, I am grateful to Sylvia E. Bowman, whose editing of my manuscript has rescued me from innumerable embarrassments, both of commission and omission.

# Chronology

1871    August 27, Dreiser born in Terre Haute, Indiana.

1879    Dreiser family separates; Theodore accompanies Sarah Dreiser to Vincennes, then to Sullivan, Indiana.

1882    Paul Dreiser arranges housing for the family in Evansville, Indiana.

1883    Family regroups briefly in Chicago.

1883-   Family residence in Warsaw, Indiana. Family separated
1887    once more.

1887-   Dreiser travels alone to Chicago for the first time, works
1889    as common laborer in a restaurant and for a hardware company.

1889-   Residence at Bloomington, Indiana University.
1890

1890    November 14, death of Dreiser's mother, Sarah Schanab Dreiser.

1892    Dreiser begins newspaper career with position on Chicago *Globe*. November, Dreiser moves to St. Louis as reporter for *Globe-Democrat* and *Republic*.

1893    Dreiser meets Sara (Sallie) White.

1894    March, Dreiser departs for the East; brief residence in Toledo, Cleveland, Pittsburgh.

1895    October, Dreiser begins residence in New York. Establishment of *Ev'ry Month* with Dreiser as editor. Beginning of Dreiser's magazine career.

1898    November, Dreiser marries Sallie White.

1899    Dreiser spends the summer in Arthur Henry's home, Maumee, Ohio; begins writing fiction, including *Sister Carrie* (first novel).

1900   *Sister Carrie* published and suppressed by Doubleday, Page and Company.

1904   July, Dreiser becomes fiction editor for Street and Smith publications.

1905   April, Dreiser becomes editor of *Smith's Magazine.*

1906   April, Dreiser becomes editor of *Broadway Magazine.* Paul Dreiser (Dresser) dies.

1907   May 18, *Sister Carrie* republished by B. W. Dodge and Company.

1909   Dreiser begins intensive work on *Jennie Gerhardt* (novel). Separation from Sara White Dreiser.

1910   October 15, Dreiser severs connections with Butterick publications.

1911   April, *Jennie Gerhardt* accepted by Harper and Brothers. In November, Dreiser travels to Europe to do research on career of Charles Tyson Yerkes.

1912   *The Financier,* first volume of *A Trilogy of Desire* (novels) published; *Sister Carrie* republished by Harper and Brothers.

1913   *A Traveler at Forty* (non-fiction) published by The Century Company.

1914   May 15, *The Titan,* second volume of *A Trilogy of Desire,* published by John Lane after rejection by Harpers.

1915   Dreiser revisits boyhood homes in Indiana. October, *The "Genius"* (novel) published by John Lane.

1916   *Plays of the Natural and the Supernatural* published by John Lane. July, *The "Genius"* withdrawn by John Lane after obscenity charges are instituted against it. *A Hoosier Holiday* (autobiography) published by John Lane.

1918   *Free, and Other Stories, The Hand of the Potter* (play), and *Twelve Men* (sketches) published by Boni & Liveright.

1919   Dreiser has first meeting with cousin, Helen Richardson.

1920    *Hey, Rub-A-Dub-Dub!* (philosophy and speculation) published by Boni & Liveright.

1919-   Residence in Hollywood. Beginning of love affair with
1922    Helen Richardson. Dreiser begins writing *An American Tragedy.*

1922    *A Book About Myself* (autobiography), second volume of projected series *A History of Myself,* published by Boni & Liveright.

1923    *The "Genius"* republished and *The Color of a Great City* (sketches) published by Boni & Liveright. Dreiser and Helen move to New York to continue work on *An American Tragedy.*

1925    *An American Tragedy* (novel) published by Boni & Liveright.

1927    *Chains* (short stories) published by Boni & Liveright. In November, Dreiser travels to Russia; remains as a visitor until January, 1928.

1928    *Moods, Cadenced and Declaimed* (poems) and *Dreiser Looks at Russia* published by Boni & Liveright.

1929    *A Gallery of Women* (sketches) published by Horace Liveright.

1930    *Fine Furniture* (long short story) published by Random House.

1931    *Tragic America* (non-fiction) published by Horace Liveright. *Dawn,* first volume of projected *A History of Myself; A Book About Myself* republished as *Newspaper Days* by Horace Liveright.

1932-   Dreiser acts as co-editor of *The American Spectator*
1934    magazine.

1939    *The Living Thoughts of Thoreau* (edited with introduction by Dreiser) published by Longmans, Green.

1941    *America Is Worth Saving* (non-fiction) published by Horace Liveright.

1942    October 1, Sara White Dreiser dies.

1944 Dreiser accepts Award of Merit from the American Academy of Arts and Letters. June 13, Dreiser marries Helen Richardson.

1945 July 20, Dreiser writes William Z. Foster applying for membership in Communist Party. December 28, Dreiser dies in Hollywood, California.

1946 *The Bulwark* (novel) published by Doubleday.

1947 *The Stoic,* third volume of *A Trilogy of Desire,* published by Doubleday. *The Best Short Stories of Theodore Dreiser,* edited by Howard Fast, published by World.

1949 *Theodore Dreiser: Apostle of Nature* by Robert H. Elias, first complete biography, written in consultation with Dreiser, is published by Alfred A. Knopf.

# Theodore Dreiser

## CHAPTER 1

# The Well of Memory: Dreiser's Youth[1]

THROUGHOUT his major novels, Theodore Dreiser reiterates
the story of individuals crippled by environment, hoodwinked
by illusion, buffeted by ill-favored circumstance, helplessly tossed
thither and yon by the blind winds of chance. In a hostile world,
man dwindles to the ignominy of an expendable pawn—and a
poorly made one at that—in a chess game played not by
responsible gods but by impersonal mechanical and chemical
forces set in motion by a cosmic accident. Yet the facts of
Dreiser's own life argue vigorously against his own philosophy
of ultimate human impotence. Theoretically, Dreiser's in-
auspicious origins and early environment should have not only
militated against his succeeding but almost foredoomed him
to obscurity.

Before Dreiser's time, American literature had been dominated
solidly by men of direct Anglo-Saxon lineage, many of them
aristocratic by birth, highly educated, financially independent
or endowed with family and friends who might secure them
salaried positions or other "grants-in-aid" to finance their
embarkation upon literary careers. Of these aids, Dreiser
possessed none: no money, no friends in power, no formal
education worthy of the name, no family tradition in letters.
Still, with every advantage apparently massed against him,
Dreiser by the force of his own will and his dogged persistence
eventually burst through all barriers. In spite, some would insist,
of a congenital inability to write at all, he produced a body of
novels second to none in twentieth-century America, an achievement we are mistakenly prone to discount, so accustomed have
we become to our Saroyans, Nabakovs, Menckens, Shapiros,
Steins, and Steinbecks, not to mention the emerging flood of
excellent Negro writers, all of whom together have obviated any

national, racial, or socio-economic tests for authorship. Snobbism is dead, so far as literature is concerned. America could not be less interested.

Yet it is well to recall that Theodore Dreiser was the first "outsider" to break into the charmed circle. Before his time the melting pot had proved so inefficient in the field of letters that Hamlin Garland was provoked into complaint. Why was the United States taking so much "longer to achieve independence of English critics than it took to free itself from old-world political and economic rule"? What was needed was a national literature simultaneously free of the imitative blight and distinguished by "such quality of texture and background that it could not have been written in any other place or by any one else than a native."[2] To Garland's call, issued in 1894, Dreiser arrived in 1900 as the nation's first full-bodied response.

It is well also for us to examine with some care the early life of this hulking German-American, who is disparaged by some as "the world's worst great writer," not only because that life illustrates the deprivations over which a number of our national geniuses have had to triumph before they might contribute to our literature, but because that life is employed so extensively in the man's own fiction. His life is woven so inextricably into the fabric of his novels that even a sketchy knowledge of it clarifies for the reader a good portion of the attitudes, characterizations, and prejudices that unify Dreiser's accomplishment. H. L. Mencken called his friend "the most matter of fact writer in the world." It is an epithet most readily apprehensible when we can compare the lives narrated in Dreiser's novels with the life lived by the author himself.

## I  An American Dream Destroyed

Dreiser's father, John Paul Dreiser, was born in Germany and had entered this country some twenty-five years before the birth of his son Theodore in 1871 in Terre Haute, Indiana. A weaver by trade, John Paul had worked westward to establish himself and had eloped with sixteen-year-old Sarah Schanab,[3] daughter of a Moravian farmer living near Dayton, Ohio. The young couple moved on to Fort Wayne, where John Paul became production manager in a woolen mill, and for a time their fortunes promised to imitate the rising graph of a Horatio Alger tale. But briefly in this new land, John Paul already was becom-

ing a man of position. Raising enough cash to build a mill of
their own, the Dreisers located in the small town of Sullivan,
where their stay was marked by continuing prosperity and by
the birth of eleven children.

In 1870 a trio of misfortunes struck in rapid sequence. Loaded
with fleeces consigned by the farmers of the region, John
Dreiser's woolen mill burned to the ground. During its rebuild-
ing, a heavy beam crashed down upon the weaver's head and
shoulders, destroying the hearing in one ear. While he con-
valesced, his guileless wife was cheated by "yankee trickery"
out of the remainder of the family's property. The father,
according to his son, was broken, "never quite the same again."

The penniless family retreated to Terre Haute, where Theodore
was born the following August 27. After him came yet another
son, Edward, bringing the family total, with five boys and five
girls surviving infancy, to an even dozen. But for the remainder
of the parents' lives, the family was never again to experience
the solidarity and affluence it had enjoyed so briefly in Sullivan.

## II  *"A Thin Grasshopper of a Man"*

John Paul Dreiser, often incapacitated and working sporadically where and when he could secure employment, stood as a
figure of grim authority to his children, a despot to be respected
only so far as duty commanded. To be feared at the slightest
transgression of what seemed to them his unreasonably confined
moral code, he never received genuine filial love from any of
them, least of all from young Theodore. Until the novelist's
later years when life had left him well-schooled "in its bitter
aspects, its grim constructive process," he regarded his father
quite frankly as a plain fool, an ineffectual nibbler at life's
banquet table, "a thin grasshopper of a man, brooding wearily."

Religious differences early built an insurmountable barrier
against understanding between father and son. John Paul, though
a devout and orthodox Roman Catholic, apparently neither
knew nor cared greatly about his Church beyond an ironclad
observance of a narrow, rigid scheme of thou-shalt-nots. Following the debacle in Sullivan, he grew increasingly fanatical with
concern for his salvation, obsessed "much more with the here-
after than the now." In contrast, his children, reared in poverty,
deprivation, insecurity, were tantalized by the prospect of
worldly pleasures—the hungry dog could think of nothing but

meat. "Material possessions," reports Dreiser, "were already the goal as well as the sum of most American life, and so one could not help feeling the state of isolation and indifference which accompanied a lack of means." To the father, mindful of his obligation for the souls placed in his care by God, his children were guileless moths enticed dangerously near the fascinating lamps of corruption. Frustrated by his inability to prevent them from plunging headlong toward their own ruin, he raged, threatened, sulked; in the end he accomplished only a deepened estrangement between him and them, a rift in the family which widened with the passing years. "Never have I known a man more obsessed by a religious belief," declares Dreiser in his autobiography; "to him God was a blazing reality."

Most of the novelist's remarks concerning his father are couched in bitterly antagonistic terms: "a morose and dour figure, forlorn and despondent"; "a narrow bigot" trapped in "the asinine teachings of his Church." And if Dreiser's frank analysis of his family is to be given credence, the total scope of the father's moral code was limited to a set of dual emphases concerning sex and thrift.

Of sex, he was ever on guard to preserve his daughters' virtue, a care aggravated severely by the girls' own disregard for it as they bloomed into young womanhood. Whether they were more drawn to men than men seem to have been attracted to them may well be a moot point. Certainly they were "boy crazy" and early discovered men to be an obvious source of the trinkets and flattery they thirsted for. Enraged daily at the sight of the rouged faces, the flashy—to him sinful—clothing with which they hoped to render themselves irresistible, the father showered them with abuse. Inevitably they evaded his guard to go walking or buggyriding with admirers, leaving him beside himself with concern. And when in due time the father's worst fears were realized in the pregnancy of one of the sisters by a brash young local aristocrat who promptly hopped a train for parts unknown, Dreiser admits in all candor, "We were a scandal."

Of money, the father was convinced "it was a sin to be in debt" and lived in perpetual fear of dying insolvent, stranding his soul in the flames of purgatory where it would scorch until cleansed of injustice. In a family never far from the rocky brink of beggary, such a tenet could not avoid becoming the source of endless exacerbation.

Religious conflict with his father was the first step in Dreiser's well-known antipathy for the Catholic Church. Surprisingly, in his novels he exercises remarkable restraint. He holds his hatred in sufficient check that it does not unduly embitter his writing, and he often deliberately avoids the Catholic issue in scenes where its presence might be anticipated. The father in *Jennie Gerhardt*, for instance, though patterned upon John Paul Dreiser closely enough to be a portrait from life, is presented as being of the Lutheran faith. And in *The Bulwark*, the most religiously oriented of the novels, the faith under scrutiny was altered in later drafts from Catholicism to Quakerism.[4] But in his non-fictional works, Dreiser's anti-Catholic bias—which was to lead him soon to atheism and later toward communism—bursts forth vehemently. The Church itself he attacks savagely as an institution of "wornout folderol," "quite lunatic theories and pretensions," "psychopathic balderdash," "intellectual dry-rot." In sum, the Church was to him "the horrible charnel house of mediaeval ideas," worthy only of his undying opposition and headed, he earnestly prayed, for speedy obliteration.

A succession of parochial schools in which Dreiser was enrolled he likens to prisons; his first nun teacher impresses him as "the Nemesis or Gorgon of the place, an outlandish figure of a woman clad in black, with a flaring white hood or bonnet"; the curriculum, "a mixed gibberish"; and the entire school system, "an outrageous survival of a stultifying mediaevalism which should be swept away to its last detail." To the various pastors he encountered in the family's endless moves he is scarcely more complimentary, one in particular being limned as a "low-browed, dogmatic little Bavarian, panoplied with the trashy authority of his church." Significantly, when he describes this priest's face as "a distorted and dictatorial cloud of narrow, Teutonic, bigoted religion and authority," he might as easily be describing his own father wearing the Roman collar.

Not until his mature years was Dreiser capable of visualizing his father in any light other than that of the religious fanatic. Then the hate softened, if not to sympathy at least into pity. "How snippy and unkind I had been," he reflected, seeing his father now no longer as an iron tyrant, but "as he really was, warm, generous . . . a poor, tottering, broken soul wandering distrait and forlorn amid a storm of difficulties: age, the death of his wife, the flight of his children, doubt as to their salvation, poverty, a declining health." Only at the end did Dreiser award

his father a due share of the compassion he had at all times
showered abundantly upon other human beings.

### III   *"The Woman Whose Memory I Adore"*

For his mother Dreiser never felt any but the most tender of
sentiments. If the father was bound rigidly by his adamant
morality, Sarah Dreiser seems not to have acquired that trait
from him. Whatever the reason—quite possibly her overriding
struggle for survival excluded all other concerns from her mind—
she simply was unconcerned with moral codes. Dreiser's
numerous pictures of her show us a woman who lavished upon
her many children every ounce of loving care she possessed
and who provided them with whatever meager opportunities
she found within her power. By nature quiet, sentimental,
sympathetic, gentle—"dreamy" is the word her son most often
chooses to describe her—she was endowed with endless strength
and patience; her enthusiasm for life faltered only when black
clouds of poverty dimmed her family's prospects to the point of
hopelessness. Afflicted through most of his life with a painful
sense of inferiority and rejection, Dreiser confessed: "no one
ever wanted me enough, unless it was my mother." In return, he
bound himself tenaciously to "the silver tether of her affection,
understanding, sweetness, sacrifice." He thought of her as "a
pale, spindling flower left to vegetate in a dark room, yet
earnestly struggling to reach the light. Yet her efforts were so
groping, and for the most part futile."

Eager to be helpful, the mother stood ready to comfort, to
encourage, often to abet the efforts of any child with whom the
father was angry. Did one of the restless girls hope to avert her
father's wrath by meeting a current beau "on the sly"? Then the
mother could be relied on to help arrange a rendezous. Did
brother Rome, "the family Nemesis," return unheralded from
vagabonding it in Michigan, Kansas, Canada, only to sail off on
a drunken spree, with a night in jail the result? Then the mother
was prepared to forgive. Did Dorsch—as Theodore was known
at home—feel the tug of the great magnet, Chicago, and burn to
make his own way in the world? Then the mother stood waiting
with her blessing and with six dollars scraped from her savings.
Sarah, early recognized by her children as the "sustaining force"
of the family, its "great comfort and strength," drew her children
close to her as powerfully as the father repelled them. All the

love withheld from the father was directed toward her, and when she died Dreiser felt for years like "a lone barque on a lone sea."

## IV   On the Move

The father's stern religiosity, the mother's flowing tenderness, the family's unceasing poverty—this trio of forces worked at shaping the young Dreiser. His recurring apprehension at the approach of winter, a dread he was powerless to shake off even in adulthood and in times of affluence, is evidence enough of the crippling scars left by poverty. To be poor was to be isolated, ignored, helpless. To be destitute in winter was a threat to survival itself. Food, shelter, heat, heavy clothing to cope with biting Midwestern cold: these were the needs. Money, or lack of it, was the key. Invariably, remembrance of the privations which winter's advent heaped onto the family's chronic miseries caused the grown Dreiser to shudder with "an indefinable and highly oppressive dread." Never in his life was the man able to "look upon crowded tenements or small, shabby cottages in cheap, mean streets, or poorly-clothed children, men or women, with grimy hands and faces and a weary, troubled or labored look" without an involuntary reversion to these earliest memories and with the wish that life "might be better organized . . . that it would not permit the untrained or the inadequate to stew so persistently and helplessly in their own misery."

The catastrophes initiated with the destruction of the family mill led now to a constant, bewildering succession of moves and separations; and these produced a family whose character Dreiser recognized as "nebulous, emotional, unorganized and tradition-less." In Terre Haute alone the Dreisers resided in at least five or six houses, each inferior to the one before. Regularly the mother, in a burst of ambition, opened a boardinghouse. Regularly each new venture failed. The reason, according to her son: undercharging and overserving. Whenever John Paul was thrown out of work, which was often, the mother would take in washing, go out as a scrubwoman, do "anything and everything which might tend to keep us from starving." So desperate grew the family's situation during these years that the younger of the ten Dreiser children might be observed gleaning lumps of coal from the ground along the railroad tracks; at times they mustered courage to steal fuel directly off loaded cars until chased by "ill natured" hands. In this, as always,

Theodore, "a most curious-minded child," was stockpiling memories which would one day be utilized fictionally.

In desperation the family was driven to admit that survival depended upon its splitting up. It was 1879; never again would they form a truly coherent unit. The oldest girls, Mame, Emma, Theresa, Sylvia, remained with their father on the assumption they could find sufficient work as governesses, waitresses, or clerks in five-and-ten-cent stores to contribute to the family's support; the younger children, Tillie, Theodore, and Edward, accompanied the mother to Vincennes, where a friend had offered shelter. Al was packed off to his mother's half-sister at North Manchester. Talented Paul, the oldest boy, had already struck out on his own as an apprentice in the minstrel shows so popular in that period. Rome, the next in line, an errant, erratic youth, had vanished for the time being to seek his fortune as a railway "candy butcher."

This painful fragmentation once agreed upon, Sarah Dreiser's optimism came springing back to its natural level once again. Past struggles were set behind her. She dreamed of starting afresh, of creating a new, more fruitful life for her children. Her friend, wife of the Vincennes fire-chief, lodged the group in quarters over the fire house; and all seemed well until it dawned upon Sarah that other sections of the building were being operated as a brothel. The mother's "colorful day-dream" evaporated "under the tarnishing power of reality." Filled for once with moral indignation, Sarah herded her children back to Sullivan, where Theodore spent what he afterward considered the three happiest years of his life, "compounded of innocence, wonder, beauty, little or no trace of knowledge of good and evil or the broodings thereby entailed."

In Sullivan the boy was free to roam the open fields and contemplate their abundance of flora, to sit by waterways and wonder at the mysteries of aquatic life. He learned much from nature, perceiving always analogies to human life. Passenger trains bearing crowds to farflung destinations caught his eye. Denver, Santa Fe, San Francisco, these were localities brother Paul had praised in relating his experiences with traveling minstrel shows. In particular, the boy dreamed of burgeoning Chicago, cynosure of hordes of young and hopeful Midwesterners.

Meanwhile, the family finances had not improved. The girls in Terre Haute found life under their father's vigilant eye devoid of gaiety or relaxation. One confided to her brother later: "I despised the idea father had of saving money and going without decent clothes in order to pay old debts." And when asked about her primary interests, she replied without hesitation, "Clothes and men!"

The third winter spent in Sullivan, "this worst of all winters" as Dreiser afterward recalled it, was one of utter destitution. Another attempt at running a boardinghouse had failed, draining the mother of hope. Then, with the irruptive impact of a *deus ex machina*, brother Paul returned after a four-year absence, splendidly clothed, already acquiring the Falstaffian corpulence which to the family was a legitimate hallmark of affluence. Rising swiftly in the vaudeville world, Paul for some time had been writing the comic and sentimental tunes which would make his fame (*On the Banks of the Wabash, My Gal Sal, I know It's True For my Mother Told Me So*); and, having "Americanized" his name in the interests of euphony, he carried with him copies of his *Paul Dresser Songbook*.

Paul's jovial, generous, assuring presence—fur coat, silk hat, altogether an inspiring success-symbol to the impoverished family —intervened at this moment to lift the black gloom from his mother and to revitalize her faith in life. His appearance stirred in Theodore a "conception of a fate or fortune in the affairs of men—an interfering hand that beyond our understanding or willing makes or mars our inconceivably petty lives." This concept finds expression throughout Dreiser's novels, in which coincidence plays a decisive role in human fate.

Best of all, the mother and children were taken by Paul to Evansville to the finest house they had occupied thus far. Paul forsook the vaudeville circuit temporarily to become star comedian at the Apollo Theatre, a decision prompted only in part by concern for his family, since he had fallen in love with Annie Brace, mistress of an Evansville house of prostitution—a circumstance apparently well concealed from his mother. The two women never met, but young Theodore soon found himself subjected to the taunts of neighbors: "What's the name of that woman your brother lives with downtown?" Talk being cheap and the family by now more inured to it than not, Dreiser remained unaffected in his attitude. He knew only that Paul had acted magnanimously, had come to his mother's rescue when she most needed help. So the incident simply merged with many other observations, all of which proved the impossibility of defining clear-cut areas of good and evil in human affairs.

From here it was an easy leap to be fully convinced of the stupidity of all established moral codes, which from an early age he considered "a curse to the individual." As for ethics, they "were being taught me by life itself." What need for school or book to teach the individual about the way life organized itself in social patterns? Did one not possess eyes and ears for that purpose? Direct observation of life itself was what was called for. Enduring lessons stood ready to be learned from "the open forge and the potter's window."

The Dreisers' life in Evansville followed a familiar pattern: temporary stability, a tentative groping for roots, then disruption, upheaval, the strain of a new beginning elsewhere. At first the children, singly or in pairs, gravitated back to the family axis, the mother. From Chicago and employment as varnisher in a coffin factory came brother Al, soon to establish himself at the same trade in a local chair factory. From Terre Haute came the father, with two of Dreiser's sisters, on a visit that lengthened into months. The two oldest girls left their Chicago jobs and joined the group, so infuriating the father with their "goings-on" with Evansville men that, were it not for Sarah's timely intervention, he would have driven them out. Even Rome was back— from God knows where: Mexico, Honduras, California perhaps —to inflict his inevitable pain, "borrowing money, drinking, passing worthless checks, and presently landing in jail." Most importantly, there was Paul, the "glowing luminary" upon whose presence—and pocketbook—this home was based. Then, as suddenly as he had appeared, Paul decamped as a result of a lovers' quarrel with Annie Brace. The family regrouped, this time turning to Chicago, familiar territory to the older children and much talked up by them as the spot to relocate.

## V  "Hail, Chicago!"

Chicago! For years the magic name had dinned into Dreiser's brain. Brother Rome, brother Paul, his sisters—all returned with exciting tales of the mecca. Taut with wonder and anticipation, Dreiser was never to forget this journey. Again and again in his stories he depicts the first entry of a young American into Chicago; each is imbued with the thrill of his own experience.

"Would that I might sense it all again!" he exclaimed, "the throb and urge and sting of my first days in Chicago!" Ecstatic with the "miracle" of pleasant sensations, the fascination of astounding, kaleidoscopic human scenes, he never felt equipped with powers sufficient to reproduce adequately the exact excitement of the city, "like a great orchestra in a tumult of noble harmonies" and himself "like a guest at a feast, eating and drinking in a delirium of ecstasy."

"Hail, Chicago!" he sang, "first of the daughters of the new world!" Later he might grudgingly admit New York to be the true heart of national activity. But first loves are powerful, and for him nothing could ever displace as a symbol the young Chicago, the lusty, brawling city of big shoulders which Carl Sandburg was soon to celebrate in verse as new and raw as the metropolis itself.

To prepare the way, three sisters preceded the family, obtained employment, and rented a six-room, third-floor apartment overlooking the Waverly Theater on West Madison. Then the mother was sent for, with the younger children. Under a plan calling for all able-bodied members to secure work and contribute to the family's support, Theodore, an impressionable twelve, became cash-boy in a West Side drygoods store, and later peddled newspapers on a street corner. All money was to be pooled in a common fund, with a generous donation from Paul taking up any slack. But well-conceived as it seemed to be, this plan was to work no better than the others. The father, thrown out of a job in Terre Haute, arrived in Chicago, reasserted his authority, and created discord. The older children began to revolt. The burden of supporting the father was one thing, but enduring his continual criticism and interference with their freedom was yet another. Having tasted independence, they submitted to his restraints only under duress. Those nearing adulthood objected to contributing toward a home in which they felt unduly shackled. Dissention followed speedily, and in the end nothing was possible but still another move, this time to Warsaw, Indiana. There was no choice, even though moving meant abandoning $600 worth of furniture purchased on the installment plan and as yet unpaid for. The father returned to Terre Haute with plans to rejoin the family later in Warsaw; the older children clung to their Chicago positions; the mother, with her younger brood, entrained for Indiana.

## VI "The Charm of Warsaw"

Now the story repeated itself—this time with more dire consequences. Rome returned, shaming the family again with his delinquency. Next came the father. Following him, two sisters, "a vivid, harum-scarum pair," outraged John Paul by their forwardness with the local swains. "Such a bold, shameless way to dress!" he raged, discovering them with lips and cheeks rouged, spit curls plastered to their cheeks, and dressed in "borrowed finery." One of the girls, returning to Chicago, soon married a New York Tammany Hall politician, but the other remained. Pregnant by the son of a leading Warsaw family, she was dispatched to her sister's in New York to have the baby, but not before the wagging of local tongues had left an indelible impression upon Theodore, driving home strongly "the chill resentment. . . . The sudden whispers, evasions, desires to avoid those who have failed to conform to the customs and taboos of any given region!" His notions of the incontestable—and generally negative—power of society were beginning to jell.

Young Dreiser had observed with great wonder and considerable dismay the powerful manner in which the sex force influenced his sisters' behavior and determined their fates. Now it entered his own life, awakening in his adolescent body like a "hot fire nature had lighted." More and more it occupied his thoughts, filling his dreams with conquests of love. Given always to introspection whose usual result was to increase his sense of inferiority, the boy convinced himself he was financially or personably ill equipped for sensual exploits. More affluent boys he envied hotly for their handsome appearances, their splendid clothes, for what he took to be their courage. As for the Warsaw girls, they surrounded him with "a stinging richness" so far beyond his grasp that day and night he felt himself tantalized by delights he might never have the force to possess.

To one in his position—penniless, inexperienced, eternally an outsider—desirable girls seemed more unattainable than stars. For years to come, he dreamed of himself as the central actor in a perfect love affair, craving always to "shine as a lover"; and his later notorious varietism might be traced to this source.[5] Eventual success with women on his own social plane—or as was more often the case, lower—left him thoroughly unsatisfied. Each experience left him feeling degraded, miserable, increasingly inferior. "Sex," he admits, "harried me from hell to hell!"

At the same time, much of life in Warsaw was rewarding. Though Theodore was learning, bitterly, the immense difference money makes in the social world—those who lack it being excluded automatically from entire spheres of activity—still he had companions aplenty. And in his spare time he was reading voraciously, albeit hampered by restriction to the use of the left eye, the right having a cast. The magic of the printed page put him under a spell. "Books! Books! Books! How wonderful, fascinating, revealing! Whenever I found it possible, I would steal away and ascend to a front bedroom on the second floor of our house, and there bury myself in the pages of first one volume and then another."[6]

Hawthorne's *The House of the Seven Gables* and Kingsley's *Water Babies* attracted him in particular, and the latter recalled happy days in Sullivan where he had explored "pools and waterholes watching for crawfish and salamanders." He immersed himself in Dickens, then in Thackeray; read widely in Shakespeare; tasted Bunyan, Fielding, Pope, Thoreau, Emerson, Twain; and tried history, Carlyle's *French Revolution* in particular, a book he lacked the background to understand. But his chief literary influences, such as Balzac, lay waiting for him to discover them.

Of all the houses in which the Dreisers lived, Theodore found the fourteen-room brick home in Warsaw the most charming, situated as it was on three acres of ground, buried in a grove of fir trees alive with blackbirds which roosted there after gorging themselves on the neighboring rice fields. Life seemed "lush, full and sweet, a veritable youth-dream of lotus land." Warsaw stood at the beginning of a chain of small lakes extending for thirty miles eastward, and this uninhabited country allowed him to walk alone for hours at a time while thinking—sometimes brooding—but continually delighted by the natural spectacle.

Best of all, Dreiser was at last enrolled in a school he enjoyed, and he had found a teacher who understood him. Mildred Fielding, gracious, sympathetic—not unlike his own mother in temperament—recognized in this awkward, self-conscious youth something of herself as a young girl and went out of her way to praise his reading and composition, to comment favorably upon his mental abilities. Gradually, Theodore came to feel he might perhaps be of some worth after all. To dream of a place in the sun might not be wholly an absurdity.

But with school dismissed for the summer, Theodore felt a latent wanderlust welling up in him. Chicago! He could not drive from his mind visions of streets "teeming with life and lights," of the river and the lake, of "steamers and large and small sailing vessels." Sixteen now, he was chafing to stamp his mark on the world. He was inexperienced, poorly endowed physically and psychologically, and painfully aware of all his inadequacies, prone in fact to magnify them; yet his spirit welled over with blind confidence. He went into the house. "Ma," he announced, "I am going to Chicago." With tears in her eyes, Sarah Dreiser scraped together six dollars for him—the train fare took $1.75 of it—and he hustled to pack his bag for the "most intense and wonderful" trip of his life. "I loved Chicago. It was so strong, so rough, so shabby, and yet so vital and determined. It seemed more like a young giant afraid of nothing." His description is apropos of the sixteen-year-old Dreiser himself.

Surely, argued the boy, somewhere in the teeming activity of Chicago there must be a place where an ambitious youth like himself might take his first steps on the road to fortune. The American Dream had taken such strong possession of him that it came as a rude shock to find no doors swinging open to welcome his presence. Soon disenchanted of the illusion that Chicago was waiting with open arms for just such a man as he, that his very presence would stir up a clamor of voices all competing for his services, the boy dropped his sights considerably. Then applying wherever he might as common labor, he discovered himself at a disadvantage competing with young fellows who were toughened by schooling in the city streets. After repeated disappointment, his fragile veneer of self-confidence cracked wide open; a sign advertising "strong boy wanted" was enough to intimidate him from even applying.

Eventually he did find employment—as a dishwasher in a fly-specked restaurant. Seething with the conviction that such labor demeaned him, he quit the moment he located a job with Hibbard, Spencer, Bartlett and Company, a large wholesale hardware store. Working there only confused and embittered him further. He felt instinctively that the native abilities of his co-workers nowhere approached his own. One small group of employees did impress him, however: these were the scions of wealthy Easterners, monied aristocrats some to study practical Western hardware methods and needs before returning as executives in their parents' establishments. These young men protected their smooth hands with gloves; under the denim collars of their work clothes one caught the gleam of silk shirts. Dreiser hated them for the disparity between their state and his. He envied them for what luck had poured into their laps. He hungered to be one of them, yet saw no route open by which he might enter their world. Forty years later he would portray young Clyde Griffiths, hero of *An American Tragedy*, thrown into emotional turmoil by an analogous predicament.

More forcibly than ever before, Dreiser discovered "the luck of being born rich . . . the insufferable difference between wealth and poverty." A mounting sense of being left out, excluded, was hardly balm for his wounded self-confidence, yet out of this comparison of his lot with others' another concept was evolving. Contrast, he saw, was what drilled one in learning how life organized itself. "Differences present life's edge and give it its zest," he realized. "We enjoy or disdain what we have because of contrast with what we do or do not have, what we do or do not endure." A series of novels would dramatize the principle. Carrie Meeber, Jennie Gerhardt, Clyde Griffiths— these protagonists all learned of life in America by observing contrasts between affluence and poverty.

## VII   *"One Dreamy, Lackadaisical Year"*

At the very moment when it appeared morbidly possible to Dreiser that he might have doomed himself to life as a "commonplace" hardware stockboy, another of life's inexplicable strokes of chance steered his fortunes upward. Miss Mildred Fielding, who had left Warsaw after teaching Theodore in his first high school year, was still haunted by concern over the boy's potentialities. In Chicago she was appointed principal of a high school. Seeking out her ex-pupil at the hardware concern, she astonished him by outlining a plan which would send him to college—a year, perhaps two—at her expense. "Read philosophy," she advised him, "and history. You will see how life works and how mistaken or untrue most beliefs are. Read Spencer. Read a life of Socrates. Read Marcus Aurelius and Emerson. You have the capacity for rising high in the world, and I want you to do it."[7]

In the fall of 1889, Dreiser enrolled at Indiana University, and for the first time in his life enjoyed a sense of genuine importance. Well aware of his good fortune, he knew intuitively that he stood at one of life's crossroads. But college never became for him the catalytic experience which he assumed and which Miss Fielding hoped it might prove to be; for, without being altogether conscious of it, he had long ago chanced upon his proper method for learning. Life itself had become his schoolroom and refused to be supplanted. Books might prove of value, but they would never supersede the direct observation which had already taught the boy so much about the human struggle. Later he revealed of his academic year spent in Bloomington, "its technical educational value to me was zero."

Characteristically, what did interest Dreiser at college was people, especially the small group of young men with whom he became friends. With Russell Ratliff he discussed philosophy, read Darwin and Huxley as Miss Fielding had urged. Howard Hall accompanied him on numerous geological explorations of the region's caves. But the most influential single figure was his roommate, Bill · Yakey,[8] who possessed every desirable trait Dreiser felt lacking in himself—cleverness, social adeptness, popularity, "looks, strength, grace, means, which made him a hero and an idol." This was the type of man Dreiser most admired and envied: a superman, a favorite of fortune. A ladykiller, at least in his own estimate, Yakey discussed girls in an easy, intimate manner, making it plain that "all of these girls yielded to him joyfully." For months Dreiser listened, eating his heart out silently over the several campus beauties to whom he himself was attracted but lacked sufficient courage to approach. He listened "greedily, enviously" and wished himself as "handsome, bold, magnetic, devil-may-care" as Yakey.

Again struck by the point of contrast which seemed ever more plainly life's method of clarifying its distinctions, Dreiser pondered over this situation. Why was Yakey so well equipped for human contrasts, breezing into Bloomington with two trunks loaded with jackets, suits, shoes the like of which Theodore could scarcely dream of possessing? Why was Dreiser himself so ill endowed? Why had nature showered everything on one and nothing on the other? "I used to look at him," says Dreiser, "and then at myself after he was gone and ask myself what chance had I?" Clothes made the man, it seemed. With fashionable clothes one might compensate for imperfections of the body or the personality, rendering them incapable of doing social harm. With suitable garments one might sweep through doors shut tightly against those unpossessed of the uniform of caste.

He found no reason why a few yards of wool or silk should assume such importance. Yet it was so; and most of Dreiser's young fictional heroes and heroines possess an instinctive awareness of the value of clothes as a "status-symbol" in an ironically schizophrenic American democracy.

A bitter pill for Dreiser to swallow was his exclusion by the Indiana fraternities from their invitations to membership. The rejection delivered a rabbit punch to his fragile ego. Again the gulf between the have and have not was underscored. Others were accepted, he felt, because they wore finer attire on their backs or came from wealthy homes or were endowed by chance with magnetic personalities. In consequence, figures of genuine— but unperceived—worth were relegated to a limbo of the non-elect.

The intensity of Dreiser's bitterness at this rejection burst into the open at the end of his freshman year when students gathered for a traditional burning of books. Always an injustice-collector, a trait which throughout his life manifested itself in hypo-chondria, he refused to attend these "silly revelries" which would serve no purpose but to remind him of "the deprivations I had endured, the things in which I had not been included, the joys which many had had and which I had not." Of those who had ignored him during his college year, he exclaimed bluntly, "They can all go to hell!"

He left Bloomington never to return.

## VIII  *"A Lone Barque on a Lone Sea"*

After a year's absence, Dreiser came to Chicago, determined to keep his sights set as far as possible above the menial labor which had heretofore been his lot. Noting the city's rapid expansion into the suburbs and the staggering amount of building planned or already underway, he went to work as a salesman in a real-estate office operated by one Asa Conklin, an ambitious but impractical man later used as the prototype for Asa Griffiths in *An American Tragedy*. The position promised much in the way of commissions which were never to materialize.

But this disappointment paled beside the sudden and critical illness of Sarah Dreiser, whose failing health in August of 1889 threw her family into a panic of apprehension. For weeks "the central centripetal star" of Dreiser's life declined, and finally all members of the scattered family who could be contacted were called home to say their farewells. Paul arrived with his theatrical troupe and installed his present mistress, "a creature of rounded arms, oval face, blonde hair," in an upper room of the house—to the sisters' indignation and to Theodore's envy and wonder how he too "might enjoy so beautiful a woman." Anxiety for his mother competed in his mind with lust for this beauty. With his mother dying, how could he be concerned with fantasies of sex? Such an apparent contradiction of interests, further complicated by an unrelenting drive to succeed in his real-estate ventures, fascinated him as an example of the complexity of the human personality dominated by powerful forces it is helpless to oppose.

On a day in November, while Theodore was helping his mother to the stool, she sagged in his arms, gave him "a most exhausted and worn look," and died. "Oh, I should have gone first!" cried the father, forlorn and exhausted. And Dreiser himself, rather bitterly, echoed the thought, yes, why not? But it was brother Al who spoke most pertinently. "Well," he told the rest of the clan, "that's the end of our home."

Al was correct. Within a year most of the children had deserted their father; and Theodore was completely on his own, a rudder-less ship without compass, sextant, or anchor. Drifting and searching—for what, he knew not. At $8.00 a week, he drove a delivery wagon for Munger's Laundry, a job which gave him entry into homes ranging from the crudest tenement and "bed house" to opulent apartments of fabulously wealthy capitalists. Henry James's argument that the writer of fiction ought to be "one upon whom nothing is lost" never received a more emphatic embodiment than it did in the career of Theodore Dreiser, whose insight into every life he touched added its bit to his store of memories. Noting that the type of reception a laundryman received corresponded scarcely at all with the economic levels of the persons he dealt with—rich and poor alike apt to insult him as a lackey or to respect him as a human individual—he developed a "fairly clear perception of the value of personality as distinct from either poverty or riches." After all, he reasoned, who could have been consistently more destitute than his own mother? Yet poverty had never altered her importance to him.

The poor, he was beginning to see more clearly, were not necessarily virtuous, nor the wealthy altogether diabolical. All human creatures were trapped in the same nets. They were bits of seaweed on an endless sea, swept this way and that by subterranean tides of chance and circumstance which they neither controlled nor understood. They were puppets, toys. "But where," he questioned, "is the toy-maker who makes us?"

These years immediately following his mother's death and the subsequent final dissolution of the family group were of tremendous significance for Dreiser, and he knew it. Now or never, he must abandon the role of "a stormy petrel hanging over the yellowish-black waves of life and never really resting anywhere" and establish himself in a career which might in some measure help realize his full potentialities. But how—and where—and when? He groped here and there for a place in life. Love, at least in the conventional sense of monogamous marriage, he arbitrarily concluded was not for him. The lure of "fame, applause, power" dominated his thoughts. One job followed another, each a blind alley in the career sense; but each poured into his brain new experiences, individuals, incidents that might later be tapped. A stint as installment collector for an unsavory concern whose salesmen possessed a genius for persuading the art-starved poor to shackle themselves with installment-plan purchases of "gaudy and junky" albums, lamps with flashy pink shades, wooden clocks weighted with lead and painted to resemble stone—this job, as no book could, taught him the gullibility, the inescapable fate of the masses of "blundering humanity" who are doomed by ignorance, stupidity, and poverty to a life spent squatting on the cellar steps of society. This wretched mass he had no desire to join. His mind echoed its constant refrain: "No common man am I." His eyes were fixed upon the "real rulers of the world"—bankers, millionaires, artists, executives; fame and wealth stirred him "like whips and goads."

No common man, to be sure—but how best to achieve uncommon status? It was during this period of decision that Dreiser first began thinking, albeit in vague, dreamlike terms, of becoming a writer. The reading habit had long since taken root in him, and the novels of Stevenson and of Tolstoi, particularly *The Death of Ivan Ilyitch,* so astounded him with their portraits of life that quite understandably he considered the possibility of emulating them. "It would be a wonderful thing to be a novelist," he thought. Such a notion is not uncommon to perceptive youths who dream of fame through accomplishment. For most it remains frozen in the snowpack of fantasy. For Dreiser, the dream was eventually to come true, though a decade and more would pass first.

## IX  *Newspaper Days*[9]

Young Dreiser took stock of himself. The possibility of his acquiring sudden wealth by any means was quite obviously out of the question. Despite the dime novels, few young Americans of his acquaintance were marrying their bosses' daughters. The prospect of emerging as a prominent novelist overnight was equally discouraging. But perhaps he could make a beginning at least by placing himself with one of Chicago's newspapers. Determined to force his way upward, at age twenty-one he set out, "long spindling, a pair of gold-framed spectacles on his nose, his hair combed *a la pompadour,* a new spring suit consisting of light check trousers and bright blue coat and vest, a brown fedora hat, new yellow shoes"[10]—an apprehensive novice's conception of what "duds" a bright young reporter might affect to bedazzle the editors. In obtaining work this sartorial splendor proved of little air. For weeks a brusque "Nothing today!" iced down every flush of hope; but at last true-blue American perseverance won out. John Maxwell, copy-reader of the city's lowest-ranking newspaper, the *Daily Globe,* accepted Theodore on a trial basis. After that his imaginative coverage of the 1892 Democratic convention won him a chance at a steady berth at a glorious $15.00 a week. For the next decade he was occupied exclusively in journalistic work: reporting, editing, publishing scores of feature articles in the popular magazines.

Young Dreiser had by now attained his full height of six feet, one-and-a-half inches. Sparsely distributed over this attenuated frame was enough flesh to tip the scales at 137 pounds. Such statistics hardly suggest a robust physique, and Dreiser himself—never given to self-adulation—summed it up this way: "you can imagine my figure." Restricted to the use of a single eye, he was further handicapped—or self-consciously convinced himself he was—by inordinately large and crowded upper teeth. He frankly confessed to "a general homeliness of feature" which he imagined kept him from appealing to women—not a comfortable sensation for one whose body was "blazing with sex."

The newspaper world fell a good distance short of the nirvana Dreiser had imagined it to be. Always a bit naïve, the man often was taken aback when his dream bubbles burst in the nippy air of reality. Only his illusion of Chicago remained undimmed: with her impressive new skyscrapers, her tall grain elevators, immense railroad yards, imposing mansions, teeming slum areas, she was for Dreiser a "whirlpool of life." But the longer he dwelt in the newspaper world, the more he found that world to be "a seething maelstrom in which clever men struggled and fought as elsewhere." And in this "slough of muck in which men were raking busily and filthily for what their wretched rakes might uncover in the way of financial, social, political returns," the young cub observed that "some rose and many fell."

The struggle for survival was fierce; the motive of self-interest predominated. Journalism revealed merely another facet of life's large image, more distinctly outlined perhaps, but otherwise identical in character to all he had observed elsewhere. Sponge-like, he was soaking up experiences, moving rapidly to con-clusions about the "fierce, grim struggle" of life; he was de-veloping intense and lasting sympathies for underdogs who, unequipped for jungle-like struggle, apparently were doomed to "hungers, thirsts, half-formed dreams of pleasures . . . gibber-ing insanities and beaten resignations at the end."

Offered a job on the St. Louis *Globe-Democrat*, Dreiser left Chicago, not an easy decision to make, but an essential one if he were to rise in the world. Though he was ever insecure as a lover, he left a broken heart behind him, that of Lois Zahn,[11] latest in a series of girls with whom he had become involved during his days at Conklin's real-estate office, while driving the laundry truck, and while working on his newspaper career. These affairs, invariably painful, always burnt themselves out to the same grey conclusion. Sometimes the girl left him—each desertion an added blow to his ego; and sometimes he left her, thus igniting in himself a conflict of emotions. If the girl wanted marriage, as Lois did, then he shied away; for he was determined that marriage had no place in his life. He wanted to be ruthless, cold in avoiding romantic entaglements; but he found it no more possible than for a lamb to shed his fleece and grow a lion's mane. In his fiction he was able to create insensitive supermen who took women and discarded them like Kleenex. But except by way of fantasy these men's lives bore little resemblance to his own.

Taking what seemed the easy way out, he left Chicago without notifying Lois; and when pathetic letters from her dogged his trail to St. Louis, they left him torn emotionally between an innate sense of duty and the determination to preserve his independence. He knew what convention dictated as the decent thing to do. He knew also that his heart of hearts petitioned for its freedom. Sometimes convention and instinct collided—and what was a man to do? When Lois wrote that unless he intervened, she was marrying an older suitor who would take her, love or no, and then appended the plea, "Ah Theo, I wish I were dead," Dreiser was figuratively torn in two. But, resisting the impulse to rush to her rescue, he remained in St. Louis and left her message unanswered. Later he purged himself of the episode in one of his better short stories, "The Second Choice."[12]

Throughout his newspaper career, Dreiser was struck forcefully by the contrast between the truth of life as he daily observed it and the illusion of life he was commanded to report in his articles. Rarely did truth and illusion coincide. Journalism, as he experienced it, was dominated by a "sweetness and light code" which presented the world as a never-land in which sin and shame were reserved exclusively for outcasts, criminals, and vagrants. This distorted representation of life he considered "the trashiest lie that was ever foisted upon an all too human world"; it was diametrically opposed to everything he had witnessed since infancy:

> All men were honest—only they weren't; all women were virtuous and without evil intent or design—but they weren't; all mothers were gentle, self-sacrificing slaves, sweet pictures for song and Sunday Schools—only they weren't; all fathers were kind, affectionate, saving, industrious—only they weren't. But when describing actual facts for the news columns, you were not allowed to indicate these things.[13]

"What a howl," he concluded, would arise should a reporter portray in story or novel a true image of life drawn from his daily observations!

Trapped in an embarrassing coincidence by printing prefabricated critical reviews of three plays which the "lightning of chance" had prevented from arriving in St. Louis on schedule, Dreiser was peremptorily sacked from the *Globe-Democrat;* and, after a proper period of remorse, he was taken on by the *Republic.* This proved a fortunate transfer, for at the *Republic* he encountered H. B. Wandell, whose literary advice was to prove invaluable. Wandell sang the praises of Balzac, a writer of whose existence Dreiser was then oblivious. "Write it strong, clear, definite," urged Wandell, "and remember Zola and Balzac." When Dreiser began to write his novels, they emerged from his pen redolent of Wandell's advice: "bare facts," plus "lots of color as to the scenery or atmosphere, the room, the other people, the street, and all that."

Now to St. Louis came Paul, traveling with a melodrama entitled *The Danger Signal*. The two brothers met for serious talk. What was Theodore doing in St. Louis? New York, that was the only place for a young man of ambition and talent, the one city where men of promise might hope to attain their full intellectual stature. Paul's representation of New York as the heart of the nation's artistic and business life took root, and before long Theodore junked his St. Louis career to set out for the East, working briefly along the way for newspapers in Toledo, Cleveland, Buffalo, Pittsburgh.

Each city provided experiences which further crystallized Dreiser's maturing social views. In Toledo a street-car strike was in progress. Without previous knowledge of the case, he leaped to the workers' defense: "I had seen enough of strikes, and of poverty, and of the quarrels between the money-lords and the poor, to be all on one side." He stored away his memories of the strike and siphoned them fresh and clear from his memory when writing of Hurstwood's decline in *Sister Carrie*. Cleveland's raucous, clattering industrial force, the tremendous steel works rising from a jungle of hovels, exemplified for him an American system which had the "little brain toiling for the big one."

In Buffalo, and particularly in Pittsburgh, this conviction grew; here was beginning a "lawless and savage" era which would see the Rockefellers, Carnegies, Fricks, Vanderbilts, and Goulds "enthroned in our democracy." The city bred multi-millionaires: "on every hand were giants plotting, fighting, dreaming." And in contrast to the mansions of these titans were the most squalid slums he had ever witnessed. How was it, he pondered, that some men might soar the heavens like eagles, while others, sparrows, were permitted to flit about on the lower levels only?

This question intensified as the years passed, and he answered it, at least in part, with his *Trilogy of Desire*, under whose surface these impressions are always visible, providing a sort of backdrop for the *mise en scène* of his story of the financier. But in the newspapers no answers to the paradox of wealth and poverty might be attempted, nor might the wounds be probed.

His editor on the Pittsburgh *Dispatch*, fully aware of which side his bread was buttered on, cautioned emphatically, "Don't touch on labor problems." Anything touching the city's demigods or festering social issues was to be handled with kid gloves. "We don't touch on scandals in high life. The big steel men here just about own the place, so we can't. . . . We have to be mighty careful what we say."[14]

"So much," commented young Dreiser, "for a free press in Pittsburgh, A.D. 1893!"

## X  "A Storm-breeding Mistake"

Dreiser had departed from St. Louis, in spite of his bright plans, heavy with a sense of failure. Perhaps it was his destiny to be "an Ishmael, a wanderer." Other youths seemed immune to the tearing up of roots and to the "jerking about the world" in search of a career that had so far characterized his own young manhood. Was it that others were complacent with less or that they found it easier to hit upon the work best suited to them?

It had been winter when he left Missouri. Now spring had given way to summer. Five months of wandering—Toledo, Cleveland, Buffalo, Pittsburgh—a few weeks here, a month there. And though the odyssey had been of value—more than he could then know—Dreiser was alone, unsure of his direction, and dismayed at his apparent lack of progress. Moreover, he was twenty-one years old and in love. An exchange of sentimental letters between himself and his "western sweetheart" convinced him that before proceeding to New York he ought first to return to St. Louis. Ostensibly the trip was for a reunion with his newspaper cronies (these of scarcely a year's standing, but the only "roots" he had). But actually Dreiser hoped the visit would unite him with Sara White, the girl he adored. The return, like so many youthful attempts to go home again, proved "a most pivotal and deranging thing, probably a great mistake." But at the time it was impossible to see the journey in any such light, for he was caught in the grip of a "chemism" he could neither comprehend nor control.

Dreiser had first met Sara White the previous summer, when the *Republic*, to boost its circulation, promoted a pseudo-popularity contest to determine Missouri's favorite schoolmarms. The votes, naturally, were coupons printed in the St. Louis *Republic*; the prizes, trips to the 1892 Chicago World's Fair. Dreiser, because of his Chicago connections, was assigned to accompany the all-state winners and their chaperones in a private pullman car, to escort them on a tour of the fairgrounds, and to make journalistic capital of their trip by sending back feature articles. He was not particularly anxious to accept the assignment because to him schoolteachers conformed to an unflattering stereotype—"homely and uninteresting"; but since the trip would permit a reunion with those of his family who remained in Chicago and would allow for a bit of puffing to his friends on the *Globe,* he agreed.

Once aboard the train, Dreiser reversed his preconception of the teachers, for most all were amazingly young and spirited, many downright beautiful. From one in particular he found it hard to avert his eyes: "She was in white, with a mass of sunny red hair. Her eyes were almond-shaped, liquid and blue-grey. Her nose was straight and fine, her lips sweetly curved. She seemed bashful and retiring. At her bosom was a bouquet of pink roses."[15] Of course, one of the flowers came loose—or so it appeared as Dreiser told the story in retrospect. Of course, in his concern over the lost blossom, he wound up on the seat beside this vision and she fastened a rose in his buttonhole. They introduced themselves. Mr. Dreiser, Miss White. Her first name? Sara—his mother's name! But everyone called her Sallie, and her school was in a small town not far from St. Louis.

In the days following, squiring Sallie beside the blue lagoons and snowy white buildings of the World's Fair or escaping with her alone to view such Chicago showplaces as the colored fountain erected in Lincoln Park by Charles T. Yerkes, the philanthropist-financier,[16] Theodore perceived in his new fascination a host of her virtues—humor, romance, understanding, patience, sympathy, the very qualities he most required. Their days in Chicago together passed in a euphoria of sightseeing, hand-holding, and tender sentiments: "It was a state of hypnosis, I fancy, in which I felt myself to be rapturously happy because more or less convinced of her feeling for me, and yet gravely uncertain as to whether she would ever permit herself to be ensnared in love. She was so poised and serene, so stable and yet so tender. I felt foolish, unworthy. . . . She seemed too remote, a little unreal."[17]

A good deal more than a holiday romance was in the making; for that fall, when Sallie had returned to her desk, Dreiser wrote to invite her to St. Louis. When she accepted, he walked on air. Always given to extremes in attire, he squandered his savings on a "most *outré*" wardrobe: overlength military coat, broad-brimmed Stetson, pleated shirts. In his yellow-gloved hands, he swung a polished cane as he had seen his brother Paul do. "Gee whiz, Mr. Dreiser!" squealed the pop-eyed office boy at the *Republic* as this splendor swept through the door. Together Sara and Dreiser went to hear Chauncey Olcott, and Dreiser was heartsick at having to send her home by streetcar instead of by the private carriage befitting such perfection.

It was love, no doubt about it; and Dreiser did not descend to earth until it was too late. Marriage was not what he craved, but possession. His "peculiarly erratic and individual" personality prized freedom above all else, and marriage could only lock him in chains which sooner or later would require breaking. It is doubtful whether any woman could have held him solely for herself for long; and, if marriage was the only route to possession, then it is unfortunate that rigidly conventional Sallie White should have become the object of his desire. One life, one love, this was her ideal. First the wooing, then the wedding, this was the pattern she clung to. Two young people more differently constituted would be difficult to imagine. Dreiser realized this, or had strong inklings of it, but not fully enough to dispel the perfumed veils of illusion that hovered about his head like mists on a mountaintop, fogging his vision. "I was as much a victim of passion and romance as she was," he afterward recollected, "only to the two of us it did not mean the same thing."

On his return to Missouri, Dreiser went directly by train to Montgomery City and to the rural home of Sallie's parents. After the teeming steel cities of the East, the simple rusticity of this region stung him with its sense of peace and gracious tradition: "The very soil smacked of American idealism and faith, a fixedness in sentimental and purely imaginative American tradition."

Clearly, Dreiser had no business here; the virtues the Whites held dear were exactly those which he considered outmoded trappings of an unenlightened era, deserving only to be swept away with the times that bred them. Yet he persisted, staying for a number of days, doing his best—and seeing himself all the while as a viper in the bosom of this trusting family—to persuade Sallie to yield. When she held back, he left, determined the romance was ended.

But five years later, having corresponded sporadically with her and wrestled mentally with his own disoriented emotions, Dreiser sent for Sallie, married her in Washington, and brought her to New York as his wife. The question is *why*. She was considerably older than he. His friends and Paul had advised strongly against the match. And he himself was already somewhat aware that "the first flare of love had thinned down to the pale flame of duty." But in love others see more clearly, at least more objectively, than those involved; young lovers only sigh and rejoin, "Ah yes, but this is different." To Dreiser, the ill-starred marriage would afterward stand as a sign of the chemic attractions which govern human actions and through which nature manages always to have her way. The catastrophe, a bitter experience, would find its way to the center of a number of novels and stories, although in later years Dreiser waxed philosophic about it all:

> As I look back on it I can imagine no greater error of mind or temperament than that which drew me to her, considering my own variable tendencies and my naturally freedom-loving point of view. But since we are all blind victims of chance and given to far better hind-sight than fore-sight I have no complaint. It is quite possible that this was all a part of my essential destiny of development, one of those storm-breeding mistakes by which one grows. Life seems thus often casually to thrust upon one an experience which is to prove illuminating or disastrous.[18]

All this is not to say that the marriage proved unhappy from the start; but even granting that both young people made an effort toward harmony, the honeymoon was brief. They were too different, clashed on too many issues of vital moment. Theodore was an artist, or hoped to be; Sallie was philistine to the core. Neither appears to have been in any event an easy person to live with; and with Sallie insisting upon the sanctity and inviolability of monogamous Christian marriage and with Theodore holding to the pagan varietism he had long since adopted, only time staved off the inevitable clash.

## XI   *"Damon Had Met Pythias"*

In his travels eastward from Missouri to New York, Dreiser had augmented his well of memory with a store of incidents and individuals who later might be tapped for fictional purposes. The panorama of American life in a highly formative era had passed before his eyes, some of what he observed being new, some corroborative of impressions formed previously; and he had stumbled onto at least one enduring and influential friendship.

The young editor in Toledo, who hired him for four days' writing, including coverage of the streetcar strike, proved to have a personality so compatible with Dreiser's that Dreiser was led to confess, "If he had been a girl I would have married him." Like Dreiser, Arthur Henry harbored literary ambitions. Dreiser was by this time thinking, albeit timorously, that he might possess talents adaptable to successful playwriting—he had tried his hand at tragic drama while on the St. Louis *Republic*—and Henry aspired to become a novelist, having already written and published a volume of poems. The two men stepped out to lunch, and so intense waxed their "varied and gay exchange of intimacies" that they did not return for three hours. They talked and talked and talked, two young men of intellectual affinity, facing each other as equals. Here at last was someone with whom serious intellectual and literary conversation might be held on some basis other than editor to cub or old hand to neophyte. In Toledo, youth spoke to youth, ambition to ambition. Dreiser thought Henry "wonderful, perfect, great." Henry, in turn, evidently thought enough of the young wandering reporter to suggest that Dreiser be prepared for a telegram calling him back to Toledo should a permanent post on the *Blade* arise.

The job failed to materialize, and Dreiser continued on to New York. Establishing himself in the metropolis was not easy. If his journalistic experiences in St. Louis had impressed him as something of a dog-eat-dog existence, New York was the human jungle magnified ten, fifteen times. To break through the barricades ringing these élite newspaper circles was more arduous than he had imagined—it was a shock to discover that, unlike Chicago or St. Louis or Pittsburgh, in New York one could not get so much as a peek at a city editor, the sanctum sanctorum of these worthies being watchdogged by "supercilious, scoffing" anteroom sentinels. A universal rebuff met all his inquiries. All the same, he was not wholly alone in the city. His sister and her family were residing on Fifteenth Street. Also, Paul, at the height of his fame in musical comedy, had recently become a partner in a promising song publishing venture.

Dreiser was elated when at last he was taken on the staff of Pulitzer's *World*, but his euphoria thinned considerably upon discovering that he was not to be a regular reporter but rather was to be hired on "space," meaning that he would in a sense free-lance and be paid by the column for whatever of his reportage the paper chose to purchase. Depressing as such an appointment was—sometimes the results of his day's work scarcely covered his carfare—the assignments carried him to every corner of the city: the East Side, the Bowery, the Brooklyn waterfront, Wall Street, the Tenderloin, Fifth Avenue. The contrasts of life in Chicago and the steel cities paled beside the spectacle of New York; everywhere his observations of city life were identical: "either a terrifying desire for lust or pleasure or wealth, accompanied by a heartlessness which was freezing to the soul, or a dogged resignation to deprivation and misery."

His dream of becoming a playwright, dormant as it may have been, had never fully deserted him; and he had been doing extensive reading in new-found authors who were to be influential: Balzac, to whose novels he had been introduced in Pittsburgh; Thomas Hardy; and Tolstoi. For the first time Dreiser began to consider the possibility of writing fiction, the short story perhaps. Time was not inuring him to the frustrations of newspaper work—his nature called for some occupation other than this rat race—and there was also the insistent stimulus to set down on paper some of his observations and conclusions about life, not as they had to be muted to suit purveyance by the timid public press but as he honestly felt them: life painted in its bold colors of indifference and injustice. But who would publish such material? Could he possibly be wrong about life? Was it actually as bright and optimistic, as neat and laden with ideals as the magazine writers insisted? He doubted it, was sure it was not. Stronger and stronger grew the need to abandon journalism entirely, to strike out on his own; and if he failed, to salvage the satisfaction of failing on his own terms; and if he succeeded, then to reap the rewards.

Brother Paul came to the rescue as dependably as he had in the past. When his publishers established a new music periodical, *Ev'ry Month*, Theodore was made editor and among the contributors was—no surprise—Arthur Henry of Toledo. Renewing his acquaintance with Dreiser, Henry nagged him to try his hand at fiction, inviting him on a number of occasions to come and stay at his own home if time and solitude were what was required.

The invitation appealed strongly to Dreiser; yet it was not possible to accept until 1899 when he and Sallie went to Ohio to spend the summer. The Henrys occupied a large white Greek revival home, the "House of Four Pillars," which from its high rise overlooked the Maumee River near Toledo. In this idyllic vacation atmosphere the two men, working together, acted as catalysts upon each other, stimulating, criticizing, praising when praise seemed deserved. Under Henry's prodding, Dreiser initiated a series of short stories and was gratified to have some of them accepted for publication. The first, "The Shining Slave Makers,"[19] fittingly portrayed the jungle world of two rival ant colonies involved in bloody conflict to the death. In its demonstration of nature red in tooth and claw and of the preservation of the mass at the expense of the individual, it portrayed a scene and theme Dreiser would handle on innumerable later occasions. Invariably he took his stand with the individual in protesting nature's unjust but omnipotent method for advancing the species. Soon followed "The Door of the Butcher Rogaum" and "Nigger Jeff,"[20] both based upon incidents observed in St. Louis.

Henry, eagerly beginning work on his novel, *A Princess of Arcady,* urged Dreiser to try something in the same form. As Dreiser put it, "He began to ding-dong about a novel. I must write a novel. I must write a novel." And pat as the story sounds, Dreiser insists that to please his friend he sat down one day in September and, choosing a title at random, wrote on a yellow sheet of paper the words *Sister Carrie*—thus turning a new page in American literary history.[21]

## CHAPTER 2

# A Waif Amid Forces:
# *Sister Carrie*

### I *The Mechanism Called Man*

BY THAT SUMMER of 1899 when at age twenty-eight he began his first novel at Arthur Henry's home in Maumee, Theodore Dreiser had matured substantially into the man he was to remain for the rest of his life; he scarcely altered at all except to become more and more emphatically himself. Having observed life at first hand with the eagerness of a young biologist scrutinizing the cadaver of a rare, grotesque specimen, he probed, dissected, analyzed until he emerged with a definite impression as to what constituted life. Like Thoreau—but with immeasurably less premeditation—Dreiser had driven life into a corner, reduced it to its lowest terms, and confronted its essential facts—both of meanness and of sublimity. It is only fair to add at once that, of the two, he saw meanness as prevailing in men's lives—stark as the raw, broad plains on which they dwelt; sublimity, if it existed at all, hovered ephemerally like a range of delectable mountains beyond the horizon.

Now, without ever substantially altering his theories, Dreiser would, decade after decade, book upon book, publish to the world his finding that life at bottom is a tragedy. Beyond this most salient of facts, it was difficult to express exactly what constituted life. It was inexplicable, of course. This granted, it was gigantic, overpowering, dizzying as sound and fury emerging apparently from nowhere, headed nowhere surely, yet thundering brutally on its way with the rage of a trackless locomotive. Life had much to do with "chemisms" and "magnetisms"; it was dominated by invincible material forces; and of these the drives for power, money, and sex were primary.

Man, standing in the eye of the storm, remained the puppet of these forces, a mere wisp in the wind, a leaf on the maelstrom which—through sheer accident, good luck or bad, taking no regard at all of man's puny hopes or efforts—cynically cast a few up and many down, thus producing wild extremes of fortune.

These things Dreiser knew from observation. They were truth incontrovertible. And while one could scarcely hope to analyze and portray such a phenomenon, Dreiser tried. In his deliberate way he worked sporadically for decades on an extensive book of essays in which he hoped to formulate his philosophical views into a meaningful sequence of forty chapters, beginning with "The Mechanism Called the Universe" and ending with "The Problem of Death." At his own death the volume, to be entitled *The Mechanism Called Man*,[1] remained unfinished and unpublished, but it scarcely mattered. Most of what he wanted to say had long since been said, implicitly or explicitly, in his novels. Dreiser's strength never lay in his power of analysis; it was not his method. Even in his non-fiction the intuitive artist in him led to a search for solution in the metaphorical:

> As yet we do not understand life. . . . But we do know that it sings and stings, that it has perfections, entrancements, shames —each according to his blood flux and its chemical character. Life is rich, gorgeous, an opium eater's dream of something paradisical.[2]

> .    .    .    .    .    .    .    .    .    .    .    .

> Life is greater than anything we know.
> It is stronger.
> It is wilder.
> It is more horrible.
> It is more beautiful.[3]

> .    .    .    .    .    .    .    .    .    .    .

> Among the forces which sweep and play throughout the universe, untutored man is but a wisp in the wind.[4]

If this formula we call life could not easily be defined, yet it could be described. And this, beginning with *Sister Carrie*, is what Dreiser set himself to do. His first novel would describe American values for what he had found them to be—materialistic to the core. The money ideal would be exposed as the great motivating purpose of life in the United States: one's relative affluence at any level of society determining the degree of creature comfort one might enjoy, the measure of prestige one might own, the extent of social power one might command. In all of *Sister Carrie* there is not one character whose status is not determined economically; there are few whom possession does not stimulate into ravenous pursuit of even more fulsome wealth.

Step by step, but not too rapidly to consume conspicuously along the trail, individuals claw their way upwards, rising by means fair or foul. With eyes so fixed on mountaintops yet to be attained, they never stop to wonder whether this way madness lies. One summit is reached only to reveal another beckoning ahead, loftier, more magnetic in appeal. And so life passes in a meaningless quest for El Dorado, with perennial dissatisfaction the symptom of the great American disease, and bliss eternally just one more easy step ahead, "up there" where homes are more palatial, clothes more splendid, carriages more sumptuous. Such a climb can lead eventually to nothing but cold, blank stone—as those who eventually possess all they desire come to realize, to their intense bitterness.

These things *Sister Carrie* says about America in a loud, clear voice; and by saying them in 1900 its author could scarcely be courting popularity. The day when a Vance Packard might label us a nation of waste-makers and status-seekers and be lionized for it was in the future, yet Packard's book does no more than underscore the topicality of what *Sister Carrie* revealed sixty years before. A few perceptive critics praised Dreiser's novel; some solid citizens were shocked, or pretended to be shocked by it; and its own publishers did their best to smother it. But it has survived to become an American classic.

## II   *A Young Girl's Odyssey*

The microcosmic quality of *Sister Carrie* anticipates the rest of Dreiser's novels. The basic story is uncomplicated. Three human leaves are caught in the winds of chance and circumstance: one tossed upward toward (but never reaching) fulfillment, another dragged downward to ruin, a third swept along briskly but at a dead level. Of Dreiser's principals, Carrie Meeber begins as "a waif amid forces" and ends as Carrie Madenda, popular favorite of the musical comedy stage; George Hurstwood we meet as the impeccably groomed manager of a prosperous saloon but leave as a ragged, penniless suicide. Charles Drouet, the single minor character whose career the novel spans, both begins and finishes a shallow but congenial salesman, a personality boy; he is so steadily prosperous that he never consciously confronts the forces which shape him.

In 1889, on an afternoon in August, eighteen-year-old Carrie, unencumbered by moral values but "full of the illusions of ignorance and youth," boards the Chicago train in Columbia City, Wisconsin. She possesses her train ticket, four dollars in a yellow leather snap purse, and no idea at all of what she may find to do in the city. She is a modern Dick Whittington with cat tucked under ragged coatsleeve; and, though she does not rise to Lord Mayor, she succeeds far beyond her expectations, and even farther—one is tempted to add—beyond anything her mediocre talents justify.

What happens to a young girl of this type under these circumstances? In the Dreiserian world, she will fall under the sway of the "forces wholly superhuman" which govern life, her overweening drive for self-interest motivating her in every instance, her rise impelled or retarded by her ability to resist any distraction from the main chance. Finally, her success or failure will depend upon the good or bad luck which chance metes out and upon her innate adaptability to new circumstances.

An hour has not passed before Carrie is reacting to these dark, mysterious forces. From the seat behind her, flashily accoutred Charles Drouet initiates a conversation, and although "a certain sense of what was conventional" warns Carrie to remain aloof, the drummer's "magnetism" prevails. Impressed by his purse choked with greenbacks, his new suit and shiny tan shoes, and his general sheen of sophistication, Carrie soon is speaking with Drouet as confidentially as if he were an old family friend. By the time they part on the station platform in Chicago, a date has been tentatively agreed on.

When Carrie arrives at her sister's meager Chicago flat, she feels "cold reality taking her by the hand." We realize by now that a dream of material beauty had prompted her to leave Wisconsin, but that dream, stimulated by Drouet, vanishes at the first grim sight of the Hansons' "lean and narrow life."

Lacking money to supply any but the barest essentials for survival, the Hansons of necessity restrict their activities to the daily cycle of early rising and long, hard hours at the job of keeping body and soul together. They are, in fact, hopefully counting on Carrie to help them make ends meet. None of this is lost on Carrie, who perceives at once the true state of affairs;

for whatever the girl lacks in intellect or experience she more than compensates for with instinct. Just as her brief encounter with Drouet flashed a glimmer of those things she must by some means acquire, she knows at once that the life lived by the Hansons epitomizes a fate she must avoid. Implications hint that Carrie has received none but the most rudimentary home training in social behavior, and so far as moral values are concerned, that training has no salutary effect upon her actions in the world. For all practical purposes, her mind blanked into a *tabula rasa* the moment she entered the Chicago coach, and since then the pencil of experience has been furiously occupied in scribbling upon it the lessons of her observation. Life's contrasts have begun their tutorial process.

A quick learner, Carrie soon knows more specifically what it is she wants from life, and what she wants is heightened by observing the dreariness of states she hopes to avoid. But how to achieve what seem the only worth-while rewards of life? To an unequipped newcomer no route appears open except perhaps that of shop girl at miserable wages: if luck is with her, five dollars a week. Carrie begins her round of job seeking, hopeful but frightened too, in the intimidating brick canyons of Chicago, sleek façades of brass and plate glass behind which lurk golden mysteries of financial conquest. She musters her courage to apply for work, but one cold dismissal follows another. Even the green hope of seeing Drouet withers when he fails to call at her sister's. Carrie is consumed by thoughts of people "counting money, dressing magnificently, and riding in carriages." Each footsore step she takes along the sidewalks of the Loop carries her farther away from this golden vision. Craving pleasure, she is offered misery in its place.

When Carrie does locate work—and she is glad to get it—it is in a shoe factory, operating a punch which cuts eye holes for laces, and is sweatshop labor of grueling hours without rest. Her co-workers disgust her. All are mired in the quicksands of poverty, and in their abandonment of hope she glimpses the specter of her own probable future. With the girls and their cattle-like stoicism Carrie finds nothing in common; the boys, in comparison with her ever more attractive memory of Drouet, seem "uncouth and ridiculous." Worst of all, her wages amount to a scant $4.50 a week, out of which she must pay four dollars board and room to her sister.

When Carrie is in despair because she has lost her job after an illness, by sheer accident she encounters Drouet on Chicago's crowded streets. Out of the sea of faces he appears, takes her by the arm, and ushers her into a splendid dining room for a feast. Sirloin—at a dollar twenty-five a plate! Carrie is overwhelmed. Without question she accepts a "loan" of twenty dollars, "two soft, green ten-dollar bills." All scruples, though she does not yet acknowledge it, are now overruled. Carrie promises to meet her Prince Charming the next morning to shop for new clothes. Now the die is cast. Because the new clothes are much too fine and expensive to be plausibly accounted for, Carrie leaves the Hansons' home in secrecy, a perfunctory note her only farewell, and moves to a room Drouet has taken for his "sister" on Wabash Street. In no time the two of them are sharing a three-room flat in Ogden Place, and Carrie is the proud possessor of all it takes, at this elementary stage, to make her happy: fine clothes, abundant money, and the attention of Drouet, in her eye the capstone of charm, elegant taste, and generosity.

But *Sister Carrie* was not to be a conventional Cinderella tale. The brutal forces governing life dictate that any achievement permitted a human creature be diluted by dissatisfaction. It is the Midas touch at work, drawing its victim imperceptibly nearer disaster. Dreiser once considered titling his novel *The Flesh and The Spirit*; he might equally well have considered *The Unsatisfied,* which states the essence of Carrie's story. Rising to one crest of affluence, man craves more, or something different. It is so in Carrie's case, for contrasts impinge from all sides to stir her into restlessness. A chance encounter with girls from the shoe factory impresses her with the security of the plateau she has reached under Drouet's protection. But this is precisely the thorn that rankles. It *is* a plateau. Carrie by nature is prompted to look upward, forward, never back; and the apparition of heights Drouet cannot possibly attain urges her to reach beyond him.

To climb a ladder, rungs are essential. Dreiser now introduces into Carrie's life the figure of George Hurstwood, manager of Fitzgerald and Moy's saloon. Drouet prides himself on his friendship with Hurstwood, with whom he has become acquainted through his patronage of the saloon. But Hurstwood is a man more successful, more polished, "more clever than Drouet in a hundred ways"; and Carrie, forming her judgments upon material appearance, cannot avoid comparing the two men.

For her, clothes very much make the man: fine suits, linens, shoes—Hurstwood's "were of soft, black calf, polished only to a dull shine. Drouet wore patent leather, but Carrie could not help feeling that there was a distinction in favour of the soft leather, where all else was so rich."[5] Hurstwood invites Drouet and Carrie to see Joseph Jefferson perform in *Rip Van Winkle,* and in the expensive box, surrounded by people of means, with Hurstwood affable, fluent, at ease in this higher realm, it is "driven into Carrie's mind that here was the superior man. She instinctively felt that he was the stronger and higher, and yet withal so simple. By the end of the third act she was sure that Drouet was only a kindly soul, but otherwise defective. He sank at every moment in her estimation by the strong comparison."[6] It is a law of physics that one bucket in the well must go down as the other rises.

Unluckily for Hurstwood, Carrie's rising esteem for him is matched on his part by infatuation. But why—granting the fresh contrast of her beauty with his wife's shrewishness—this untutored country girl with scarcely an idea in her head should so captivate a man of Hurstwood's polish and experience is never satisfactorily explained. Dreiser does not attempt it—he simply informs us it is so. Perhaps he is wise not to try. For Carrie, far from being a breath-taking beauty, has nothing of the siren in her, nor could her background in any sense render her a fit social companion for this sophisticate twenty years her senior. She is innocent of the rudiments of fashion or social etiquette. Her speeches are confined to such profundities as "I know," "I don't know," and, for variation, "I wonder why." But attract Hurstwood she does, and fatally. Such mysteries Dreiser is willing—eager—to attribute to his indefinable, overpowering "magnetisms," chemical affinities which are part and parcel of his vast governing forces.

At the same time, one must grant Carrie credit for doing what little she can to suit herself for Hurstwood. Possessed of a sharp eye, she learns rapidly: from Drouet's comments about other women she discovers a host of detailed refinements concerning dress and demeanor that augment a woman's charm. Carrie's neighbor, Mrs. Hale, plays her part in opening the girl's eyes to the decorum of those towering above her on the social ladder. But even with these considerations it remains difficult on any realistic basis to account for Hurstwood's passion. Better, perhaps, to leave it in Dreiser's terms, the allure of the flame for the moth.

From the beginning, Carrie's life is motivated by strong desires for security, for wealth (and particularly clothes, wealth's emblem), and for pleasure. The first of these she has achieved through Drouet, but his removal of her fears of poverty ironically leaves Carrie free to dwell upon her other desires. Drouet also has given her money, as much as is essential, and clothes suitable to her position. Yet in riding out with Mrs. Hale north along Lake Michigan toward Evanston and in witnessing the mansions there, some private carriages, with footmen, the broad lawns, the rich interiors glowing with lamps, Carrie's unsatisfied yearnings rise again. "She was perfectly certain that there was happiness. If she could but stroll up yon broad walk, cross that rich entrance-way . . . oh! how quickly would sadness flee."[7] This invariably is Carrie's lot—a plaintive reaching out for the will-o'-the-wisp of lasting happiness and final satisfaction.

In appeasing Carrie's yearning for pleasure, Drouet fails dismally. And what is pleasure? Material comforts, of course. Beyond that, entertainment, stimulating companionship. Above all, variety. This last need Drouet fails even to perceive. He leaves Carrie too often and for too long alone, allowing her time to think and to brood. Drouet's little apartment, after her cot at the Hansons, had once seemed elegance itself. Now, in contrast to what she has glimpsed of the life enjoyed by the wealthy, it pales into "comparative insignificance." She is ripe for change, awaiting only a "magnet," a lightning stroke of chance, to draw her away from Drouet as Drouet drew her from her sister's. This becomes Hurstwood's function; and he, a dupe of fate, sacrifices himself in the process.

### III  *"The Idea of Hurstwood"*

It is not uncommon to speak of *Sister Carrie* as a love story; but although the surface events of the novel appear to parallel those of many a tale of passion, love as it is conventionally understood plays no genuine role in Carrie's life. Other needs, other drives are too all-consuming. She feels affection, tenderness even, but her heart never rules her head. Whatever element of love or passion is involved in the novel is furnished by Hurstwood, who finds himself more and more deeply enmeshed.

A man of forty, married to a shrew, father to two indifferent and insufferably snobbish children (the entire family, very like Carrie, is crazy for wealth and status), Hurstwood—when he meets Carrie—stands at the apex of his career, solidly established in a fine position, an esteemed member of monied circles "the first grade below the luxuriously rich." He has (considering Carrie's inability to love) little to gain and a whole world to lose. Dreiser was interested always in the power of society to mold, to create, or to smash at will. Often in his fictional works the fragility of the human position is treated, but never more pointedly than in his description of Hurstwood's fall. Forgetting the vulnerability of a man his age, in his position, Hurstwood imagines himself the youth of twenty years past, free to court the object of his passion openly. "A man can't be too careful" had in former days been his usual remark to express a lack of sympathy for compatriots who slipped and were trapped by their mistakes.

Now Hurstwood, blinded by his passion for Carrie, throws caution to the winds and makes his own fatal mistakes. Unknowingly, he is seen at McVickar's Theater with Carrie and Drouet. He is spied riding in an open carriage with Carrie. Attending an amateur theatrical in which Carrie participates, he rashly explains his wife's absence by insisting she is too ill to attend. Her husband's indiscretions being duly reported to Mrs. Hurstwood, there follow rapidly vehement accusations on her part, an inept handling of the situation on his, and ultimately a scandalous suit for divorce.

The solution to Hurstwood's predicament occurs in an action of the most crucial relevance. In dramatizing man's ultimate helplessness against the forces which prod him, Dreiser's handling of the theft at Fitzgerald and Moy's ranks among the half-dozen most telling scenes in all his work. This incident was so pertinent to his philosophy of life that with variations it was used again twenty-five years later at the heart of *An American Tragedy.* A perfectly balanced combination of motive and accident leads Hurstwood into perpetration of the crime whose result will be his own destruction. "When Waters Engulf Us We Reach For A Star," the label Dreiser employs for this episode, expresses epigrammatically the clouding of vital self-interest in moments of panic by any apparent solution that suggests itself. For the moment, illusion overwhelms reality. A man takes one false step and his life is forfeit—the way of the transgressor.

Intensely motivated by anger and by the impending notoriety which threatens to cost him his managerial position, Hurstwood's balance is lost. Alone, he is closing his saloon for the night, dreading the next day when his wife's lawyers threaten to file suit in court. How will his employers react? Will he lose his family, his property, his position—and, because of these, Carrie as well?

By accident the bar's safe has been left unlocked. Hurstwood glances idly inside. Ten thousand dollars in ready money. He removes the bills, then puts the money back, paces about the room, his brain afire. "Surely no harm could come from looking at it!" He takes the money from the safe again, decides he will abscond with it: "Why, he could live quietly with Carrie for years." He goes so far as to stuff the money into his hand satchel, bills and loose change alike. No! Scandal, the police, himself a fugitive from justice! Prison bars! Faced by such prospects, he recoils, self-interest reasserting itself. He lays the money back in the safe, is about to snap the door shut when he realizes the bills and change have been replaced in the wrong boxes. He lifts the boxes out and shifts their contents. While the money is in his hand, the lock clicks. "It had sprung. Did he do it?"

Now panic takes over. As inept in covering his "crime" as Clyde Griffiths would be twenty-five years later in *An American Tragedy,* he rushes to Carrie's flat; on the pretext that Drouet has been hurt, he persuades her to board a train with him. The next morning they are in Montreal. But so, almost at once, is a detective hired by Hurstwood's employers. Within a few days, Hurstwood has been intimidated into returning all but $1,300; in exchange, Fitzgerald and Moy agree not to prosecute. With this remnant, he and Carrie—she oblivious to theft and reparation alike—board the train for New York.

From this climactic episode, the novel chronicles the steady decline of Hurstwood and the corresponding rise of Carrie. The tone is set at once:

> Whatever a man like Hurstwood could be in Chicago, it is very evident that he would be but an inconspicuous drop in an ocean like New York. . . . The sea was already full of whales. A common fish must needs disappear wholly from view—remain unseen. In other words, Hurstwood was nothing.[8]

Whether it is true that Hurstwood dominates *Sister Carrie,* stealing the thunder from the title character, is a matter of dispute which cannot be settled except by personal taste. Surely Dreiser does document the man's fall in long and infinitely detailed sequence, yet it is precisely through this extended contrast that a reader sees both Carrie and Hurstwood in a more clearly defined light. They serve each other as foils. Both are walking the high wire in this precarious, material world: one looks down and loses his balance, the other keeps her eyes on the tether ahead.

Hurstwood retrenches. Instead of battling to rise, he gazes back upon the ruin of his previous career and, obsessed with all he has forfeited, strives only to safeguard his reduced position against further loss. In this fight, luck turns against him. When he invests his capital in a saloon partnership, the building in which he holds his lease is sold to make room for a new edifice.

Stranded without funds, he hunts for employment as manager, then as clerk, finally as anything he can obtain. It is a winter of mass unemployment, and the search proves futile. His self-confidence deteriorates like a sand castle in the rain. He withdraws farther from the battleground of economic life, his natty appearance by degrees becoming untidy, then slovenly. He and Carrie move to ever tackier quarters. He resorts to gambling, forgetting that in former years he played for his own amusement —a vastly different position from playing in desperate hopes of winning enough for subsistence. Soon, of the seven hundred dollars he possessed when his saloon closed, only the dregs remain. The handwriting on the wall has long since been evident.

Carrie, convinced she has recklessly immolated herself by sticking with her lover through his long dark jobless months, grows irritable. When it is clear the man's money is all but exhausted, she puts her clever mind to work, recalls the amateur dramatics which afforded her a moderate success in Chicago, makes the rounds of the theaters, and at last locates an inconspicuous position in a musical comedy chorus. Before long, she has, through good luck, become the breadwinner; Hurstwood remains at home unshaven to do the chores, shop for groceries, squabble with the butcher, pay the coal man. Carrie senses a trap analogous to that which in Chicago had threatened to doom her to the shoe factory and life with the Hansons; and her escape is similarly managed. One evening Hurstwood returns from tramping the streets to find a brusque note:

> I'm going away. I'm not coming back any more. It's no use trying to keep up the flat; I can't do it. I wouldn't mind helping you, if I could, but I can't support us both, and pay the rent.

I need what little I make to pay for my clothes. I'm leaving twenty dollars. It's all I have just now. You can do whatever you like with the furniture. I don't want it.[9]

The denouement of Dreiser's story follows Carrie and Hurstwood to the logical dead ends of their respective routes. For Hurstwood there is an accelerated lapse into beggary, his total abandonment by the life-force, a final "What's the use?" as he opens the gas jets in a fifteen-cent flophouse, and eventually a plot in Potter's Field—an unmourned, nameless hulk whom luck deserted and chance denied.

As for Carrie, she "found her purse bursting with good green bills of comfortable denominations.[10] . . . She could look about on her gowns and carriage, her furniture and bank account."[11] Gone are the days when she sat in her rocking chair and dreamed "Ah money, money, money! What a thing to have. How plenty of it would clear away all these troubles." She has reached the bucket at the end of her rainbow—and found it empty; the baubles which so recently seemed essential are "now grown trivial and indifferent." Drouet, reintroduced, is unchanged, still selling, still prosperous, still chasing skirts. Carrie dismisses him, puzzling as to what she could ever have seen in him to begin with. She has changed, but exactly in what way is unclear. The road ahead is dim. Another man, Bob Ames, an engineer, has "pointed out a farther step," the possibility of a career in straight dramatic roles. Somehow, somewhere, there must be more to life than Carrie has so far tasted, things to be had beyond "the tinsel and shine of her state" that will bring her to final happiness. She struggles to know what they might be and how she may attain fulfillment.

## IV  Rocking to Dreamland

Throughout *Sister Carrie*, Dreiser employs the rocking chair to symbolize the restlessness, the feverish activity which transports Carrie to no satisfying destination. At her sister's flat she had rocked by the window, dreaming of escape with Drouet from the humdrum life of West Van Buren Street. As Drouet's mistress in Ogden Place, she sat in her rocker hungering after luxury, refinement, applause. Living with Hurstwood in New York, she sits rocking to and fro, thinking how "commonplace" her pretty flat is compared with "what the rest of the world was enjoying"—

*the rest of the world* obviously applying to the only ones who matter, those in better circumstances than she. For Carrie always anticipates, discarding and leaving behind her like a locust husk whatever has served its purpose and is no longer of use.

By way of contrast, Hurstwood, after losing his saloon, resorts to the rocking chair merely to brood over days gone by, positions lost, strength waned, funds exhausted. In the steady ebb and flow of the chair's repeated motion, he finds an opium dream of security.

Our last view of Carrie is appropriate. Rocking in her chair, successful but unhappy, accomplished but unfulfilled, she dreams of further conquests which will—*must*—bring her lasting joy; yet she is driven to acknowledge for the first time that happiness may possibly never be for her, that perhaps her fate is "forever to be the pursuit of that radiance of delight which tints the distant hilltops of the world." In Dreiser's universe, life takes on the aspect of "a fierce, grim struggle in which no quarter was either given or taken, and in which all laid traps, lied, squandered, erred through illusion." And even those who survive the struggle to become king of the hill are left without trophy.

Carrie has arrived in her quest at the empty terminal which, Dreiser points out, so many Americans finally reach, particularly those who clamber up from lowly beginnings and are hoodwinked by the life about them into believing the money ideal to be all in all:

> Unfortunately the money problem, once solved, is not the only thing in the world. Their lives, although they reach to the place where they have gold signs, automobiles and considerable private pleasures, are none the more beautiful. Too often, because of these early conditions, they remain warped, oppressive, greedy and distorted in every worthy mental sense by the great fight they have made to get their money.
> Nearly the only ideal that is set before these strugglers . . . is the one of getting money. A hundred thousand children . . . are inoculated in infancy with the doctrine that wealth is all—the shabbiest and most degrading doctrine that can be impressed upon anyone.[12]

Carrie cannot escape her lot. By her adoption of the illusory values of the social system that she enters when she boards the Chicago train, she becomes fully as much a victim as Hurstwood. Their bankruptcies differ only in kind, and Carrie's is by far the more ironical. It is a pure case of "winner take nothing" which Dreiser would pound home strongly in novels yet to come.

## V "Madame Bovary—c'est moi"—Flaubert

From what casting bureau did Dreiser obtain the principal actors for this story? Much has been written concerning the use of his sisters as models, and surely, considering their craving for adulation, their love of finery, their starvation for material possessions, and their numerous love affairs, any one of them could have suggested a good deal of Carrie. But accepting as typical the one sister's ready admission that her principal interests focused on "clothes and men," Dreiser has curiously failed to combine these twin drives in Carrie until we realize that, in his eyes, just as marriage burdened a man with hostages to fortune, sex for a woman was a trap in which the loving were altogether at the mercy of the loved. His sisters had suffered mightily in this respect, infatuation being the Achilles heel through which, in affairs of the heart, they were repeatedly victimized. Dreiser would dramatize this aspect of his sisters' lives, but not through Carrie. Had Carrie ever truly fallen in love, her fortress of self-interest would have weakened disastrously; its walls, once breached, would have crumbled to rubble. Accordingly, in Carrie the sex drive is—if not wholly nonexistent—subordinated.

On the other hand, the sisters' yearning for clothes Dreiser does make central to his book; Carrie's acute sensitivity to apparel is underscored in the first chapter when Drouet's showy garments impress her sufficiently to break down whatever reserve she feels about conversing with male strangers. Alongside Drouet's finery, her own respectable but plain blue dress seems shabby, her shoes worn. By his clothes alone Drouet is made master of the situation. Clothes to Carrie remain direct, tangible representations of her desires for material comfort, wealth, and power.

Job hunting, Carrie inquires after positions in Chicago department stores where she wanders spellbound through Elysian acres of finery—a wonderland of dainty slippers, stockings, delicate skirts and petticoats, laces, ribbons, purses; and simultaneously she senses every shop girl's eyes ridiculing "her individual shortcomings of dress." Contrast of apparel is also the first step in her rejection of Drouet in favor of Hurstwood. And in New York, strolling down Broadway for the first time with her sophisticated friend, Mrs. Vance, Carrie feels "stared at and ogled. . . . on parade in a show place—and such a show place!" "She could only imagine that it must be evident to many that she was the less handsomely dressed of the two. It cut her to the quick, and she resolved that she would not come here again until she looked better."[13]

As Hurstwood's fine clothes had influenced her initial estimate of the man, so the degeneration of his outward appearance parallels her gradual rejection of him during his economic decline. Sartorially perfect, he is a god; unkempt, he is a tramp. Only at the novel's denouement when, having been granted the coveted Midas touch, Carrie finds herself satiated with finery and display, does it begin to dawn upon her that clothes have been a mirage.

When fashioning Carrie, Dreiser appears to have made particular use of an older sister's story, though solely for the bare bones of the plot. This girl had come to Chicago and lived for a time with an architect; but, falling in love with a man fifteen or more years her senior, the manager of Hannah and Hogg's restaurant, she eloped with him. The manager embezzled fifteen thousand dollars from his employers and took the girl, by way of Toronto, to New York, where they lived together on Fifteenth Street, Dreiser visiting them there in the early 1890's.[14] In most basic respects, this story provided an outline for *Sister Carrie;* where Dreiser departs from fact, the changes are significant. Unlike Carrie, his sister was the ultimate victim in the affair, tied to circumstances in which her husband experienced a tumble comparable to Hurstwood's, flagrantly betrayed her with other women, then all but deserted her. The couple produced two children, to whose survival the sister was chained. In contrast, though Carrie for nearly five years is mistress to ardent males, she bears no children. It is not as if Carrie were explicitly presented as barren; the novel contains not the slightest implication that offspring might be a possible result of such unions. Unrealistic as it may be, this procreative immunity is in harmony with Carrie's asexuality, with her use of men, not as love-objects, but as the most logical stepping stones toward her real goals. More important, being childless, her self-interest remains unimpaired; and it allows her creator to display her even more patently for what she is: a human bark single-mindedly impelled by winds of vanity toward an illusory harbor.

Dreiser points out that Drouet is "a type of the travelling canvasser for a manufacturing house," but the traits with which he endows his salesman are those of Bill Yakey, his roommate in Bloomington:

> Good clothes, of course, were the first essential, the things without which he was nothing. A strong physical nature, actuated by a keen desire for the feminine, was the next. A mind free of any consideration of the problems or forces of the world and actuated not by greed, but an insatiable love of variable pleasure. His method was always simple. Its principal element was daring, backed, of course, by an intense desire and admiration for the sex.[15]

In Dreiser's rooming house, Drouet-Yakey had sat for his portrait many times. The future writer had observed this handsome, devil-may-care paragon in innumerable attitudes: choosing from his bottomless trunk of clothes the proper raiment for conquest; energetically exercising his well-knit body, even coercing his spindly roommate into calisthenics; boasting with every other breath of his irresistible appeal to women. Since college Dreiser had often been reintroduced to Yakey in the persons of reporters in Chicago and in St. Louis, so that in writing *Sister Carrie* he had merely to alter the man's occupation—which never is of moment in the novel—to produce his lusty "masher" in full perspective.

Dreiser knew Hurstwood less from particular experience than from a general observation of both affluence and poverty. Surely Hurstwood, as a reader first sees him, is one type of man Dreiser had every opportunity to observe—the highly polished, successful, socially prominent man of the upper middle class. He is exactly the kind of man to catch the curious, admiring eye of an ambitious young cub who felt himself unjustly lacking —for the present, at least—in status, but who would question constantly: How did this man rise? How might I match his level of success?

Of fallen men Dreiser was even more pointedly informed, having not only the ineradicable memory of his own father's fortuitous ruin to draw upon, but scores of similar cases he had observed in his travels and journalistic work. In St. Louis there had been Clark of the *Republic,* a capable-looking man with "something of the manager or owner or leader about him"; but a man, if one judged by the positions he had formerly held, already on the way down. Within a period of a few short months Clark, through drink, completed his tumble; and, when Dreiser met him again in the gin-mill and tenement section of the city, he did not recognize the face behind the "short, matted, dirty black beard." Clark's natty appearance had disintegrated (like Hurstwood's): his hat looked as if it had "been lifted out of an ash-barrel," his clothes and shoes were filthy, and his ragged coat "was marked by a greenish slime across the back and shoulders, slime that could only have come from a gutter." He had been in the hospital with pneumonia (like Hurstwood) and was now reduced to begging (like Hurstwood). So shaken was Dreiser by the encounter that he hastened to seek the civility of the lobby of the Southern Hotel in order to shake off "that sense of failure and degradation which had crept over me."[16]

Shortly before writing *Sister Carrie,* Dreiser had completed an article for *Demorest's* magazine, "Curious Shifts of the Poor,"[17] which vividly pictured the breadlines and bedlines to which Hurstwood resorts in his indigence. The Toledo streetcar strike which had so moved Dreiser was trotted out, refurbished, and transported to New York so that Hurstwood might figure in it. In his autobiography, Dreiser recalls the precise crystallizing stimulus for this character.

During those first days in New York Dreiser's spirits were at low ebb. An accumulation of discouragements plagued him. He was jobless, disillusioned with the journalistic world which had in no wise lived up to his colorful expectations, disheartened at the icy reception which greeted his hunting a position with the local newspapers, further jarred by the intensified "every man for himself" pace of life in the metropolis, struck anew by the fragility of the lines separating triumph from ruin, and alarmed lest he himself be doomed to be "an Ishmael, a wanderer." In such a mood, Dreiser strayed down toward City Hall Park, a drain where the dregs of the social system collected:

> About me on the benches of the park was, even in this gray, chill December weather, that large company of bums, loafers, tramps, idlers, the flotsam and jetsam of the great city's whirl and strife to be seen there today. I presume I looked at them and then considered myself and these great offices, and it was then

that the idea of *Hurstwood* was born. . . . I turned my steps
northward along the great, bustling, solidly commercial Broadway
to Fifteenth Street, walking all the way and staring into the
shops. Those who recall *Sister Carrie's* wanderings may find a
taste of it here.[18]

The despair which drove Hurstwood to his dark finish was not
unknown to Dreiser, "a guy with a total of 15 cents left," whose
wife had returned to Missouri to live with her parents and whose
pride and anger had reduced him to a state where he had
"*cursed* life and gone down to the East River from a $1.50 a
week room in Brooklyn to a canal dock to quit."[19]

But much as Dreiser drew upon his observations in creating
the *dramatis personae* of *Sister Carrie,* the personages derive
largely from Dreiser himself, each depicting a separate facet
of the writer's own nature. Thus Drouet is endowed with the
personality traits Dreiser most envied in others and coveted for
himself—the easy poise, firm assurance, happy-go-lucky nature,
freedom from moral inhibition. Drouet's unshakable confidence
in his ability to succeed means that he rarely is occupied in self-
analysis, indeed in any mental concern transcending the
immediate moment. Neither brooding over the past nor scaring
himself with thoughts of the imponderable future, he is a free
creature, an opportunist. If Drouet will never move upward
appreciably, he will always remain the unruffled master of the
present, will always "make the grade." Had Dreiser been born
with this man's immunity from inhibition and concern for the
forces that mockingly pull the strings backstage of life, he would
have counted himself the most fortunate of mortals.

Conversely, Hurstwood dramatizes Dreiser's ambitions and
fears. If Drouet is what Dreiser yearned to be in personality,
Hurstwood bestrides the economic levels Dreiser was groping
to achieve. At the same time he is everything Dreiser most
feared to become: a total failure, a man whom frivolous chance
had spurned and society condemned. Of Clark he had wondered,
"Could people really vary so greatly and in so short a time?
What must be the nature of their minds if they could do that?
Was mine like that? Would it become so?" Into Dreiser's already
dark broodings, failure cast large and more terrifying shadows.
The specter of Hurstwood was his companion, in one guise or
another, throughout his life; Hurstwood pointed always to the
"way of the transgressor"[20] of established codes.

Above all, Dreiser mirrors himself in Carrie. A number of parallels are apparent at once, beginning with their sharing the same birth date, 1871. Carrie arrives in Chicago late in the summer of 1889, cutting her ties with home and past. This corresponds with Dreiser's arrival in the city from Bloomington and the subsequent loss of his mother, the one stabilizing influence on his family, after whose death he was permanently on his own. Both he and Carrie are eighteen when this decisive break with the family occurs. Carrie's father is a miller, as was Dreiser's, a fact the novel mentions but once, and then only in passing. Carrie's mother is never specifically described. For all the thought Carrie gives her parents or the connection she retains with them, they might as well be dead or irrevocably estranged, as were Dreiser's.

The reversals by which Dreiser instinctively clouds the autobiographical origin of his heroine are simple, direct, and easily noted. The boy Theodore is first transvested into the girl Carrie. Then his residence is shifted to Wisconsin so that Carrie's entry into Chicago may be effected from the northwest to contrast with Dreiser's southeasterly journey from Indiana. These reversals accomplished, Carrie's aspirations and experiences parallel those of her author, albeit from the feminine point of view. Dreiser interestingly sticks to fact in providing for his heroine's needs. In her purse Carrie has four dollars; when he first came to Chicago alone, Dreiser had six (out of which was deducted $1.75 for his fare). Carrie's wonder and bewilderment at the city itself, her growing fear of inadequacy in the face of the savage competition for employment, her labored search for a job, the repeated blows to her ego until she is overjoyed to accept any work at all, her disparagement of her co-workers at the shoe factory, as Dreiser had disparaged his at the hardware concern—these superficial parallels are numerous.

We might add and add, citing direct correspondence between Carrie's apartments in Chicago and New York and addresses where Dreiser himself had resided,[21] her interest in theatricals so obviously suggested by Dreiser's experience as a drama critic and the knowledge of show business made available to him by Paul, his use of the Toledo streetcar strike from his newspaper days, and Carrie's instinctive leaving of notes (to her sister and Hurstwood) to avoid face-to-face confrontation in difficult farewells, resembling Dreiser's desertion of Lois Zahn when he left Chicago for St. Louis.

These are parallels which would lack pertinence were it not that interiorly the two people resemble each other so profoundly. "No common girl am I" is Carrie's dominant thought, seldom verbalized but inexorably motivating. Carrie's hopes are young Dreiser's hopes, her admirations his, her experiences in essence his, her frustrations his. Young Dreiser dreamed of "fame, applause, power"; his heroine dreams of "scenes of luxury and refinement, situations in which she was the cynosure of all eyes, the arbiter of all fates."

Carrie's reliance upon clothes as a yardstick for measuring worth and attainment is surely Dreiser's own, though by 1899 he was wise enough to recognize the inevitability with which such criteria lead to the blank wall Carrie faces at the novel's end. But Carrie's life is far from finished at that point. We might say it has only begun. She stands poised on the threshold of change. What and where are undetermined, but whatever path she choses in her quest for ultimate happiness must transcend the purely material; for she is beginning to see that she has chased the horizon in her rocking chair. "The world which Hurstwood and Drouet represented no longer allured her. . . . though often disillusioned, she was still waiting for that halcyon day when she should be led forth among dreams become real."[22]

We leave Carrie where we properly should, on the brink of the immense and soul-rending discovery that she, no less than George Hurstwood, has been made the victim of the American system. It would be a mistake, though an understandable one, for Carrie—or her readers—to believe that she has charted her own course; for Dreiser warns that "the illusion of the self-made is one of the greatest of all."[23] Carrie is Carrie still, a waif amid forces, enticed into the quicksands of materialism by "mirages of success that hang so alluringly in amethyst skies!"

CHAPTER *3*

# The Washerwoman's Daughter:
# *Jennie Gerhardt*

### I   *"'Tis a Sad Story, Mates"*

NOT FOR A DECADE after *Sister Carrie* did Dreiser publish another novel, the most compelling reason for this long silence being his disheartenment over the suppression of his first. American letters, as the twentieth century dawned, were still mired hand and foot in the tarpits of nineteenth-century gentility. Realists—and naturalists in particular—had a hard row to hoe against William Dean Howells' dictum that Americans by nature should be expected to portray the sunny side of life and publish for public consumption nothing which could not be "openly spoken of before the tenderest society bud at dinner."[1]

Popular writers of the era, novelists like the Reverend Harold Bell Wright and Mrs. Gene Stratton Porter (a fellow Hoosier against whose astronomical sales records Dreiser's old Warsaw neighbors assessed his relative literary insignificance) dominated the best-seller lists with tales in which virtue was its own defense, truth crushed to earth was bound to rise again, and life generally was characterized by swift administration of poetic justice.[2] Stories hinting that the wages of sin might be success or the way of the transgressor denuded of thorny retribution were perhaps compatible with the jaded palates of a decadent European audience whose corrupt appetites glutted on Balzac and Zola, but Americans wanted it made clear that life this side of the Atlantic thrived on fresher, purer, more wholesome fare.

In this atmosphere *Sister Carrie,* glorifying a heroine who sinned and prospered, seemed a calculated affront to public morals; it was not to be condoned. The account of the book's suppression, told and retold, varies in its details according to the teller; but Dreiser's own version, surely no less reliable than another, does double service by casting substantial light on the literary situation then prevailing:

I took the book to Doubleday, Page & Co. At that time Doubleday had newly parted from McClure and had employed Frank Norris as a reader of manuscripts. It was Norris who first read the book. He sent for me and he told me quite enthusiastically that he thought it was a fine book, and that he was satisfied that Doubleday would be glad to publish it. . . . About a week or ten days later I had a letter from Walter H. Page, the late ambassador, who asked me to call. And when I came he congratulated me on the character of the work and announced that it was to be accepted for publication, and that he would send me a contract which I was to sign. Also, because he appeared to like the work very much, he announced that no pains would be spared to launch the book properly, and that—(the glorious American press agent spirit of the day, I presume)—he was thinking of giving me a dinner, to which various literary people would be invited in order to attract attention to the work and to me.

. . . Frank Doubleday, the head of the house, was in England at the time. In my absence he returned and hearing, as I was afterwards informed, that the book was much thought of, decided to read it or, at least, have it read for himself. Accordingly . . . he took the book home and gave it to his wife. Being of a conventional and victorian turn, I believe—(I have always been told so)—she took a violent dislike to the book and proceeded to discourage her husband as to its publication. He in turn sent for me and asked me to release him from the contract which had already been signed. . . . And Doubleday finding that I wished to stand by the contract, announced very savagely one day that he would publish the book but that was all he would do. I returned to Norris, who said in substance—"Never mind. He'll publish it. And when it comes out I'll see that all the worthwhile critics are reached with it."

. . . When the book came out Norris did exactly as he said. He must have written many letters himself for I received many letters commenting on the work and the resulting newspaper comment was considerable. However, as Mr. Thomas McKee, who was then the legal counsel for Doubleday afterwards told me, Doubleday came to him and wanted to know how he could be made safe against a law suit in case he suppressed the book— refused to distribute or sell any copies. And McKee advised him

that he could not be made safe—that I had rights under the
contract which would be enforced by me if I were so minded.
Nevertheless, as he told me, Doubleday stored all of the 1,000
copies printed—minus three hundred distributed by Norris—in
the basement of his Union Square plant, and there they remained
. . . until 1905.

. . . At the time of my last conversation with Frank Doubleday
I referred to the fact that not only Norris but Mr. Page was
heartily for the book, and that Mr. Page had told me that
not only would he be pleased to publish the book but that he
had proposed . . . getting up a dinner for me. This seemed
to irritate Doubleday not a little, and walking into the next room
where Page was sitting at the time at his desk, and asking me
to follow him, he said, "Page, did you say to Mr. Dreiser that
you really like this book very much and that you intended to
make a stir about it and give him a dinner?" And Mr. Page
calmly looked at me in the eye and replied, "I never said anything of the kind."

He was a man of about forty-five years of age, I should have
said, at that time. I was just twenty-nine and not a little overawed
by editors and publishers in general. In consequence, although
I resented this not a little, I merely got up and walked out.[3]

Others have pointed out that perhaps Dreiser's admitted resentment may have colored his later recollection of the episode, and
surely his correspondence with the publisher reveals that he was
aware for some time that the company might be reluctant to
publish the novel, that he had, in fact, suggested to Arthur
Henry that the manuscript be submitted elsewhere secretly in
case Doubleday, Page & Company chose to back out of the
agreement. Page himself had written of dissatisfaction, criticizing
the mention of real names and places and the choice of characters, whom he found not the kind of people to "interest the
great majority of readers." Although he found much to praise,
he advised finally that *Sister Carrie* was "not the best kind of
book for a young author to make his first book."

Notwithstanding Dreiser's having been given advance warning,
to suggest that he was disappointed at the publisher's action
is an understatement; he was staggered. Sharply as his newspaper days had alerted him to the timidity of the American
press, he received a severe jolt to find censorship so blatantly
operative in the field of fiction as well. Now began his long
warfare with the censors. It was to endure, hot and cold, the

rest of his life; and his vigorous, aggressive fulminations against
self-appointed watchdogs of the nation's bookshelves played a
considerable role in an eventual breakthrough into the permis-
siveness characteristic of American writing in midcentury. When
on the offensive, he rarely minced words:

> We run with the pack. Some mountebank Simon in art, literature,
> politics, architecture, cries "thumbs up," and up goes every
> blessed thumb from the Atlantic to the Pacific. Then some other
> pseudo-ratiocinating ass calls "thumbs down," and down go all
> thumbs—not a few, but all. Let a shyster moralist cry that
> Shakespeare is immoral and his plays are at once barred from all
> the schools of a dozen states. Let a quack nostrum peddling zany
> declare that the young must not be contaminated, and out go all
> the works of Montagne *[sic]*, Ibsen, Hauptmann, Balzac, on the
> ground, forsooth, that they will injure the young. Save the
> sixteen year old girl, if you must make mushheads and loons,
> absolute naturals, of every citizen from ocean to ocean.[4]

Dreiser's protests against suppression of his novel having
produced no perceptible effect, *Sister Carrie* remained in
quarantine in Doubleday, Page's basement. Its author was
destitute, intensely moody, broken in spirit. There was no money
to live on; and Sallie, partly in consequence of the financial
straits but also because the honeymoon fires no longer flared
with any brilliance, returned to Missouri until her husband
could establish himself. But Theodore sank even deeper into
despair, existing alone in a tiny tenement room and contemplating suicide before the nervous breakdown he was enduring was
recognized for what it was. At the timely intervention of Paul,
the Egdon Reddleman of the Dreiser family, there followed a
period of months at a "rest camp," then a stint of physical
labor on the railroad—occupational therapy aimed at restoring
body and mind.[5]

As soon as he felt able to resume the literary life, Dreiser
realized he must act to settle the most agonizing conflict that
can afflict a producing writer. On the one hand, he might write
to please himself alone. He could turn out manuscripts which
depicted life according to the naked truth as he saw it. But
even supposing he located a courageous publisher, to so defy
current literary convention was only to invite a repetition of the
*Sister Carrie* debacle. On the other hand, he might join the

pack, give the public the sugar nostrums it craved, and make a fast, determined drive for the quick dollar.

Rarely has a writer been presented with more clear-cut alternatives. Dreiser's passion for truth, coupled with his contempt for the nauseous falsifications of life typical in the fiction of his day, militated strongly in favor of preserving his literary integrity. But his desperate psychic need for security and status was more overpowering. He hesitated only briefly at this crossroad, then made an arbitrary choice. He would go for the main chance.

Unless he were allowed to write about life truthfully, he preferred not to write at all. Instead, he would edit and market the writing of others. In this way, his own immediate need might be satisfied, while the public would continue to be given the dreams it demanded. What seemed at the time a tenable solution to Dreiser's dilemma was, fortunately for American letters, to prove only briefly feasible.

Having reached his decision, Dreiser encountered no difficulty in establishing himself solidly in the magazine field.

In 1904 he went to work for Street and Smith, publishers of dime novels. The next year he rose to the editorship of the company's new *Smith's Magazine*; in 1906 he moved to the *Broadway Magazine* at a very respectable sixty-five dollars a week. His remarkable success with these periodicals led to an invitation to supervise the Butterick publications, a combine of three magazines at that time constituting a minor empire in the field, the *Delineator* being placed under his direct editorship. In a word, he had arrived.

At $7,000 a year, Dreiser's financial worries seemed a thing of the past. He was well on his way to becoming an influence to be reckoned with. Strangely—and yet understandably, too, considering his bitter experience with *Sister Carrie* and the paralyzing dread of poverty he could never slough off—upon accepting this responsibility, Dreiser fell temporarily into lock step with the genteel tradition. He set a policy for his magazines that stood in obvious contradiction to his personal belief and practice:

> We cannot admit stories which deal with false or immoral relations or which point a false moral, or which deal with things degrading, such as drunkenness. I am personally opposed in this magazine to stories which have an element of horror in them,

or which are disgusting in their realism and fidelity to life. The finer side of things—the idealistic—is the answer for us, and we find really splendid material within these limitations.[6]

William Dean Howells with his "smiling aspects of life" could not have wished for more explicit acquiescence.

It was only a matter of time until such a patent conflict of interests would erupt. Although Dreiser's salary rapidly soared to an unbelievable $10,000 a year, he could not long remain contented in the Butterick harness. By 1909 he was moonlighting, editing a magazine of his own, the *Bohemian*, which allowed him to range with more freedom and variety. His personal life also was in turmoil, his marriage to Sallie White smashing up as he became ever more convinced of their basic and irremediable incompatibility. Perhaps he had been correct in the beginning and should never have married against his conviction that monogamy was not for him. Now he felt tragically mismated; he was fettered to a woman he no longer cared for, a wife who did not understand his work or way of life, and who would never accede to his compulsive dalliance with other women. As he and Sallie drifted into a separation which was to become permanent, Dreiser became involved with the daughter of an employee at Butterick's. The girl's mother threatened to expose him publicly, fomenting a ruinous scandal. To avoid this, he announced in October, 1910, that he was severing his connections with the Butterick organization.

## II  *Sister Carrie's Sister*

From now on Dreiser would work for no man but himself and would devote himself to his writing. He had not been idle in the ten years since *Sister Carrie* had been suppressed, for writing was in his blood and no amount of commercial success, however heady, could kill his instinct for expression. A number of projects had occupied him: a novel, eventually to become *The "Genius,"* of which he wrote thirty-two chapters in 1903; sections of what would eventually be published as *Dawn*, the first volume of his autobiography; sketches for *Twelve Men*, including the portrait of his brother Paul, who had died in 1906.

His spirits restored somewhat by the British success of *Sister Carrie* and by the book's reissue in 1907 by B. W. Dodge & Company to at least a modicum of critical acclaim, Dreiser felt prepared to submit more of his writing to public scrutiny. The major work commanding his attention during this decade had been another novel, which he was tentatively calling *The Transgressor,* taken from the phrase "the way of the transgressor" so often quoted in his works and, in its own way, the theme of every novel he wrote. After breaking with Sallie and resigning his position with Butterick's, he turned his full attention to readying this manuscript for Harper & Brothers. Published in 1911 as *Jennie Gerhardt,* the book was praised by Dreiser's new friend H. L. Mencken as "the best American novel ever done, with the one exception of *Huckleberry Finn.*"

For *Jennie Gerhardt* Dreiser returned once more to memories of his sisters for material, but this time he had other fish to fry. Carrie's driving self-interest assured her survival, for instinctively her feet found the route of material advancement. This was far from being the whole story; turned over, the coin would reveal another face:

> There is a type of mind or intelligence that seems to leap into the world full-armed and as though equipped by previous experience elsewhere to move without error or faltering here. On the other hand, there is a lesser order of force, equally intuitive and possibly even more sensitive, which, like some of the hardy though none-the-less gorgeous flowers, requires special nurture in order to bring it to its proper stature and value. The hardy weed that fights and in the face of obstacles and oppositions comes to such beauty as is in it, we can admire for its courage as well as forgive its defects. But of the sensitive soul that requires both shelter and aid in order to be all that it might be, and yet fails of the same, what shall we say?[7]

If Carrie is a weed equipped to thrust its way sunward against the hostility of its environment, Jennie is the fragile blossom that, deprived of care and protection, will be trampled underfoot. She is all love and affection; Carrie is all ambition. In his sisters Dreiser saw much of Jennie. Even more so, in his mother —the fountain from which they sprang—he found every virtue with which Jennie is endowed: compassion, gentleness, a yielding softness, generosity, selfless love, and fidelity which "would follow love anywhere."

Because *Jennie Gerhardt* appeared twenty years after the death of his mother and the dispersion of the family, Dreiser felt under less constraint in drawing upon these early experiences. Accordingly, where Carrie's novelistic life begins only after she has parted from her family, Jennie's family circle dominates the first half of her story. And it is the Dreiser family to the life, no doubt about that, transplanted to Columbus, Ohio. One by one the members reveal their identities. There is John Paul Dreiser in the guise of William Gerhardt, a glass-blower out of a job, a Lutheran of near-fanaticism with whom "religion was a consuming thing," God a tangible personality, "a dominant reality." There is the mother, gentle, resourceful in poverty, concerned first, last, and always with her children's welfare, reduced to scrubbing stairs and taking in washing to keep body and soul together. And there, gleaning lumps of coal beside the railroad tracks, are the children, not so numerous as their real-life counterparts, to be certain, but quite a house-filling brood nevertheless—six of them, equally divided into boys and girls, like the Dreisers. Sebastian (Bass) and Genevieve (Jennie) are the two eldest and the only ones who play sub-stantial roles in the story.

Bass will take Carrie's road. At nineteen he has already "formulated a philosophy of life. To succeed one must do something—one must associate or at least seem to associate, with those who were foremost in the world of appearances. . . . Clothes were the main touchstone. If men wore nice clothes and had rings and pins, whatever they did seemed appropriate."[8]

Bass will get on in the world. His self-interest will protect him like a coat of mail as he encounters the "tremendous forces among which we walk." But Jennie, "poor little earthling, caught in the enormous grip of chance," wears no such armor. Like Hurstwood, a transgressor of society's values ("Its one test that of self-preservation. Has he preserved his fortune? Has she preserved her purity?"), Jennie will follow along Hurstwood's road, although not to the same bitter conclusion.

*Jennie Gerhardt* is based more explicitly upon the Dreiser family than any other of the author's novels (*The "Genius"* is more revelatory of the author's young manhood), and the destitution Drieser shared as a boy is utilized to full impact. The Gerhardts exist beneath the shadow of poverty as under a precipitous cliff of shale which threatens with the slightest earth tremor to thunder down upon them. With every action colored by lack of money, life is lived breathlessly in a day-to-day battle for survival.

## III  *When Lovely Woman Stoops to Folly*

William Gerhardt is ill and out of work. Mrs. Gerhardt, reduced to desperation, musters her courage and seeks work as a charwoman at Columbus' most imposing hotel; there the manager, out of pity, assigns her to scrubbing the marble stairs. Emboldened by this turn of fortune, the mother pushes her luck one step further. Might she also take in laundry for some of the gentlemen guests of this "palace"? The clerk makes inquiries. Yes, one guest, a Senator Brander, has washing to be done. This triggers a series of events. Eighteen-year-old Jennie delivers the packet of laundered shirts and linens, and the senator, deeply affected by the girl's beauty and poverty, tips her with a ten-dollar bill. What eventuates is no more than natural, and in his *Dawn* Dreiser records the family episode from which the novel's action derives:

> During one of the most desperate periods of the family's finances, when my father was out of employment, my sister Eleanor, who was then only fifteen or sixteen, met a Colonel Silsby (the name is fictitious), a prominent lawyer and office-holder in Terre Haute. The meeting came about through no less a personage than the family doctor, who met the Colonel outside the family gate one day as he was leaving. Later, seeing her eyeing longingly the hats in a milliner's window at Eastertide, and knowing the family's financial state, this same Colonel asked Eleanor if she wouldn't like to have one.
> "Indeed I would!" she replied.
> "Then you take this ten dollars and see if you can get one!" After some persuasion she took the money. And so began a friendship which ended in intimacy and what by some might be deemed seduction. . . . My mother, being without moral bias or social training . . . entered into this arrangement to the extent of permitting the child to keep the money. Afterwards, when misfortune pressed most severely, this man's beneficences were accepted—unknown to my father, of course. When Paul was in jail for the second time, it was this same Colonel Silsby who got him out.[9]

When Jennie is pregnant, Senator Brander dies unexpectedly of typhoid in Washington before he can fulfill his promise of marriage. "Why this sudden intrusion of death to shatter all that had seemed most promising in life?" The forces of chance and accident are at work again to "seize and overwhelm one as does a great wind." The strict Lutheran father, horrified at the breach of his religious code, turns his back on Jennie and drives her from the family home. After Jennie's daughter, Wilhelmina Vesta, is born, he relents somewhat; but he thaws with such glacial slowness that father and daughter are not reconciled until enough years have passed for him to learn that, of all his children, Jennie can least be said to have "gone to the bad."

Bass, in Cleveland working for a cigar store, sends for Jennie, and before long the mother and younger children join them there—a parallel to the Chicago adventures of the Dreiser family —and the father remains in Ohio, where he has located a position. The exactitude of Dreiser's adherence to biographical fact is evident in his summary of the Cleveland domestic arrangement with its centripetal action around the mother, its pooling of resources for common survival, its infinite concern with the dollars and cents which are its foundation:

> Bass, originally very generous in his propositions, soon announced that he felt four dollars a week for his room and board to be a sufficient contribution from himself. Jennie gave everything she earned, and protested that she did not stand in need of anything, so long as the baby was properly taken care of. George secured a place as an overgrown cash-boy, and brought in two dollars and fifty cents a week, all of which, at first, he gladly contributed. . . . Gerhardt, from his lonely post of labor, contributed five dollars by mail, always arguing that a little money ought to be saved in order that his honest debts back in Columbus might be paid. Out of this total income of fifteen dollars a week all of these individuals had to be fed and clothed, the rent paid, coal purchased, and the regular monthly installment of three dollars paid on the outstanding furniture bill of fifty dollars.[10]

Jennie is hired as a maid by the wealthy Bracebridges, where she meets their house guest, Lester Kane. Lester, Charles Drouet drawn on a larger scale, is endowed with wealth, position, and infinitely finer discriminations; he strongly suggests Dreiser's roommate of the Bloomington year. A bachelor of thirty-six, Lester possesses enough charm and self-assurance so that—feeling "magnetically and chemically drawn" to Jennie—he can declare bluntly, "You belong to me." He trusts his own irresistibility: "He had only to say 'Come' and she must obey; it was her destiny."

As for Jennie, "horrified, stunned, like a bird in the grasp of a cat," she too is at the mercy of life's "chemisms," and of course her poverty dictates a good share of her response. Lester easily persuades the girl to accompany him to New York, once the trip is condoned by the mother, who sees in Lester's magnanimous gift of $250 "the relief from all her woes—food, clothes, rent, coal—all done up in one small package of green and yellow bills." Lester's first act is to take Jennie on a shopping trip such as that to which Drouet treated Carrie; and, admiring her new finery in the mirror, Jennie is struck by the transformation:

> Could this be really Jennie Gerhardt, the washerwoman's daughter, she asked herself, as she gazed in her mirror at the figure of a girl clad in blue velvet, with yellow French lace at her throat and upon her arms? Could these be her feet, clad in soft shapely shoes at ten dollars a pair, these her hands adorned with flashing jewels?[11]

Until this scene the careers of Jennie and Carrie seem roughly parallel; for each, Cinderella tatters have blossomed into silks. Here the similarity ends. Impressed as Jennie is with her adornment, it is not the clothes themselves which she cares about but Lester. Clothes are far from becoming any sort of an end in themselves. Even though, being human, she feels a quick spontaneous joy in their possession, Jennie's elemental happiness springs from satisfaction in being dressed suitably for her position as Lester's mistress.

When Jennie and Lester's North Side Chicago "love nest" is discovered by his sister Louise, the Kane family is scandalized—not because Lester in indulging in a love affair, but because this particular one bears dangerous implications of permanence. In their anxiety for Lester to assume his filial obligations toward the family enterprises, they regard marriage with a woman of his own class as imperative. They do everything in their power to persuade him to break with Jennie. Under tremendous social pressure, and with ostracism from society as an imminent retaliation for his obstinacy, Lester persists in his refusal to desert the girl.

All things considered, Jennie is most fortunate in her choice of lovers—or is it they who are fortunate in her? Jennie strongly resembles the heroine of Anton Chekhov's "The Darling"; both are creatures of love and devotion to whom their various husbands are all in all. Since a woman can bestow no greater flattery upon the man she loves than to live entirely for him, reciprocation on the husband's part is encouragingly human. Olenka's Vantichka and Vassitchka would never in their wildest dreams willingly part from their darling, and Lester, to his credit, has no intention of relinquishing the treasure he has found in Jennie. On this score her worries are nil.

The serpent that eventually spoils Jennie's Eden (and Olenka's) is the force of circumstance: in Brander's case, the accident of death; in Lester's, the coercive strength wielded by society and economics. Against such powers love may hold out for a time but eventually stands defenseless. Lester may choose to violate the decorum of the world he was born into, but if he does so choose, retribution will follow as the night the day:

> In this world of ours the activities of animal life seem to be limited to a plane or circle. . . . A fish, for instance, may not pass out of the circle of the seas without courting annihilation; a bird may not enter the domain of the fishes without paying for it dearly. . . . In the case of man, however, the operation of this theory of limitations has not as yet been so clearly observed. . . . When men or woman err—that is, pass out from the sphere in which they are accustomed to move—it is not as if the bird had intruded itself into the water, or the wild animal into the haunts of man. Annihilation is not the immediate result. People may do no more than elevate their eyebrows in astonishment, laugh sarcastically, lift up their hands in protest. And yet so well defined is the sphere of social activity that he who departs from it is doomed. Born and bred in this environment, the individual is practically unfitted for any other state.[12]

If Lester is ready to stand by Jennie, come what may, she is prepared to step out of the picture gracefully in order to minimize his forfeitures. In a stormy scene, her renunciation is refused; and Lester moves with her and Vesta to a home in Hyde Park and brings old Gerhardt, now a widower, to live with them. Now Lester learns part of the price he is to pay for his transgression. It occurs to him that for some time old friends have avoided his company, and when by chance he encounters them on the streets, their ambiguous remarks slice like razors, sharply but almost indetectably, till blood is drawn. His family hardens against him. The newspapers get wind of the story and mercilessly lay it bare in the tabloids, complete with photographs and the headline: THIS MILLIONAIRE FELL IN LOVE WITH THIS LADY'S MAID. Although the press's approach is kindly—the Cinderella aspects of Jennie's life being stressed—the ensuing wreckage of Lester's social hopes is total.

## IV  *Handfuls of Borrowed Jewels*

The death of his father forces Lester to a decision. Archibald Kane has provided in his will that Lester must leave Jennie or marry her; he is to receive $10,000 a year for life if marriage is the decision and a normal share in the fortune if he leaves her. Economics is a powerful force; it rules the circles into which Lester was born and now tempts him beyond his endurance. He is forty-six, and the ardor that once kinged it over all other drives in his nature has cooled with age. With the cards on the table, Lester, to his family's relief chooses the practical route—but not without feeling simultaneously "that painful sense of unfairness which comes to one who knows that he is making a sacrifice of virtues—kindness, loyalty, affection—to policy." True to her nature, Jennie is eager to make Lester's decision as painless as possible; she is also fully aware that "she had been living in a dream. . . . humble, out of place, holding handfuls of jewels that did not belong to her." To relinquish, to renounce—this she had always been prepared to do. Now in her magnanimity she is willing to hand Lester over to the society woman who has loved him since girlhood.

The surface life, appearances, what people think—these never interest Jennie. "Affection was what she craved. Without it she was like a rudderless boat on an endless sea." Nothing else matters. So long as she is positive of Lester's affection, Jennie is satisfied to free him and let appearances take what shape they may. "They would be dead after a little while, she and Lester and all these people. Did anything matter except goodness—goodness of heart? What else was there that was real?"

Jennie, dangerously near as she comes to being a soap-opera heroine of the Stella Dallas stamp, manages to rise above mere sentimentality and to take shape as a recognizable human figure. What might have been soggily maudlin becomes poignant, and

Jennie far outruns Carrie in achieving a philosophical position where genuine happiness is not only possible but within human grasp. As for Lester, in his weakness he reiterates the familiar Dreiser position, explaining lamely to the girl he is in fact deserting: "All of us are more or less pawns. We're moved about like chessmen by circumstances over which he have no control."

Jennie's vindication arrives when Lester, now near sixty, calls her to his side in his final illness. Dying, he desires only her; and, despite all his neglect, this last unmistakable token of his affection compensates. She is happy, even though Lester's world—the circle which by the accident of his birth was empowered to determine his fate—will have none of her. As she stands in the dark shadows at the railroad station watching Lester's coffin being loaded, she ponders:

> Was not life a patchwork of conditions made and affected by these things which she saw—wealth and force—which had found her unfit? She had evidently been born to yield, not seek. This panoply of power had been paraded before her since childhood. What could she do now but stare vaguely after it as it marched triumphantly by? Lester had been of it. Him it respected. Of her it knew nothing.[13]

The novel's ending, though it leaves Jennie suspended between present and future, is replete with implications of happiness—or at least peace, contentment—which render it a far more optimistic work than *Sister Carrie*. Where the prognosis for Carrie, in her futile pursuit of satisfaction, is overwhelmingly negative, a reader senses Dreiser's reluctance to paint as black a future for Jennie.

The novel's ending as originally planned, as a matter of fact, would have made Jennie Lester's wife. Evidently it was Dreiser's impulse to reward his lovable girl even though such a denouement would do incalculable violence to his tragic vision of life. We can be forgiven a sigh of relief that he resisted that impulse, for it is quite obvious—and not unnatural, considering her prototypes—that Dreiser is himself emotionally involved with his creation. It is difficult in reading *Sister Carrie* to detect any such affection on the author's part. Interest, yes, to the point of fascination. Sympathy and compassion, by all means. But Dreiser does not greatly admire his "little pilgrim," who does what she feels she must do to prosper in her headlong pursuit of riches and fame, nor does he feel for her a spark of the tenderness which characterizes every paragraph of Jennie's tale. Dreiser's "pet heroine"[14] is left, not destitute, but occupied with the rearing of two orphan children she has adopted (her own Vesta has died of typhoid some years before—another borderline skirmish with sentimentality).

"And then what?" asks the author. The question is pertinent, for while Carrie's inevitable frustration was quite explicitly forecast, Jennie's future is left open for the reader to surmise— an ambiguity which by itself is a sizable concession for a master naturalist to make. But Dreiser's dilemma is clear. On the one hand, he sees Jennie as eminently deserving of the best life can bestow; on the other, he is committed to his view of life in which the worthy are unjustly thwarted by circumstance. It must have pained him, in his adamantly honest approach which obligated him to uphold his life-vision, to refrain from showering Jennie with the rewards he clearly saw to be her just desserts. With his emotions too strongly engaged in both directions, his clouding the denouement in irresolution was perhaps the only tenable answer.

And then what, indeed? Jennie will not be immune to loneliness, to disappointment, or to further rejection by society. Yet she cannot help but prosper in her own way. "We live in an age in which the impact of materialized forces is well-nigh irresistible; the spiritual nature is overwhelmed by the shock," announced Jennie's author in explaining Lester Kane's position. It is to Jennie's everlasting credit and well-being that she manages consistently to resist these forces. She invariably asks the right questions. Carrie inquired only, What is there to be had? How can I best get it, and quickly? Jennie asks, Why? Why has all this happened, and why am I the way I am and others the way they are? Carrie is oriented to the exterior life; Jennie, to the interior. And this will be her salvation. Like Chekhov's Olenka, she surely will encounter an object on which to lavish her treasure of love and devotion, for givers are few and takers many.

"Did anything matter except goodness—goodness of heart? What else was there that was real?" By posing the question rather than answering it, Dreiser reveals his own deep skepticism; for the method by which his world has organized itself leaves scant room for natural affections and holds goodness of heart very cheap indeed. In a jungle society, gentleness invites the predator. In a society of caste and class, passivity dooms one to fruitless waiting outside doors that will never yield. Many of Dreiser's succeeding novels would show goodness of heart trodden into the dust under the greedy human stampede toward materialistic rewards.

## CHAPTER 4

# Financier, Titan, and Stoic:
## *A Trilogy of Desire*

### I *"The Discovery That Even Giants Are But Pygmies"*

A HELL OF A FINE NOVEL is going to be written about some of these things one of these days," remarked John Maxwell of the *Globe* to Theodore Dreiser. The two men—editor and cub reporter—were speculating on the drama of the current scene in their Chicago, as they observed machinations little different from what prevailed in other burgeoning American industrial centers where "cat-like" dynasty builders, financiers, "the coldest, the most selfish, and the most useful" of beings maneuvered frenetically to erect their thrones of power in the American agorae.

In Dreiser's city one man in particular was dominating these early 1890's: Charles T. Yerkes, a financial wizard nonpareil who recognized no law but the self-decreed, was "bestriding the narrow Chicago world like a colossus," tooling his way into supremacy over the city's street-railway networks, buying city councils and mayors as he would bonbons at a confectionery counter, and generally remolding the financial life of the raw, midwestern metropolis to promote his own grandiose schemes.

Twenty years later, after Yerkes had abandoned flagging Chicago lodestock for richer bonanzas in England only to be stricken down a hairsbreadth short of victory, and after Dreiser also had deserted Chicago for New York City and achievement as a novelist, life was breathed into editor Maxwell's idle remark by the publication of "a hell of a fine novel" indeed, the first volume of Dreiser's auspicious *Trilogy of Desire*, based closely upon Yerkes' life and called *The Financier*. Hard upon its heels appeared the second volume, *The Titan;* but not for another thirty years did the final book, *The Stoic*, reach the press.

This triple-decker, ranking in any estimation among Dreiser's major achievements, concerns the Philadelphia boyhood and rise to power of a born financier, one Frank Algernon Cowperwood, rapacious, classically Machiavellian, a wolflike superman who devours unsuspecting sheep by the flock and fattens on their succulent flesh to ever more massive economic girth. Temporarily checkmated in his native Philadelphia and hungry for new worlds to conquer, Cowperwood invades Chicago; there he consolidates the street-railways into a monopoly and approaches absolute power before that city's populace rises to check him; then he adroitly shifts to England with a program for snaring control of the London subway system. Death striking on the eve of conquest, Cowperwood's properties, mortgaged to the hilt, fall into the hands of receivers to be devoured by "legal vultures." Coterminous with this chronicle is the running account of Cowperwood's amatory adventures—two unhappy marriages and the most amazing chorus line of mistresses in American literature—which prompted critic Stuart P. Sherman to epigrammatize the trilogy as a "huge club sandwich composed of slices of business alternating with erotic episodes."[1] The comment is on target. As a work of art, the *Trilogy of Desire* is flawed, and the author's preoccupation with infinite details of business and sex may finally have much to do with the lack of satisfaction experienced by its many sympathetic readers and friendly critics.

## II "Giants Fighting, Plotting, Dreaming"

With the *Trilogy,* Dreiser leaves "fallen women" to focus upon the American Croesus, a drastic shift of interest which might appear abrupt except for considerations which, once understood, render his change of subject not only plausible but inevitable.

Although Dreiser was anything but a slavish follower of fashion, the *Trilogy* plunged into a main current of existing topical interest. Since the Civil War, America had watched, half-dazed, half-entranced, while finance and enterprise flourished on an unprecedented scale, forming huge corporations, industries, utility combines, all marked by common characteristics: massiveness, concentrated wealth, octopus-like tenacity and reach, untold power seized through piratical methods and legislative corruption, and a fundamental contempt for public opinion. The great mass of the people was cut out of the card game completely, kibitzing while financiers fought among themselves over the divvying up of the kitty. "The swordfish were among the bluefish slaying and the sharks were after the swordfish. Tremendous battles were on, with Morgan and Rockefeller and Harriman and Gould after Morse and Heinze and Hill and the lesser fry."[2]

As the implications of this unbridled power struggle in the land of the free slowly dawned upon the citizenry, and particularly upon the writers, "the shadow of the muckrake" fell over the land. Captains of Industry were unmasked as Robber Barons. Condemnations of big-business monopoly cropped up in the press; magazines and newspapers found the exposé so profitable that few areas of public life were left undisturbed. Oil, slums, factory conditions, child labor, insurance, wheat, beef, railroads, city government—all were subjected to microscopic examination. *McClure's Magazine*, to which Dreiser himself contributed shortly after the turn of the century, marshalled angry writers like Roy Stannard Baker (*The Subway Deal*), Lincoln Steffens (*Chicago: Half Free and Fighting On*), Burton J. Hendrick (*The Making of Great Fortunes*), and Ida Tarbell (*History of the Standard Oil Company*). A favorite of Dreiser's was Gustavus Myers' multi-volume *History of the Great American Fortunes*, which accomplished in non-fiction what Dreiser was attempting in fiction. Imaginative writers joined their voices with the chorus of professional muckrakers who were deploring the evils rampant in the mushroom growth of industrialism. Frank Norris in *The Octopus* and *The Pit* raged against the railroad's stranglehold on wheat farming. Jack London and Robert Herrick swelled the group, and Upton Sinclair produced the most influential of all muckraking novels with his polemic on meat-embalming factories, *The Jungle*. In such an atmosphere and with established writers selecting from the grab-bag their particular demon of American industrial life, staking out their claim, and portraying its corrupt face for the press, it is small wonder that Dreiser should slip his hand in with the rest.

Yet the muckraking instinct, though by no means inconsequential, played the least part in Dreiser's choice. In both of his published novels, and in volumes yet to come, his concern with the individual's relationship to society was primary—a society often the villain and generally the victor. Carrie Meeber recognized early the futility of struggling against the deep currents into which society had organized itself: believing she had discovered an answer, she joined the crowd; and by adopting its values, she invited for herself the bankruptcy to which these values lead. Jennie Gerhardt transgressed the arbitrary codes of conduct established by society and was crushed by its prejudices. For Carrie no harbor seemed possible; for Jennie, no harbor safe.

But, while Dreiser respected and feared the omnipotence of society, he did not believe—as *Sister Carrie* and *Jennie Gerhadt* had seemed to imply—that nature intended society always to win. Dreiser dreamed of powerful, magnetic, dominant individuals untrammeled by codes or caste. He was far from being such a man himself. Most of his fellows, he was fairly certain, were, if anything, more intimidated and inhibited than himself.

Where was the man with strength enough to rise boldly to his full stature and tell society to go to hell, to choose his own battlefields on which he might challenge society's massive power—and win? Inclinations toward such a giant had already entered his writing. Drouet was the palest beginning; the drummer remained relatively oblivious to society, went his own way uninterested in what it thought or said or did. But Drouet set his sights too low. Handicapped by a lack of capacity, a modicum of pleasure and of security were enough to surfeit him. He was a dwarf, and a titan was called for. Hurstwood might have served had not paralyzing fear doomed him to be a minnow among whales. Lester Kane wanted to fight society and keep his Jennie, and for a time he did so; but he always fought defensively, never on the attack. He lacked ambition and stamina and was far too genteel to fight nature's way, tooth and claw.

More than any of the men, Carrie Meeber most clearly foreshadowed Cowperwood; but Carrie had crippling limitations of her own and was unable to see beyond the point of her pretty nose; she was less a dynamo than a mouse in a maze conditioned to respond to stimuli and to avoid mistakes. Writing the *Trilogy* would allow Dreiser to argue that society need not be succumbed to. But before it could take shape, he needed a central figure to play superman; someone who would not, could not knuckle under. And the only place he saw one available was in the market place.

III   *"The Pathology of the Genus Financier"*

It saddened Dreiser that only in the field of finance could America exhibit to the world exceptional individuals who compared favorably with the products of other lands.[3] Why this should be so, Dreiser did not understand; and he deplored the fact that his country did not shine as brightly in the arts, philosophy, or even politics.

What was this rare breed of financiers? How were they set apart from mortal men? To begin with, they were born, not made; and they seemed the darlings of the gods. One could no more become a financier by wishing it than he could add an inch to his natural height. The genius for organizing an enterprise was a gift, just as a great voice, a woman's beauty, a painter's talent are gifts. Once chosen by Nature, the financier was known for his single-minded intensity—"shark-like" is Dreiser's image for it. He might be destructive in his avidity, yet Nature used him as she would any other implement—and often in ways too devious to be discerned by ordinary men—as a great constructive force in opening the resources of uninhabited areas, laying railroads, building cities and utility systems. In the long haul, seeming evil produced positive good. For democracy the financier had no use; a Constitution, a Bill of Rights, or any law in fact existed merely to be violated. Paradoxically, in producing and disseminating goods, the financier might well serve as a useful implement for achieving democracy.

Ethics did not concern this breed. His reverence for the "thine and mine" concept applied strictly to things "mine." Sex was less a matter of morality than a question of convenience and animal desire—or the acquisition of a lovely status symbol. Where his own interests were concerned, any trick or snare was justified, pettiness no deterrent so long as it played its part in achieving success for whatever project his enthusiasm had seized upon. At the same time, he was capable of immense and seemingly contradictory benefactions; but these were designed always to promote his own popularity. The perpetuation of his own fame was a continuing concern.

How then were these titans prevented from dominating the world? The same way that political and military leaders have eventually been subdued, by the same process that had thwarted the ambitions of Darius, Alexander, Napoleon. Nature in her inscrutable plan for the wc..ld had provided a set of checks and balances which, while allowing generously for change and progress, assured the stability of the total system. By means of what Dreiser terms "the equation inevitable," willful individuals are born to promote change and reorganize life into new patterns; but at the same time there are born other individuals with opposite tendencies and with the will and the power to resist.[4] Between the two equilibrium is maintained.

Far from repealing the law of survival of the strongest or intimating that the race does not go to the swift, Nature's arrangement assures only that "no thing is fixed. All tendencies are permitted apparently. Only a balance is maintained." The financier, then, while seemingly omnipotent, is essentially a tool used by Nature to achieve a specific end; and, by remaining always under the control of Nature, it is quite possible for a man to "be a Colossus and bestride the world without upsetting the equation ultimately." Deriving these ideas from his thinking, Dreiser felt compelled to agree with Nietzsche that "it is folly not to wish that the significant individual will always appear and will always do what his instincts tell him to do."

Nature's way, for Dreiser, was invariably the right way; the difficulty came always in perceiving amid the confusing welter of human activity what Nature's way might be—and then ridding one's self of emotional involvements sufficiently to adapt. Since in Nature's plan the mass was all, the individual nothing, in the final analysis the world suffered no permanent harm from allowing a financier his temporary clutch on conditions.[5]

As a specimen of *Genus Financierus Americanus*, Frank Cowperwood is created free of any of the limitations Dreiser placed upon his previous figures. Unhandicapped by fear or by lack of scope or ambition, he is heavily armored for the fray: vital, crafty, completely amoral, driven by desire without limit, supremely confident of his own destiny. Cowperwood runs no risk of the disillusionment which plagued Carrie, because his soul is "as bereft of illusion as a windless moon." For him the illusion *is* reality. Untold sucking in of wealth, ever greater and greater power, these for him are life itself, the only ends worth spending a life attaining. Against him, individual men are trifling as gnats. He is in every sense a lion set loose in the streets. Society en masse can draw blood, but the protean superman parries their thrusts with swift maneuver and retaliates with telling blows of his own. Outnumbered, he withdraws to strike elsewhere, aware that discretion is the better part of valor. When he slips—which is seldom—he learns from his mistakes how to win in another place, at another time, recouping every loss and advancing. Over such a man, one force alone—Nature with her "equation inevitable"—wields decisive power.

Dreiser was also driven to depict the financier by his insatiable curiosity about those few favored ones upon whom Nature had lavished all the gifts she had withheld from himself—a fascination already apparent in his idealization of his college roommate and others. In his frankness he lamented, "Alas, I haven't the least faculty for making money, not the least," but he admired those who did, and he was intrigued with the ways in which they were able to do it.

The same was true of his relationships with women, in which insecurity shadowed him always. "I am a great coward when it comes to women. Indeed, their least frown or mood of indifference frightens me and makes me turn inward to myself, where dwell innumerable beautiful women who smile and nod and hang on my arm and tell me they love me. Indeed they whisper of scenes so beautiful and so comforting that I know they are not, and never could be true. And so, in my best moments, I sit at my table and try to write stories which no doubt equally necessitous editors find wholly unavailable."[6]

By inverting his own personality, Dreiser manages to create his Cowperwood by making him as unlike himself as possible. He sets the tone early in the first volume of the *Trilogy*:

The appearance of young Cowperwood at this time [was] prepossessing and satisfactory. His hair was rather a neutral shade, dark brown. . . . His head was large, shapely . . . and fixed on a square pair of shoulders and a stocky body. Nature had destined him to be five feet ten inches tall. . . . He walked with a light, confident, springy step. Life had given him no severe shocks nor rude awakenings. He had not been compelled to complain of illness or pain or deprivation of any kind. His family was respected; his father well placed. . . . His handsome body, slowly broadening, was nearly full grown. His face, because of its full, clear, big, inscrutable eyes, had an expression which was almost babyish. . . . He looked like a young warrior . . . with his even teeth, his square jaw.[7]

Contrast this paragon with the self-portrait of the author: a skinny, beanpole figure, and a face with receding chin, splayed teeth, and cast eye. Compare this life with the author's own life, its poverty, defeated father, and chronic hypochondria.

Where Dreiser felt himself swept along with the tides of chance, Cowperwood resists these tides, grapples with them, turns them often to his own benefit. Where young Dreiser trembled at the prospect of testing himself with women, Cowperwood, "no trembling novice quailing at every thought of the moral law," has the utmost confidence in his magnetism and takes a prodigious series of mistresses, far exceeding even that hinted at in factual accounts of Yerkes' sybaritic life.

Dreiser's family moved frequently, always to more destitute quarters; Cowperwood's family moves frequently but always to a richer neighborhood, a more palatial home. In contrast to Dreiser's financial ineptitude, Cowperwood "from the very first" knows which path leads to the lodestock. Strongly possessed by the same motivations toward money, power, and sex with which he endowed his financier, Dreiser blamed the arbitrary unjustness of Nature for not equipping him with the means of satisfying his desires: "How often have I looked through the windows of some successful business firm and wished I had achieved ownership or stewardship, a position similar to that of any of the officers and managers inside! To be president or vice-president of something, some great thrashing business of some kind. Great God, how sublime it seemed."[8] On a cloud of fantasy, Dreiser rode with Cowperwood the money king into dream worlds of finance and love which he might never experience so long as his feet were mired in reality.

## IV   Mr. Yerkes-Cowperwood

Why Dreiser selected Yerkes instead of one of the better-known financiers whose meteoric careers fascinated him is not difficult to ascertain. Frick, Vanderbilt, Gould, Rockefeller, Astor, Carnegie—any of these might possibly have served as model; Dreiser had his eye on each of them, and Gustavus Myers' volumes would have provided him with documentary evidence aplenty on their acquisitive methods. But circumstance had familiarized him with Yerkes' manipulations, had thrown the two men together as if for a purpose, first in Chicago and then in New York. While Dreiser was struggling to locate his place in the Manhattan sun, Yerkes was ensconced in a Fifth Avenue mansion from which he worked back and forth across the Atlantic on his London underground deal. The newspapers had never ignored Yerkes—nor did he intend them to, reveling in the publicity and quasi-recognition they awarded him; and when he died in December, 1905, the press in all its forms lavished front-page space on accounts of the funeral, speculation on bequests, and the actual reading and interpretation of the will.

Reporters, prying into the great man's private affairs, ransacked the press morgues for details of his past affairs, spied on his mansion for family secrets, and bribed his servants for any morsel of information. The headlines indicated their success:

MRS YERKES RELENTLESS[9]
EMELIE[10] LOSES LAST TRICK[11]
YERKES DUAL LIFE THAT OF SYBARITE[12]
YERKES WILL NOT READ[13]
YERKES WILL IS READ[14]

For another five years feature articles detailed the legacies this multimillionaire left behind him and the fierce legal battles contesting the estate. When news was lacking, muckraking articles like Edwin Lefevre's "What Availeth It?"[15] and Charles Russell's "Where Did you Get It, Gentlemen?"[16] in *Everybody's Magazine* took over to keep the story breathing. In 1910 the headlines read "YERKES ART TREASURES UNDER THE HAMMER," the palace and all its fabled hoard going to the highest bidder. Soon after, Mrs. Yerkes died, and the year had scarcely passed before Dreiser, having mulled the project over in his mind for a long while, as was his habit, set to work on the *Trilogy*.

It was clearly advantageous that, while most of the great financiers were just hitting their full stride, Yerkes' life could be scrutinized in totality. The Greek saying "count no man happy till he has died" was applicable to him but not to many others of his ilk. Across the country, papers caught the implication of Croesus' fall; the headlines even in far hamlets such as Ottumwa, Iowa, were set to declare: DEATH THE GREAT LEVELLER. Probably this more than any other was the element which had already caught Dreiser's attention, the direct application of "the equation inevitable" by which Nature could allow its superman to gain the world and yet restrain him from upsetting the final balance.

Whether Yerkes lived or died, the world would remain the same. What useful things he had bludgeoned into existence would live after him. The people of the cities would ride his transportation networks without a thought for the builder. The rest, the treasure trove he had guarded more carefully than any dragon, would be dispersed to the four winds. And Dreiser, having built a superman upon his own inverted image, could handily destroy the fantasy he had created, bring the dream empire tumbling back to earth again to demonstrate the principle he never relinquished: that Nature cares naught for the trees but only for the forest. High though the redwood grows, it must sooner or later come down, splintered, to moulder in the dust for compost. Winner still takes nothing.

To make this statement is the function assigned *The Stoic*. In his entire *Trilogy*, Dreiser has two theses to prove. The first— that Nature creates these supermen who will dominate and reshape the world against any societal resistance—is argued in *The Financier* and again in *The Titan*. The second—that Nature, having used her implement to accomplish whatever purpose he was created for, discards him on the rubbish heap—is *The Stoic's* task. Nature retains control. Man remains a creature of illusion.

Not only did Yerkes' life dovetail into Dreiser's philosophy, but that life, by great good chance, proved a microcosm. Other financiers might be wealthier, more powerful. One had risen more dramatically out of obscurity perhaps. Another was craftier. But Yerkes possessed every trait Dreiser associated with the genus; he was, to subvert the modern cliché, "well-rounded." He was, in fact, ideal.

For what fiction demanded was the construction of a powerful, dominant prototype as a universal symbol of the age of Big Business. To so act, with the ruthlessness of the giants of that age, required a single-mindedness and a lack of sentimentality which would leave him free to trample on whom and what he must.

The boy Cowperwood is furnished early with the proper ethic. At the age of ten, when passing a fishmarket near his home, Frank spies a tank in which a lobster has been paired off with a squid: predator and prey, the jungle in a tub of water. The lobster, heavily weaponed, aggressive, considers the squid his natural victim. The squid, unarmored, without any defensive equipment aside from the speedy movement not useful in an aquarium and a prematurely depleted supply of "smokescreen" ink, is doomed. It is only a matter of time before the race goes to the swift, the battle to the strong. Frank Cowperwood ponders this object lesson; it answers for him the riddle of the way life is organized. If lobsters lived on squids, and men lived on lobsters, then what lived on men? A little observing, a little thinking, and the answer arrives: "That was it! Sure, men lived on men."

Too bad, but true. Human society, he sees, is but an extension of the jungle; and the same laws that obtain there must govern men also. Once Frank has absorbed this lesson, accepted its principle, and made up his mind to be one of the strong, he has, perhaps without fully willing or realizing it, sloughed off whatever might weaken his chances in the struggle before him—sentiment, Christian morality, concern for anyone except himself, and satisfying the overpowering drives which a few short years will develop in him.

## V   A Lion in the Streets

Before he is out of his teens, Cowperwood knows all the desires which are to ride him until death looses their hold: for success, for women, for beauty, for art, for acceptance and prestige, for immortality. The route to gratification in each area is firmly substructured by an intuitive Machiavellianism apparent to observers of the American financial scene. In 1906 Ida Tarbell was preaching in *McClure's*:

> There has always been a trace of Machiavellianism in American life, but never in the history of our country has the formula been applied and openly defended, until the last two decades. . . . Four hundred years ago it was a state to which the Prince aspired to control, today it is a great business—a national product like iron or coal or oil, a great food product like beef, a great interstate transportation line like the railroad. . . . These are the kingdoms for which modern man sighs.[17]

To the builders of these kingdoms, success in money stood head and shoulders above any secondary aim. To Cowperwood, "Money was the first thing to have—a lot of it. . . . Then you secured the reputation. The two things were like legs on which you walked."[18]

In the money game, conventional morality or ethics played no part, not because the rules were to be broken, but because the world of the financier was a universe apart. The Golden Rule, the thou-shalt-nots of the Ten Commandments could not possibly apply here. Yet, because the financiers were compelled to mingle with their terrestrial cousins, the illusion of conformity was to be maintained at all cost. Miss Tarbell, in her updating of *The Prince*, does not overlook the pertinence:

> Success is the paramount duty. It can be attained in the highest degree only by force. At times it requires violence, cruelty, falsehood, perjury, treachery. Do not hesitate at these practices, only be sure they are necessary to the good of the business. . . . Although a Prince must do evil when required to preserve and strengthen his domain, he must, above all, preserve the appearance of doing good.[19]

The financier must then put up a convincing front, so that his undercover operations may pass unquestioned. The ambiguity through which a man becomes simultaneously a buccaneer and a philanthropist has ever fascinated and perplexed observers of American financial history, notwithstanding the fact that the principle is as old as man himself. And Cowperwood needs not consult *The Prince* to understand that "the thing for him to do was to get rich and hold his own—to build up a seeming of virtue and dignity which would pass muster for the genuine thing."[20]

As he slashes his path through life, cutting down his opponents with no more mercy or remorse than a reaper feels for the individual stalks of grain, Cowperwood always takes pains to preserve this semblance of conformity in his personal and business affairs. One way to create the mirage is well known; it is the method by which the Rockefeller family has in the last half-century washed its name so clean that one of its members can be suggested without mockery as a serious prospect for the American Presidency: public benefaction. Cowperwood's first such gift, the donation of an observatory to the University of Chicago, is motivated by a need to enhance his reputation with other financiers and thus to facilitate the loans he is seeking in New York and in London where as yet he is little known: "On such repute (the ability to give a three-hundred-thousand-dollar telescope out of hand to be known as the Cowperwood telescope) he could undoubtedly raise money. . . . The whole world would know him in a day.

. . . The gift was sufficient to set Cowperwood forth in the light of a public benefactor and patron of science."[21]

At strategic points in his career, Cowperwood sees that circulation is given to his plan for donating his mansion and his art collection to the city of New York as a monument to his memory and reveals the stipulation in his will providing for the building of a gigantic free Cowperwood Hospital. Both proposals, of course, evaporate after his death; but they have already served a good share of their *sub rosa* purpose.

Secondary to the acquisition of wealth is a mounting desire in Cowperwood for the possession of art—paintings, sculpture, tapestries. This familiar trait of the multi-millionaires of the era has served to furnish the halls of more than one public museum, and while in itself the obsession with art may be praiseworthy, it is a recurrent oddity of the money king's psychology. Nor is one surprised to discover that this acquisition of art, like public benefaction, is ambiguous at bottom and tainted with the Midas-touch. Lewis Mumford was on the right track in explaining:

> This hunting for pictures, statues, tapestries, clothes, pieces of furniture, for the epidermis and entrails of palaces and cottages and churches satisfied the two capital impulses of the Gilded Age: it gave full play to the acquisitive instinct, and, with the possible rise and fall of prices in even time-established securities, it had not a little of the cruder excitement of gambling in the stock market or in real-estate. At the same time, it satisfied a starved desire for beauty and raised the pursuer an estimable step or two in the social scale.[22]

Although Cowperwood is first inspired by what he feels—at least hopes—is an authentic interest in art for art's sake, he instantly reverts to type when his dealer suggests that, since great pictures invariably increase in value, an investment of a few hundred thousand cannot help but result in a profit of millions. His financial acumen tells him that the dealer is correct; in both value and social distinction he is bound to gain.

Accordingly, with one beady eye on the cash register and another on aesthetics, Cowperwood crams his lavish mansion with the conspicuous loot of his travels until it is far more a museum than a home. Little would be required but the stationing of an attendant at the front door to convert it at once into a public gallery—which is, in fact, intended to be its ultimate function in the master plan. William Randolph Hearst later set what must be a permanent record in piling up sheer Matterhorns of art treasures, but Cowperwood's prototype did all right for himself too. In magazines of the time, we may scan pages devoted to photographs of the Yerkes palace with its white marble staircase, its indoor palm garden complete with bubbling spring, its orangery, and its pair of immense art galleries hung with Watteaus, Turners, Gainsboroughs.[23] An approximation of what this home must have resembled in its heyday can be gained from a stroll through the Frick mansion on Fifth Avenue; like that of Cowperwood-Yerkes, it is a Renaissance palace furnished with the cream of world art. It is not easy to imagine human beings conducting their daily affairs in such edifices, but they serve to illustrate the status consciousness of genus financier.

Considering the motives which these collectors could not transcend, it is not surprising that, when the Yerkes collection was auctioned, it set an all-time high for receipts. Turner's "Rockets and Blue Lights," purchased for $78,000, had appreciated to $129,000; Corot's "Fisherman" brought $80,500; Franz Hals's "Portrait of a Woman," $137,000. In all, 198 paintings drew a total of $1,693,350. Frederick Lewis Allen sums up the moral: "When Yerkes, the Chicago traction magnate died, his canvas by Troyon, "Coming from the Market," had already appreciated $40,000 in value since its purchase, according to the newspapers. This was a fact which any speculator could appreciate; perhaps there was something in art after all!"[24]

Thus Cowperwood embodies every essential trait of the financial titans who, like brontosauri stalking through the ooze of the first industrial age, dominated the final quarter of the nineteenth century: success an end in and for itself, great wealth gained through Machiavellian practices and preserved through force and chicanery, an awakening desire for beauty and art, and the dream of self-created immortality as a philanthropist.

But post-mortem establishment in the hearts of the people as a national demigod does not fully satisfy the financier. Being first of all in this world and of this world, he must wrench from the social dictators that status which is food for his ego. He must be accepted. His drive for prestige here and now demands it. For what avail money and power unless one can use them as a crowbar to force entry into the Four Hundred and a fitting locale in which to flaunt material success through possessions, clothes, lavish entertainments? Once one has appeased his financial appetite by gnawing chunks of living flesh from his opponents, these same maimed princes must be made to pay obeisance to the new king.

Cowperwood's efforts, largely thwarted, to have his cake and eat it too require a partner. What is a host without a hostess, adorned from head to foot in the best money can buy, to receive his summoned guests? Cowperwood's program is put in the hands of his second wife, who, like her husband, has her basis in real fact. Rumors surrounding Yerkes' divorce from his first wife suggest a Philadelphia beauty who stuck with him through his conviction and ensuing incarceration for embezzlement. Aileen Butler Cowperwood is this woman; and, aside from the titanic figure of her husband who dominates all but the final pages of the *Trilogy*, hers is the most realized portrait in the three volumes. Since Aileen's original model is found only sketchily in the sources, she is more the product of the artist's creative power than is Cowperwood; and she is fully drawn and completely believable. The rash, headstrong daughter of a Philadelphia politician, young, gay, colorful, exuberant, she is magnetically drawn to Cowperwood, and her desires for material success tally with his. Like Lester Kane, but with the force to persist, she deserts her natural circle for love and becomes the financier's mistress.

After his release from prison, Cowperwood marries Aileen. They set out for Chicago to start afresh, blazing with financial stratagems in which the harvest will be bountiful, but determined as well to penetrate to the heart of a "brilliant society that shone in a mirage." Following an initial flourish of entertainments which, because they are well attended, the Cowperwoods mistakenly interpret as tokening acceptance, their false spring of hope dies in a bitter winter of rejection. Society barricades its doors, partly in retaliation for Cowperwood's buccaneering forays and partly because Aileen's high spirit and flair threaten to burst the mold set by the frigid leaders of Chicago's social empire. One financier describes Aileen as "Charming, but she's hardly cold enough, I'm afraid; hardly clever enough. It takes a more serious type. She's a little too high-spirited. These old women would never want to get near her; she makes them look old. She'd do better if she were not so young and pretty."[25]

Aileen's most appealing traits are thus turned into spears against her; and, when hints of her previous irregular relationship with Cowperwood are whispered around the city, she finds her new mansion empty, fewer and fewer callers peopling her at-homes. So long as she has her husband, Aileen can endure the debacle of her social life, but it is not long until she must face the bald fact that she no longer possesses him solely. His wandering eye has strayed to delights in neighboring pastures. As he flits from woman to woman, she is left at home alone without company aside from a small army of semi-occupied servants.

In an effort to arouse Cowperwood's jealousy and so win him back, Aileen turns to other men—only to find that her husband is happy to have her so occupied, thus leaving him free to dally. An attempted suicide only deepens the gulf between them; at the same time Aileen, growing older, heavier, less attractive sexually, clings tenaciously to her name as his wife and to the wealth which has come to represent only blasted hopes. The bitterness of her Chicago failure is repeated when the Cowperwoods erect their auspicious citadel on New York's Fifth Avenue, and Frank's death finds the two of them estranged, her acrimony venting itself in a last obstinate refusal even to allow his body to be brought into the house. Servants must be bribed to smuggle the coffin in under cover of night so that its lying in state may perpetuate the façade of domestic harmony.

## VI  "A Huge Club Sandwich"

The alienation of Frank and Aileen Cowperwood results from the final controlling desire in the financier's life. Next to self-interest, which to Dreiser always ruled supreme, sex was the most tremendous of forces goading the human creature; and here Frank Cowperwood is as precocious as he is at coining money. At thirteen he wins his first girl, the twelve-year-old daughter of Quaker neighbors, with the gift of a licorice stick; and, although the result is no more momentous than a surreptitious kiss or two stolen at parties or in darkened hallways, Frank rapidly moves on to other girls, to Dora Fitler and to Majorie Stafford. At this point Dreiser waxes coy: "Shall the story of Marjorie be told? It isn't as innocent as the others. But no, let it go. There will be more than sufficient without it."[26]

Prophetic words. Whether Dreiser spoke earnestly or in jest, there are many more than sufficient. And invariably, whether to underscore the illusory magnetism of love Dreiser so keenly felt in his relations with Sallie or to make it plain that no one woman could hope to hold the quicksilver attentions of this superman, or both, Cowperwood selects the wrong woman.

Enamored at nineteen of one Mrs. Semple, five years his senior and recently widowed, Cowperwood marries without the least perception that his wife and he are temperamentally incompatible. So long as he acts with his brain, Cowperwood is as invincible as human flesh can be. Unfortunately perhaps, one is prone to choose women, not intellectually, but on an emotional, passionate basis. He knows only that Lillian Semple's clear skin and fragile beauty charm him like something painted by Bourne-Jones. Desiring her, craving her, he therefore must have her. Soon tiring of Lillian, who ages quickly and, losing her beauty, loses her hold on him as well, Cowperwood turns to Aileen Butler, thus exhibiting an ineptness of choice which is to dog him all his days. For Aileen is the daughter of a financial colleague upon whose good will Cowperwood depends; and, when Edward Butler is apprised of his daughter's seduction, he relishes taking a hand in Cowperwood's ruination.

In Chicago, Frank begins taking mistresses again. They parade one by one through the pages of *The Titan* in sequences neatly arranged to evoke the "club sandwich" effect that peeved Stuart Sherman.[27] Once only, when he seduces his secretary, does Cowperwood show any degree of common sense in his choice; for his usual mistresses are summoned from among the wives and daughters of associates. Rita Sohlberg, wife of an artist friend; Stephanie Platow, daughter of an influential furrier; Cecily Haguenin, daughter of an editor, until then his most earnest journalistic supporter; Florance Cochrane, daughter of the president of the Chicago West Division Company; Carolyn Hand, wife of a wealthy director of a number of principal mercantile and financial institutions in the city, a man in a position to do Cowperwood genuine harm.

All of these affairs are more or less explicitly detailed, yet they tell much less than the full story; a book, even be it six hundred pages long, can contain only so much, and what remains must be summarized: "he had been intimate with other women for brief periods, but to no great satisfaction—Dorothy Ormsby, Jessie Beele Hinsdale, Toma Lewis, Hilda Jewell; but they shall be names merely."[28] The last of the series, the final jewel of Cowperwood's harem, becomes much more than a mere name.

Berenice Fleming, daughter of a Louisville brothel madame, is barely sixteen when her blonde beauty catches Cowperwood's eye. Then he decides that of all the women in the world—and he has known a good share of them—this is the one he wants, the one he must have, the one destined for him. Yet in a weakly supported turn of character, in no way foreshadowed, Cowperwood determines not to seduce Berenice; instead he will wait stoically for her to come to him or not, as she will. Perhaps Cowperwood's age has something to do with this decision, or perhaps this is the author's device for making his financier appear more human, his shrewdness in business being set off against his crassness in love. Again, it may be Dreiser's "chemisms" at work, making illusory fools of men, deceiving them like roaring fires built by wreckers to lure vessels onto the reefs. Berenice goes to Cowperwood in the first place because, word of her mother's past having leaked out, her chances of marrying well in the East are ruined. And while she is faithful to the financier, she schemes at the same time to have herself set up securely; as she herself puts it, she far prefers unhappiness in wealth than happiness in poverty. Berenice figures prominently through half of the *Trilogy,* and is the only major character active in the last third of *The Stoic.* Yet she fails to achieve a cubit of Aileen's stature as a fictional creation; and, like so many of the persons and events in the story, the incidents of her life are based upon fact.

## VII   *Fact and Fiction*

The use Dreiser made of his sources regarding Berenice and the other *dramatis personae* reveals a good deal about his method of writing. Previously, he had dealt with materials closely linked with his own life, but from which he stood at enough distance to achieve some measure of objectivity. Now, turning to the story of Charles Tyson Yerkes, he had to rely primarily upon research. Interviews and the ransacking of newspaper files yielded richly, and he traveled to Chicago, to Philadelphia, even to Europe to absorb background and to see the world as Yerkes himself had so recently seen it.

In transforming fact into fiction, the realist has a number of means at his disposal. He may remove his story a generation or two from the original or, like Lewis and Faulkner, either alter the location of events or create an entirely new, even fictional, location behind which reality may dodge. Dreiser apparently has only contempt for these devices. Every significant detail in Yerkes' life is presented to the reader, and never is fact cloaked in more than the barest minimum of fiction. In most cases a simple substitution of names yields Yerkes' biography. At times even the names are but slightly altered, as when the first Mrs. Cowperwood becomes Mrs. Semple instead of her real-life counterpart, Mrs. Gamble.

Places and dates are scrupulously adhered to. Charles Yerkes was born in Philadelphia in 1837; Cowperwood is represented as being born in the city in the same year. Both men are of Quaker extraction, both are ruined in the panic following the Chicago fire of 1871, and both are imprisoned for several months after misusing city funds and refusing to give preference to the city over other creditors. Both recoup their fortunes in the Jay Cooke failure of 1873; and, after scattered investments in Minnesota and the Dakotas, Cowperwood and Yerkes settle in Chicago, where they establish grain-commission offices, gradually edging into control of the city's streetcars. When Yerkes donates the Yerkes Observatory to the University of Chicago, Cowperwood must donate an observatory, costing an identical sum, to the same institution. Yerkes' battle with Governor Altgeld over long-term franchises is reproduced practically without fictional draping. One sequence at least—Yerkes' attempt to bribe Altgeld at a time when the governor was in dire financial straits following ruinous investments in the Unity Building skyscraper—is given in the novel detail for detail as newspapers had recorded it.[29] At Yerkes' death, the New York *Tribune* divulged details of a meeting at the Chicago home of Philip D. Armour, at which a combination of financiers attempted to break Yerkes. He, entering unabashed, began his upset of the plot with the casual opening gambit, "I never before saw so many straw hats at a funeral."[30] Except for Mr. Armour's not altogether convincing metamorphosis into Mr. Arneel, this identical scene is spliced into *The Titan* as closely as a stenographer's dictation.[31]

The remainder of Cowperwood's story can easily be documented by newspaper records, for by now Yerkes was a celebrity, big news. In New York he lived in his Renaissance palace at 964 Fifth Avenue, the precise street number given Cowperwood's mansion. Because Yerkes bought Turner's "Rockets and Blue Lights" for $78,000, Cowperwood must be pictured as purchasing the same picture for the same sum, and this attachment to fact might be duplicated for the bulk of paintings in the Cowperwood gallery. Both men are stricken at sea with Bright's disease, both rushed home and quartered in the Waldorf Astoria after the wives—estranged to the end, in vengeance for the "shameful" treatment each has received—refuse entry into the home. Both men are interred in an elaborate mausoleum in Brooklyn's Greenwood Cemetery, the novel's funeral account paralleling newspaper records practically verbatim. The real and the fictional wills are, to the smallest bequest, identical, both as regards persons and amounts, including $190,000 to endow the Yerkes-Cowperwood Observatory and a philanthropic gift of $800,000 to erect a Yerkes-Cowperwood hospital in the Bronx, to which patients shall be admitted regardless of race, color, or creed. Details of the estate's final and dispiriting dissolution, after costly litigation, correspond also in both fact and fiction.

Whether such adherence to source material makes for good writing or inhibits it is a matter of opinion which has been hotly argued, but one thing is certain: to transcend the merely biographical, a writer must add something of his own, a personal ingredient, an element of meaning and form and interpretation that will produce a novel out of an obituary. What Dreiser adds—besides the impressive characterizations of Frank and Aileen and the fully scaled cradle-to-grave cycle of the financier's life, both of them achievements of merit—is the picture of life itself. This life is seen from a new vantage point, but it is still illustrative of Dreiser's philosophy.

## VIII  *"The Glitter Tarnishes"*

The assumption that the *Trilogy* was intended as a celebration of Nietzsche's superman was understandable after the publication of *The Financier* and was still valid after *The Titan* appeared, even though the *Macbeth* allusions ending those novels implied disasters to come: "in the glory was also the ashes of Dead Sea fruit. . . . To have and not have! All the seeming, and yet the sorrow of not having!"[32] The elements of that superman are undeniably present; the power, the craft, the anarchy that raise Cowperwood so far above ordinary men that only titanic and inevitable forces can crush him, huge events like the Chicago fire, the rising of a citizenry en masse, or the cold hand of death itself. But had Dreiser been bent only on canonizing the financial titan, there were sufficient whose lives had ended more happily, whose plans remained unblasted, whose fortunes, in fact, endure and prosper to the present day.

Always in his observations of wealth and power, Dreiser rang in the contrast of poverty and helplessness which were their corollaries. He was angry that life did not better organize itself so that even though the strong must rule the weak, the big brain dominate the little one, there might be "just a slightly less heavily loaded table for Dives and a few more crumbs for Lazarus." Efforts toward this equilibrium are made by Dreiser's insistence in his fiction that even the superman be the ultimate victim of circumstance. The winds of chance do blow fortuitously through the *Trilogy*, rendering man helpless. The Chicago fire smashes Cowperwood's dreams of conquest in Philadelphia; the failure of the house of Jay Cooke re-establishes him as a power. His own inopportune death, coming as it does with the worst possible timing, demolishes his empire and scatters its ashes.

And the Cowperwoods do not escape personal disillusionment. Frank's first marriage ends badly. His second, to Aileen, although built upon grandiose hopes and rosy promises, also breaks on the rocks of circumstance. Their aspirations to social prestige burst like soap bubbles. Only Cowperwood's money remains and, through it, his power. Aileen is more cruelly dealt with than her husband. Having staked all on her marriage, she loses all. Dreams of social conquest fade quickly; her husband abandons her for other women; her luxurious home loses whatever meaning it might have attained: "The sum and substance of all those years and efforts was that she lived alone, was visited by no true friend, legally defeated in one honest claim after another, until she at last fully realized that the dream of grandeur which this house represented had vanished into thin air."[33]

Aileen's final disillusionment arrives as her chauffeur drives her past the Fifth Avenue palace from which collectors bear her auctioned treasures. A photograph exists which might embody Dreiser's judgment of the ultimate end and achievement of the Cowperwoods' lives.[34] Taken in 1910, it pictures the Yerkes mansion, on whose corner has been fastened a billboard reading:

AUCTION SALE
THIS ELEGANT PLOT
TO BE SOLD
MONDAY, APRIL 11

No one today visits the Yerkes-Cowperwood public art galleries. No one today is nursed in the public Yerkes-Cowperwood free hospital that was to be. Rich or poor, high or low, "chance blows all our dreams away."

What remains? Edwin Lefevre suggested an answer to the puzzle a full year before *The Financier* appeared in print. Noting the savagery with which Yerkes' estate was looted in death, as the money baron had himself looted in life, he concluded interestingly enough: "The Great American Novel can be nothing but pages taken from the lives of Americans Who Do Things. Only in death is the moral of their tale plain. You read 'Finis' and then you begin to think. The glitter tarnishes; the jingle of the dollar ceases; envy is stilled. What remains. . . . nothing!"[35]

## IX  *Berenice*

Lefevre was not entirely correct. A good deal remains, more in the novel than in the life. And what does remain explains to some degree why *The Stoic* is the weakest section of the *Trilogy*. Ideally, a trilogy should be so constructed that a dramatic "build" is maintained, rising to a culmination in the third volume. Instead, the first, *The Financier,* is the most absorbing of the three. It is much more intriguing to watch the youthful Cowperwood grow and expand, attempt and fail, learn and succeed, until he lands on top of the heap.

Once there, his fight to remain king of the hill, while of interest, lacks the involvement of the early struggles; besides, we have been there before. The reader is already jaded. And it is more engrossing to follow a man's rise or fall than to observe him striding along a plain. *The Stoic*, with its ironic smashing of Cowperwood's dreams—potentially the greatest material, surely much more vital than that of *The Titan*—is a definite falling off. It lacks the zest of the other volumes. Some blame, considerable probably, must be laid on the circumstances surrounding its completion. Finished in Dreiser's last days when, exhausted, he made a final attempt to get it between covers, the volume was never really completed at all in the ordinary sense. Everything was at least sketched in, but no time remained for revision and final polish. The final chapters, left in summary, had to be put together by others. Four days before his death, Dreiser wrote to James T. Farrell, his friend and self-chosen critic: "I simply stopped writing at the end because I was tired."[36]

What remains in *The Stoic* after Cowperwood's demise is Berenice; and Dreiser makes a fatal—but probably unavoidable —mistake in shifting the emphasis to her. This may well be the result of his intensified social consciousness between 1914, when *The Titan* appeared, and 1945, when he applied for membership in the Communist Party. Convinced that the *Trilogy* as it stood did not hammer home its point forcefully enough, and left with only Berenice to act upon a stage emptied now of principals, Dreiser invokes a lightning bolt of conscience which, striking Berenice with force sufficient to bring about "the dawn of a spiritual awakening," transforms the girl from an empty-headed, self-centered odalisque into a yoga-practicing social worker bent on improving slum conditions in New York's Harlem.

She becomes the worst kind of unknowledgeable do-gooder. After the years spent in India which convert her to mysticism, she blossoms out in full-feathered philanthropy, putting her Park Avenue home—a gift from Cowperwood—on the market to raise money. With this sum, augmented by whatever she can finagle out of influential friends, Berenice intends to build the Cowperwood Hospital her lover had dreamed would stand as his monument. In the end she becomes Dreiser's spokesman, mouthing the words he wanted the *Trilogy* to say. Not having said them elsewhere, he found her a convenient megaphone: "Her entire life, as she realized—with the exception of the past few years—had been spent in the pursuit of pleasure and self-advancement. But now she knew that one must live for something outside of one's self, something that would tend to answer the needs of the many as opposed to the vanities and comforts of the few, of which she herself was one. What could she do to help?"[37] Very little is the only answer possible.

What Dreiser could do had already been done. The story of the financier, of life itself, had been told in all its grandeur and misery, its hope and futility. He knew that it had its merits and its defects. The latter are readily discernible. The books are too long; they tell us far more about the intricate shenanigans of the financial jungle than we ever wanted to know or could possibly absorb; and, if everything in Cowperwood's life is relevant, then there is too much of the relevant. The impression grows that, rather than selecting his timber and sculpting it carefully with the full intricacy of his genius, Dreiser has been content here to hew down the entire tree with crude axe strokes and to allow its massiveness to stand as its own testament.

But crude or subtle, the job has been done; and the first merit of the *Trilogy* is that it is there, complete, for America to read. It possesses other merits. It has, undeniably, life and breath of its own, for American society at the turn of the century impinges upon the consciousness with a verisimilitude which only the born writer can achieve. Perhaps the best—and truest—compliment which can be paid the effort is to say that Dreiser achieved his avowed purpose to "draw the man as I see him—And when I get through with him he'll stand there, unidealized and uncursed, for you . . . to take and judge according to your own lights and blindness and attitudes toward life."[38]

When this achievement occurs in a work of literature, little else can be demanded.

## CHAPTER 5

# Self-Portrait of the Artist:
## *The "Genius"*

*"always the special individual, the genius of any kind, will be curbed and restrained if not actually pushed into the background."*

## I

IN ANY ESTIMATION of Dreiser's accomplishment, *The "Genius"* must rank among the weaker novels; but it is seen at particular disadvantage because it comes between two high points in his career—after the first two volumes of the *Trilogy* and before *An American Tragedy*. Considered in sequence of writing rather than of publication, it would appear more of an achievement; for Dreiser was working on the novel as early as 1903 and had in fact completed it before he published either *The Financier* or *The Titan*.

What makes this novel, which should ideally have stood among Dreiser's masterpieces, less engrossing than *A Trilogy of Desire* and less compelling than *Sister Carrie* is more a matter of execution than conception. Substantial blame for the failure can be attributed to the circumstances of composition. Dreiser could weave fine work from the threads of his own life—would be lost, in fact, without that basic experience; but to do so he needed the distance of time, a point of perspective from which real events might be assimilated into his larger experience and contemplated somewhat dispassionately. The best previous example of this is the two- and three-decade lapse between his early boyhood experiences and their emergence in the fictional portraits of his father, mother, and family in *Jennie Gerhardt*. Objective distance might be achieved also by deliberately selecting an extrinsic subject (Yerkes); in this case, the compiling of sources, the mulling over, the selecting and the formulating demanded a period of calendar time briefer than the autobiographical sources, yet sufficient for the loaf of fiction to rise properly in the oven.

In writing The "Genius" Dreiser had the benefit of neither safeguard. Dealing with the most intimate and immediately personal material in any of his novels, he began putting pen to paper almost before the events he was describing had terminated. The book deals to an extent with his childhood experiences, and these invariably are done with effect; but it also concentrates upon the period of his marriage and employment with the Butterick organization—roughly 1900 to 1910. It had been labored on intermittently during these years and completed in 1911 while Jennie Gerhardt was in press. Its autobiographical emphasis is prophetic of the method Thomas Wolfe later adopted, and it exhibits the same weaknesses as Wolfe's work; a massive all-inclusiveness and a difficulty in imposing form and meaning on recently transpired events.

To structure his novel, Dreiser relied on experiences which had characterized his struggle out of boyhood poverty into a position of at least moderate affluence, groping always to locate his proper niche as an artist. Having married with misgivings, more out of duty than passion, he had seen that marriage fail from its inherent defects as surely as a newblown vase flawed by imperceptible cracks will finally shatter. He had produced a work of art, suffered a breakdown when that work was ill received. Seduced by the need for money into a passion for wealth, Dreiser attempted a marriage of business and art which in time proved as incompatible as his marriage to Sallie White; and, though his editing career braked to a halt ostensibly because of his indiscretions with a young lady, the true causes cut deeper and were cumulative. Altered, but never by more than the most eggshell-fragile veneer of fiction, this sequence is reported in the novel, the story relying on theme and character as unifying elements.

The theme is as powerful as any Dreiser dealt with, and he understood it well—the conflict between artistic dedication and the carnivorous distractions of the unbridled sex drive and of materialism. The character is Eugene Tennyson Witla, painter, and fighter for a degree of artistic freedom which many might label as license. Character and theme are strong supports which have served to buttress many a work of fiction which might otherwise sag. In this case they prove impotent in preserving *The "Genius"* from its flaws.

## II   *"The Perfection of Eighteen"*

Helen Richardson Dreiser identifies the central figure of *The "Genius"* as a composite of Everett Shinn, whose veritist paintings hung with those of Sloan, Glackens, and Luks in the Macbeth Galleries in 1908; a young art editor employed by the Butterick company; and Dreiser himself.[1] But it is apparent upon juxtaposing the novel with the author's life that the other two men are little more than tools for transmuting writer into painter and that Dreiser himself serves as principal model throughout.

The reader encounters Eugene Tennyson Witla as a young lad emerging from the cocoon of childhood in Alexandria, Illinois, an obscure hamlet on the prairies, akin to Dreiser's own Warsaw or Sullivan, yet as likely a spot as any other for inscrutable Nature to engender genius. At seventeen, not yet a painter, Eugene's artistic bent manifests itself through "an intense sense of beauty" that foreshadows the source of many of his later difficulties: "He admired girls—was mad about them —but only about those who were truly beautiful. . . . He invested them with more beauty than they had; the beauty was in his own soul. But he did not know that."[2]

For the next 750 pages, the reader observes Eugene lured toward disaster by this "illusion," this "mirage" of beauty. Any confrontation with a beautiful girl whose manner suggests even the most remote possibility of her being approachable is sufficient to tumble Eugene off his precarious perch into an abyss of utter infatuation. When he is seventeen, it is Stella Appleton whose "beauty like a tightened bow" shoots love's barbs deeply into his susceptible male heart. In rising head and shoulders above the common herd, Witla and Cowperwood the financier share common traits, and Eugene swiftly takes possession of a series of mistresses which threatens to rival Cowperwood's harem.

In rapid order these girls succumb to his passion. Margaret Dunn, Ruby Kenny, Angela Blue, Christina Channing, Frieda Roth, Carlotta Wilson, Suzanne Dale are some of those dwelt upon in the story. But with the exception of two—Christina

Channing, the opera singer, and Carlotta Wilson, the brash divorcée—each is cast from the same mold. Always eighteen, theirs is the breathtaking loveliness of that age when girlhood's bloom bursts out with "the sweetness of perfume of spring fires." Round these flames of eighteen-year-old beauty Eugene flits like an excited moth singeing his wings; struggling on the edge of doom with unendurable tensions; believing ever, like Poe's rider to Eldorado, in the ultimate fulfillment of the mirage. But each illusion leads only to vast deserts of disillusion on whose horizon shimmers yet another dream of perfection. Never relinquishing entirely his search for the one girl who will be all-in-all, Eugene moves toward stoicism and the admission that "this is the way things are."

Added to the tantalizing search for perfect beauty is a sharp and enduring contest between art and business. This tug of war tears Eugene apart between the magnets of fame and money, which Dreiser depicts as mutually exclusive. One cannot be all things at once, as even Cowperwood discovered in his drive to capture power and social status simultaneously; and Eugene Witla discovers this truism too late to avoid a sequence of violent reversals. These vicissitudes constitute a major weakness in the novel. Overnight—we are asked to believe—Eugene can plunge from a fully productive artist to a helpless neurotic, shorn of any ability to put brush to canvas. Inexplicably he passes from the threshold of immense wealth to the sub-basement of destitution—and may as unbelievably snap back again. When Dreiser writes of Witla: "He first gorged the spectacle of life and then suffered from mental indigestion," he is describing the characteristic pattern of the artist's career. Prodded by his uncurbed appetites, lacking the least semblance of self-discipline, the painter gluts upon his illusions. But Dreiser throughout defends the natural right of the artist to absolute freedom. He protests with vehemence the cruelty of indifferent Nature and the dark prejudices and empty ideals of society which curb the creative genius.

The novel is divided into three books. The first, "Youth," parallels in part Dreiser's own early life (Eugene's father is a sewing-machine agent of moderate means) retold as elsewhere, but softened, as it traces the boy's progress from Alexandria to Chicago to New York and his initiation into the spheres of art and sex. We are scarcely surprised, for instance, to feel the automatic racing of Eugene's youthful pulse at discovering

Chicago for the first time. It was the last occasion on which Dreiser was to present this precise scene in a novel, though later books contain parallel experiences; and he rises to the occasion with a Whitmanesque prose-poem rhapsodizing the Midwestern "magnet":

> This vast ruck of life that had sprung suddenly into existence upon the dank marshes of a lake shore. Miles and miles of dreary little houses; miles and miles of wooden block-paved streets, with gas lamps placed and water mains laid, and empty wooden walks set for pedestrians; the beat of a hundred thousand hammers; the ring of a hundred thousand trowels! Long, converging lines of telegraph poles; thousands upon thousands of sentinel cottages, factory plants, towering smoke stacks, and here and there a lone, shabby church steeple, sitting out pathetically upon vacant land . . . the great broad highways of the tracks of railroads, ten, fifteen, twenty, thirty, laid side by side and strung with thousands upon thousands of shabby cars, like beads on a string. Engines clanging, trains moving, people watching at street crossings—pedestrians, wagon drivers, street car drivers, drays of beer, trucks of coal, brick, stone, sand—a spectacle of raw, necessary life![3]

There is, as we come to expect with a Dreiser hero, the blow of revelation hardening Eugene's attitudes as he observes in some directions the conspicuous, almost sinful display of luxury—splendid clothes, fine homes, all the trappings of social prestige—and in others the despair, the shabbiness, and the gloom of squalor. "You could fail so easily. You could really starve if you didn't look sharp—the city quickly taught him that."

It is one lesson among many which Eugene, like all Dreiser's young Americans, must learn for survival—just as he must discern that life, despite its wonder, can be bitter as wormwood; that if one is to avoid persecution he must achieve some modus vivendi with the codes of convention; that money is the basis for all society's favors, every object and position being attached firmly to a price tag; that the individual means little enough to the universe at large and nothing at all to "the shifting, subtle forces of nature"; and that one is saved only by early realization that life is unfair. Eugene absorbs these lessons, but he could scarcely be described as being saved by learning them.

Book Two, "Struggle," opens upon the most fateful error in Eugene's life, one which plagues him for the rest of the book:

his marriage to Angela Blue. In all important respects, this marriage tallies with Dreiser's to Sallie White. It is a mismating to which Dreiser-Witla agrees for all the wrong reasons: bowing to convention, to the opinions of others; marrying more out of duty or pity than love, the heat of passion having cooled long before the couple approached the altar. Angela is older than Eugene, the bloom of eighteen has passed (actually, Eugene is more attracted to her sister than to her); she is earthbound where he longs to soar the skies unfettered. Angela worships staid monogamy, the sphere of home and children constituting her natural universe; Eugene burns to dwell in whatever Bohemia his passions impel him to create for himself. And in the jigsaw puzzle of life among artists and sophisticates cultivated by Eugene, Angela is an odd piece. Her few efforts to adjust are inept. She flames with wild jealousy against every friend her husband cultivates. Dreiser's story "Marriage," lifted bodily from the overgrown manuscript of The "Genius," lays bare the flaws that doom this union of artist and Philistine.[4]

Aware of the unsuitability of his bride for him, and of him for her, but at the same time censoring this knowledge from his conscious thoughts, Eugene proceeds with the marriage, deluding himself with the insistence—contrary to all evidence—that everything will work out for the best. Dreiser once considered calling his story of Clyde Griffiths Mirage, but that title would have suited Eugene's story as well (certainly it might serve for any of Dreiser's novels, misled by illusion as his humans are).

Acknowledging that life is at bottom tragic, bitter, and deceptive, Eugene nevertheless persuades himself—or attempts to—that "there was happiness and peace in store for him probably. He and Angela would find it together living in each other's company, living in each other's embrace and by each other's kisses. It must be so. The whole world believed it—even he, after Stella and Margaret and Ruby and Angela. Even he."[5]

Rarely has American literature witnessed such an indictment of romantic love as Dreiser presents in The "Genius." If the moonlight-and-roses notion, the "they married and lived happily ever after" nonsense that once pervaded literature had not yet received its death blow, Dreiser did his utmost to put it in its grave with every novel he wrote, but particularly with this, his most personal document.

If Eugene's marriage to Angela complicates rather than

solves his sexual problems by forcing him into the duplicity of pretended faithfulness while in reality he retains his freedom, so the couple's life in New York tears Eugene between the determination to follow his own genius to artistic integrity and the gnawing desire to grab for himself a lion's share of the money whose presence tantalizes him. Here Dreiser recaptures his own feelings during the days of bitterest struggle when, next to penniless himself, New York seemed a sea of whales worth one, fifty, a hundred million dollars. At this time, Eugene is twenty-six. His art has brought him little return, either in money or in recognition. The feeling grows that, without fame, art is nothing. Fame is all that is worth having. And with fame, money will flow into his pockets. Didn't his observations prove this true? All famous people dressed splendidly, ate richly, dwelt sumptuously. "He felt an eager desire to tear wealth and fame from the bosom of the world. Life must give him his share. If it did not he would curse it to his dying day."[6] Dreiser had already depicted the tarnished trophy cup which fame had extended to Carrie, wealth to Cowperwood, and of Eugene's burning hope he can only reiterate: "The hope of fame—what hours of speculation, what pulses of enthusiasm, what fevers of effort, are based on that peculiarly subtle illusion!"[7]

## III  *" 'Thank God for a realist!' "*

At the studios of Kellner and Son, through the efforts of M. Anatole Charles, the manager, who has seen Eugene's paintings and has instantly recognized the talent that produced them, Eugene is granted his first one-man show. The canvases themselves are a far cry from the romantic scenes so popular at the time. Though he has made his hero an artist, Dreiser guides Eugene's talent along his own realistic line; no mountain panoramas, no formal gardens, no Sundays on the Grande Jatte are for him. In their place are eloquent raw slices from real life.

Wrenched from the streets of New York—as surely as are Dreiser's own prose sketches in *The Color of a Great City* which, translated onto canvas, might substitute for Eugene's paintings and cover the walls of Kellner and Son—come scenes of industry and the lower classes: Fifth Avenue in a snowstorm, with unkempt, bony horses tugging a shabby bus along the snowswept streets;[8] Greeley Square in a drizzling rain, catching "the exact texture of seeping water on gray stones in the glare of various electric lights"; breadlines in which the destitute slouch like open sores on the body of society; milk trucks lumbering from the docks at four in the morning; an East Side push-cart street swarming with immigrant children; great locomotives of the type Whitman had chosen for recitative, plunging through freight yards amid plumes of smoke.

Very little of Whistler, Abbey, Inness, Sargent here. And, as if to insist upon Eugene's obvious and altogether conscious kinship with the emerging "ash can" school of art, there is the portrait of a great hulking Negro, bundled in tatters against the January cold, dumping a can of ashes, paper, and garbage into an iron wagon. Eugene's pictures cry the same raucous tune that Dreiser's novels shouted to the world, the barbaric yawp: "I'm dirty, I am commonplace, I am grim, I am shabby, but I am life."

"Thank God for a realist!" exclaims M. Charles. But whether such paintings, shocking and grim as they are, will sell is another question. Dreiser's novels had not sold—at least not in terms of best-sellerdom, and *Sister Carrie* had not been allowed to try—but the exhibition of veritist paintings at Kellner and Son is an unqualified success. Against the advice of a number of the critics, the obstinate public comes to gaze and remains to buy. Feeling at last that he is crossing the threshold of a significant career, Eugene sails with Angela for Paris, where he plans to paint, paint, paint. He will do for Paris what he has done for New York, mirror its face on canvas in a series of illustrations that shout their strong, uncensored message of life.

## IV   "A Sudden Glittering Light"

In the French capital Eugene suffers the first of the violent alterations which cumulatively shake a reader's faith in the novel's verisimilitude. The sole foreshadowing of the precipitous tailspin into which Eugene hurtles is the tag end of a laudatory review of the Kellner exhibit in which Luke Severas predicts a grand career for Eugene "if he perseveres, if his art does not fail him." *If his art does not fail him*—these seven syllables, we are told to believe, haunt Eugene until, despite his prodigious output, his glow of success, his undeniable triumph in New York, abruptly "one day at his easel he was seized with a peculiar nervous disturbance—a sudden glittering light before his eyes, a rumbling in his ears, and a sensation which was as if his body were being pricked with ten million needles. It was as though his whole nervous system had given way at every minute point and division."[9]

Some explanation of the crack-up is called for, and Dreiser attempts one. He attributes much of the nervous breakdown which incapacitates Eugene for five or six years to a "riot of indulgence" through which he and Angela attempt to save their marriage. "He had," suggests the author, "no knowledge of the effect of one's sexual life upon one's work, nor what such a life when badly arranged can do to a perfect art." This coming from Dreiser is a hard pill to swallow; yet he insists on outlining the effects of sexual excess upon the artist: how it can "distort the sense of color, weaken that balanced judgment of character which is so essential to a normal interpretation of life, make all striving hopeless, take from art its most joyous conception, make life itself seem unimportant and death a relief."

To ask a reader to accept this nonsense, in the face of Cowperwood, to whom sex was an essential spur to full living, is asking a good deal indeed. But it is asking much more to swallow it in the face of Dreiser's own life which, if we are to believe the legends he himself inspired, directly refutes everything he says about Eugene. Dorothy Dudley, who was on the scene and who should know, reports that the first and automatic question arising upon the mention of Dreiser's name during the most productive years was "What woman is Dreiser living with now?"[10] The remark's accuracy is attested to by others, including Dreiser himself. And when Eugene's breakdown is presented with such abruptness and oversimplification, Dreiser is asking too much by far. The reader feels that he has been done violence.

Eugene abandons art to recuperate as a day laborer. He works in a small town outside New York City as a railroad hand, then in a carpenter shop. Occupational therapy seems the remedy, although sexual abstinence apparently is not a part of the prescription; for Eugene regains his equilibrium rapidly enough to indulge in an extended affair of passion with the daughter of his landlady. When this duplicity is discovered by Angela, Eugene finds that "the hells of love are bitter and complete," but the revelation appears to retard his recovery not at all. He is poised for the struggle once more; feels his talents on the rise again; and, as an interim measure, assumes a position on the advertising staff of the New York *World*. This is the first step in a miraculous ascent more headlong, more inexplicable, and more unbelievable than his breakdown.

Practically overnight, Eugene vaults from wages of nine dollars a week on the railroad and a room at Mrs. Hibberdell's boardinghouse to a salary of $5,000 a year with the Summerfield Advertising Agency and a plush Riverside Drive apartment. The ladder he climbs is Algerian: from Summerfield's to Kalvin Publishing at $8,000, then $12,000; to Swinton-Scudder-Davis at $18,000, with swift promotion to $25,000. Installed in a white, blue, and gold office—rosewood desk and chairs, bouquets freshening ornate vases—as Managing Publisher of United Magazine Corporation, Eugene is "making good" in a big way. He owns stocks aggregating $30,000 and two lots in Montclair worth $6,000. A real-estate speculator interests him in developing a semi-swamp tract on the Atlantic into a resort for millionaires. All it will require is a little time, a little money. The prospect of a fortune dazzles Eugene's eyes. In a little while—tomorrow, next year perhaps—he will liquidate, retire on his profits, and return to his easel. But first the fortune.

Book Three, "Revolt," opens with Eugene an apparent favorite of fortune, on the high road to riches and loved by another beautiful child. In eighteen-year-old Suzanne Dale, daughter of a friend of his employers,[11] he has found—as he had in so many of her predecessors—everything a man might desire in a lover. He spies her first across the room at a reception Angela is giving; and, "with the irresistible attraction of an iron filing for a magnet," he is drawn to her, and she to him.

Oval-faced, radiantly healthy, ripe-lipped, and with chestnut hair curling above blue-gray eyes, Suzanne, to Eugene, puts to shame the glory of dew-sprinkled roses; "if he could only, once more in his life, have the love of a girl like that!" But in love Eugene never advances beyond the image of Stella Appleton of Alexandria. He is stalemated forever in the eighteenth year, the "only one true place of comfort" for him anywhere, "the spring time of love."

> So powerful was the illusion of desire, the sheer animal magnetism of beauty, that when it came near him in the form of a lovely girl of his own temperamental inclinations he could not resist it. . . . It was as though the very form of the face, without will or intention on the part of the possessor, acted hypnotically upon its beholder. The Arabians believed in the magic power

of the word Abracadabra to cast a spell. For Eugene the form
of a woman's face and body was quite as powerful.[12]

Although he realizes that taking Suzanne constitutes an adventure
of maximum hazard, so powerful is the illusion that he is ready,
eager, to wager all for love. Wife, position, money lose all
meaning. Only Suzanne counts. "For the first time in his life
he was to have a woman after his own heart, so young, so
beautiful, so intellectual, so artistic. With Suzanne by his side, he
was about to plumb the depths of all the joys of living."

For a time, paradise seems well within reach. "Surely the
gods were good. What did they mean? To give him fame,
fortune and Suzanne into the bargain?" In a Dreiser novel?
Hardly. For Eugene is fully as much a waif of illusion, every
bit as victimized by Nature's "dark forces moving aimlessly" as
Carrie or Jennie or Hurstwood or even Frank Cowperwood;
and he is equally as doomed to the bursting of the perilous
bubble, the shattering of the spell.

The dazzling light of Suzanne Dale blinds Eugene to the
antagonistic forces bent upon thwarting his hopes. To bind her
husband to her and depending on duty to accomplish what
love can not, Angela conceives a child. Mrs. Dale discovers
the Eugene-Suzanne liaison and spirits her daughter away to
Canada, but not before informing Eugene's employers of his
varietism. A niagara of blows falls, one upon another. The Sea
Island project is facing a crisis, and Eugene pours every available penny of capital into that ill-starred venture. Still blindly
confident of Suzanne's adoration, he sacrifices for this mirage
the position which has made his investments possible—and is
stripped of both. Suzanne is soon persuaded that mother knows
best, that her romance was no more than a "passing fancy,"
the chemism of her makeup having caused her to "make a fool of
herself with Eugene." The lamp of illusion, stubborn as it is,
is eventually extinguished. Angela dies in childbirth, leaving the
Genius with a daughter to raise and the possibility of a slow,
rational return to the art from which he should never have
strayed.

Piecing together the shards of his life, Eugene leaps from one
belief to another in a search for meaning. For a time Christian
Science seems the answer. Then he becomes convinced the
world is ruled by a devil, "a Gargantuan Brobdingnagian
Mountebank" of malicious intent. He at last arrives at the

position his author had outlined in "The Equation Inevitable," a state described as "not of abnegation, but of philosophic open-mindedness or agnosticism." Observing the universe, the human being shrinking smaller than a mote among swirling galaxies of stars, amid the play and interplay of cosmic forces, who was to know what to believe? Apparently anything was permitted, nothing remained stationary. "Perhaps life loved only change, equation, drama, laughter." In this huge chaotic system the individual came and went, acting his part, stung with delight by favorable illusions, crushed by the vagaries of circumstance, and altering nothing in the system itself, which remained as before, fixed, inscrutable and eternal.

In his gift of "genius," in his disregard for convention in pursuing the phantom of love, in his final failure to upset the equation of Nature, Eugene Witla prefigures Frank Cowperwood. He is not so strong, nor so clever, nor quite so ruthless and intent upon the main chance; but all the same he is an early attempt to portray the superman, as well as the nonentity, who fails in a universe where the mass is all, the individual a cipher. If the novel fails to ring the bell loud and clear, it is nevertheless a magnificent attempt. The conception, flawed though it be, is large; the theme, strong. Dreiser was not the first, nor would he be the last, writer whose materials were shattered by the dynamite of events too close to the man to be shaped by the artist.

## V   "A Band of Wasp-like Censors"

The "Genius" may not have been top-drawer Dreiser, but it did provoke a number-one battle with the censors, official and unofficial. The smog of trouble had hung in the air since the winter of 1914 when Harper's having printed The Titan and brought the volume to the binding stage, informed Dreiser with the suddenness of a lightning crackle that it was being withdrawn from publication. Whether the portrait of Emelie Grigsby (Berenice in the novel), Yerkes' last mistress, was so patently drawn from life that her powerful friends pressured Harper's into suppressing the book, or whether the novel in toto simply proved too strong meat to risk serving to a public more used to pabulum, will probably never be known.

Dreiser found himself facing a repetition of the Sister Carrie suppression. This time, rather than insisting upon his contractual rights, he went searching for a publisher with fortitude enough to see the book onto the stalls. The Century Company was afraid to touch it, although it had been given Dreiser's *A Traveler at Forty*. Scribner's refused it without a reading. George H. Doran would have nothing to do with any manuscript bearing the name Theodore Dreiser; and Dodd, Mead & Company wrote candidly that if the book was "too strong for Harper's it would surely be too rich" for them.

Finally John Lane and Company, after considerable debate and soul-searching, accepted *The Titan* and published it, to their surprise, without incident. Reassured, Lane the following year issued *The "Genius,"* although not without misgivings concerning subject matter and treatment. If *The Titan* was too rich for America's major houses to risk purveying, then surely *The "Genius,"* with its more explicit presentation of the erotic and its harsher indictment of American society for abetting the destruction of its artists, would meet with an outcry. Indeed, the *Little Review*, after hailing the book, declared "a howl will go up" from the critics and printed imaginative prophecies of the book's damnation as "sensually depraved and degenerate," as "striking at the bed rock of public solidarity, of home happiness, of everything decent and worth while."[13]

Dreiser and Lane braced themselves for the storm, but it did not break for another year. Instead, while many reviewers did howl, and loudly indeed, branding the novel Dreiser's "ugliest," the "epic of a human Tomcat," other critics compared the author favorably to Rolland, Dostoevski, Tolstoi, and other famous writers. The public was quiescent. Customers bought the book in modest quantities and, presumably having read it, formed no lynch mobs.

In July, 1916, the New York Society for the Suppression of Vice launched its attack upon *The "Genius."* Founded in 1873 by Anthony Comstock, this organization had amassed an impressive record in purging the country of obvious pornography, after which it turned its guns on the classics, banning, expurgating, attacking. Rabelais, Boccaccio, Shakespeare, Swift, Balzac, Zola, and Hardy came under fire. *Jude the Obscure* was banned; *Leaves of Grass* condemned. But Dreiser's novel was the first major work of an American contemporary to be threatened. The initial action came from an offshoot of the Comstock group, the Western Society for the Suppression of Vice who, finding *The "Genius"* "filled with obscenity and blasphemy," succeeded in removing it from most bookstores in Cincinnati. In New York, John S. Sumner, successor to Anthony Comstock, confronted the John Lane Company with "75 lewd and 17 profane passages" in the novel; and, ordering them deleted, he frightened the publisher into withdrawing the book temporarily in order to assess the situation and to plan a course of action.

Dreiser instinctively suggested an immediate counterattack. "A fight is the only thing and I want Lane to fight," he wrote his good friend H. L. Mencken. The plates of the book, to prevent their being seized and destroyed, were shipped out of the state. The United States postal authorities had been appealed to in the Comstock Society's next move to gain official sanction for its attack; and, under threat of the book's being banned from the mail, Dreiser wrote Mencken- of his intention to mail a copy personally. He declared he was "perfectly willing to break the postal laws and go to jail myself. It will save my living expenses this winter."[14]

From this rashness Mencken dissuaded him, prudently pointing out that while such a move would bring the case the notoriety Dreiser anticipated—indeed, craved—and would immediately line up the nation's authors and critics in his defense, the anti-German feeling running riot in wartime could not help but prejudice any defendant bearing a German name—and particularly one accused of criticizing American society and corrupting public morals. Any such dramatic act became less urgent to Dreiser in August when the Authors' League of America bolstered his defense with a public statement declaring *The "Genius"* to be "not lewd, licentious or obscene" and further deploring the "narrow and unfair" test of the vice society in its attempts to suppress works. Such tests threatened to "prevent the sale of many classics and of much of the serious work which is now being offered" to the public.

To the press Dreiser was vociferous; on more than one occasion he employed the give-'em-hell style lately associated with Harry S. Truman: "If my name were Dreiserevsky," he growled, "and I said I came from Moscow I'd have no trouble. But I come from Indiana—so goodnight!" And Mencken worked tirelessly in his friend's behalf, circulating leaflets and letters until 478 signatures had been obtained, many of them from authors or critics who signed to defend the principle even while deploring that the censorship battle must concern what they felt was a book not fully defensible. This, in fact, was Mencken's own attitude; yet he fought for the book as if it were the Great American Novel.

Among the signatures defending *The "Genius"* against suppression were those of E. W. Howe, Amy Lowell, Opie Read, Frank Harris, Ezra Pound, Sherwood Anderson, Robert Frost, Booth Tarkington, Gertrude Atherton, Ida Tarbell, Samuel Hopkins Adams, and Zoe Akins. From England the John Lane Company received a cable reading "We regard *The "Genius"* as a work of high literary merit and sympathise with the Authors' League of America in their protest against the suppression." It was signed by Arnold Bennett, Hugh Walpole, and H. G. Wells, among others.

But there were important dissenters also, some fully anticipated and some inexplicable. Brander Matthews, Nicholas Murray Butler, William Lyon Phelps, Bliss Perry, and Agnes Repplier all refused aid. A shock drove through the Dreiser forces when Hamlin Garland—the veritist and early defender of realism, he who had lately defined art as "an individual thing—the question of one man facing certain facts and telling his relation to them"—charged the entire movement with being "a piece of very shrewd advertising" promulgated by the John Lane Company. And when Dreiser, knowing William Dean Howells' wariness, urged that petitions be sent to the respected dean of American letters only after a massive weight of opinion had already been gathered, Howells too refused to lend his substantial prestige to the effort.

Dreiser's next step, since his publishers had not mustered the courage to reissue the novel at the risk of prosecution as he felt they had promised, was to bring a friendly suit against the John Lane Company for failing to fulfill contract stipulations. The case—heard in May, 1918, before the Appellate Division of the Supreme Court—was strongly argued by both defendant and plaintiff. FIVE JUDGES WILL DECIDE IF *The "Genius"* IS GENIUS, TOMMYROT, OR PLAIN FILTH was the headline featured by the Brooklyn *Daily Eagle*; and these five judges, apparently insufficiently impressed by the 478 signatures and the English cable presented by the defense, refused to rule for Dreiser.

For five more years, until Horace Liveright republished it, the novel stayed off the market; yet the battle, seemingly a defeat, was in actuality the first stage of victory. By awakening authors and critics to the very genuine threats to literary freedom which existed and by acquainting the public with the issues involved in suppression, the case of The "Genius" broke the ice for more favorable decisions to follow—the *Jurgen* trial of 1919 and the *Ulysses* trial of 1934 being cases in point—as bit by bit the tide of public sympathy shifted to support of the author, until today, as for instance in the case of *Lady Chatterley's Lover*, trials for suppression of reputable literary productions have become little more than formalities. The decisions are as predictable as they were in the days of *The "Genius"*—but of a more salutary nature.

CHAPTER *6*

# "Society Should Ask Forgiveness":
## *An American Tragedy*

### I  *"The Way Life has Organized Itself"*

IN HERKIMER COUNTY, New York, in 1906 a young man named Chester Gillette found his pregnant sweetheart an intolerable barrier to his hopes for rising in the world, lured her with the prospect of a lovers' outing to Big Moose Lake, and drowned her. The victim's name was Grace Brown, and her murderer was almost immediately discovered, apprehended, and executed. The crime was not unique. It closely paralleled the case of Carlisle Harris whose involvement with a poor girl threatened his marriage to a girl of wealth. Fumbling for a solution, Carlisle supplied his lover with pills salted with poison. An identical predicament ended in death for Avis Linnell of Hyannis, Massachusetts, when her lover, a Reverend Richardson, found her an obstacle on his way to advancement.

The mind of Theodore Dreiser, mulling over plans for a new novel, a big one, heard a familiar note running through these cases. There was a thread of similarity and meaning—he had been aware of it ever since his early newspaper days in St. Louis thirty years before—a pattern which might serve admirably as the framework for this story he had in mind. There was, Dreiser recognized, something distinctly—and frighteningly—*American* about the nature of the murders. Like genus financier, they constituted a peculiarly national phenomenon. And exactly as he had investigated the careers of a dozen American money kings before writing *The Financier* with Charles T. Yerkes as archetype, Dreiser studied a group of his "American tragedies"—more than fifteen in all—before he selected the Linnell-Richardson case for his model. Then, in his characteristic trial-and-error method, he laid the manuscript aside after completing six chapters; he had decided that the circumstances of the Gillette-Brown murder were more ideally suited to the book he wanted to produce.

Abstracted, the murders followed lines that might be predicted with near-scientific exactness, so closely did their basic facts agree. And their import tallied with Dreiser's own solidly established notions of an American society materialistic to the core, glittering with blandishments for the young—what Kenneth Lynn has called "The Dream of Success"—yet barring the castle of wealth with a portcullis invisible but iron-strong. Democracy or not, plates of bullet-proof glass seemed effectively to isolate one American economic class from another. If a superman of Frank Cowperwood's caliber might smash his way through at least the economic barriers, light years of frigid space still separated the classes socially. As for those born without Cowperwood's financial acumen, they could beat themselves insensible like storm-crazed sparrows fighting to get through the windows of closed rooms. If money was the first requisite for penetrating the stratified levels of status, wealth could not always provide a key to the parlors and drawing rooms of the mighty—as witness Aileen Cowperwood's fruitless at-homes. Yet other routes did exist. Of these, marriage seemed the most feasible. By such a route money and status might possibly be gained in one fell swoop.

In the existing system, society itself, it seemed to Dreiser, played the villain's role. It built irresistibly enticing parks where green thoughts might be contemplated in a green shade; then it spiked the sward with KEEP OFF THE GRASS signs. Yet America had been nurtured on tales of the office boy who married the boss's daughter. Dreiser himself had employed a variation on this theme in *Sister Carrie*, wherein men of steadily higher station ease the heroine's ascent to wealth and fame. But Carrie was able to jettison her lovers by packing a valise or by pinning a brusque note on a bedspread. In this way she preserved her mobility and could take advantage of whatever new opportunities arose.

For a young man the problem differed. Not only were a man's chances for a wealthy marriage infinitesimal compared to the Cinderella possibilities for a girl possessed of beauty and charm —and this notwithstanding the florid optimism of the dime novels—but when the young man had gotten himself inextricably involved with a poor girl, his difficulties multiplied. Such a girl could in no way advance his career. And then, if the girl found herself pregnant? If this situation were compounded by the young man's simultaneously catching a glimmer of hope from an heiress, frustration might build to explosive proportions. If the pregnant sweetheart refused to be set aside, murder might easily result; and often, Dreiser noticed, it did. Undoubtedly, if one were to base an estimation only upon the number of cases that came to public attention, it occurred more often than people realized.

The patently false but widely accepted American notion that an ambitious boy may rise to wealth with comparative ease seemed to Dreiser a primal cause of such crimes. Once again life was illustrating graphically the intense and cruel attraction wealth exerted upon the young. The power of the "money ideal" overwhelmed the poor. Continued observation merely underscored the truth of Dreiser's concept of man: "His feet are in the trap of circumstance; his eyes are on an illusion." For most, the dream of power, wealth, luxury was to prove of no more substance than a mirage; and *Mirage* became the working title under which Dreiser began writing.

## II  *A Tree Grows in Union Square*

Exactly when Dreiser first contemplated writing *An American Tragedy* is difficult to establish; but certainly, as with his other books, the idea teased his mind long before he wrote it. "I carry my plots around with me year after year before setting pen to paper," he answered an interrogator. "By the time I am ready to write I see the book as plainly as if it were a tree rising up before my eyes. Root, trunk, branches, twigs, so to speak, are all there; it is only the leaves that require to be sketched in."[1]

The "sketching in" of the *Tragedy's* foliage was underway by 1922.[2] Dreiser in 1919 had met a distant cousin of his, Helen Richardson, recently divorced from her first husband. Tumbling head over heels in love with her—only partly, we suspect, as a consequence of her youthful beauty and charm, and perhaps more so because of her obvious hero-worship and dedication to the novelist's work—he followed her the next year to Hollywood. Theatrically ambitious, she began as an extra and eventually established a minor career as a "starlet" in pictures such as *The Flame of Youth* and Valentino's *The Four Horse-men of the Apocalypse*. Still married—chained, he would cry—to Sallie White, though estranged from her for a decade now, Dreiser begged Helen to be his, and she agreed. Thus began the most permanent relationship in Dreiser's life, not unmarked by jealousy and stormy separation, to be sure, yet culminating eventually in marriage and meanwhile providing that ideal combination of youthful freshness and compatibility of interests which until now had possessed no more substance than the illusory dream of eighteen that he shared with his fictional heroes.

While in Hollywood he worked on a number of continuing projects, primarily on a book of autobiography he called *Newspaper Days* (issued in 1922 by Liveright as *A Book About Myself*), which chronicled his life following the death of his mother until his move to New York in the 1890's. By 1922 the desire to complete *Mirage* was overriding. With twenty chapters written, Dreiser could not rest until the skeletal tree in his mind was leafed out with words and the book was seen through the press. In order to do this, he had once again to set aside the manuscript of his long-delayed *The Bulwark* to gather first-hand materials on the Gillette-Brown case. In October he and Helen took the train for New York, where they rented a small studio where he could write through the winter. The following summer the two drove northward into Herkimer County where, seventeen years earlier, the murder of Grace Brown had occurred.

Already at Dreiser's disposal were the official court records of the Gillette trial and numerous newspaper reports dating from the event. But he wanted to view the area at first hand, the way he had dogged Yerkes' trail to Philadelphia, Chicago, New York, and Europe. Stopping in Cortland, New York, which was to become the Lycurgus of the novel, Dreiser toured the various sections of the city to obtain a firm impression of the locale: The impressive residential area in which he would locate Wykeagy Avenue, home of the wealthy Griffiths; the factory section where the collar plant might feasibly be set; the middle- and lower-class regions where Mrs. Cuppy's boardinghouse and Roberta Alden's lonely room would be located. No movie producer, scouting a "location" for a multi-million dollar enter-prise, ever took more pains to establish the authenticity of a scene. Near South Otselic—to become Blitz, Roberta's home in the book—Dreiser and Helen drove down the dusty road which had led to Grace Brown's country home, described vividly in the novel when Clyde Griffiths stops there by accident and is forced to request road information from Titus Alden.

Finally there were Old Forge (Gun Lodge in the book) and Big Moose Lake, the scene of the crime, which Dreiser was to rename Big Bittern. Here they rowed out upon the lake, drifting into quiet, isolated, tree-lined inlets, any one of which might have supplied the remote waters into which Roberta sank and from which Clyde escaped dripping and panic-stricken. The actual bend where the murder took place was pointed out by a boatman. Questioned by Dreiser, he replied that he remembered the Gillette boy, and went on to describe him as "dark and swarthy, young and good-looking," the way he appears in the novel. And drifting on Big Moose, Dreiser heard for the first time the ominous cry of the "weir weir" bird which haunts his murder scene.

After working through the summer in a lake-district cabin, Dreiser and Helen returned to New York in a spirit of estrangement. She entrained immediately for Los Angeles in a jealous fury at having discovered herself not, after all, the sole possessor of her lover's affections. After many months of separation, the two were reconciled. They returned to New York, where Dreiser took an office in the Guardian Life Building near Union Square where he could continue his arduous task without interruption. Two friends, J. G. Robin and Arthur Carter Hume, tenants in the same building, were equipped to supply him with technical information concerning points of law in the trial scenes of his book.

Time was growing short. A great deal of writing had already gone into the manuscript, but much more was to be done. The mass of paper was beginning to shape up into a story, and Dreiser gave his undivided attention to completing it as soon as possible. Of his work during these days, Helen Dreiser writes:

> He was like a sculptor working on a figure which had grown so large that he seemed to be throwing his clay high to the top with a mighty hand. He modeled, chiseled, formed and reformed until one could see and feel the whole structure coming to life. There was so much mass material and so much modeling to be done before it was acceptable to him—writing, rewriting, revising, four, five or six times.[3]

It was 1925 now. Spring gave way to summer, summer to fall, and still Dreiser was writing. His publisher, Liveright, was clamoring for the final manuscript. Sections of the book were already being set up in type and proofs circulated privately among selected readers. Opinions began coming in. Some damned, some praised. Some questioned the title, which Dreiser had changed from *Mirage* to *An American Tragedy*. How arrogant! Pompous, really. "How in the world can Dreiser call a book *An American Tragedy*?" asked Thomas Smith, Liveright's closest literary adviser. The author held firm. Liveright had promised him freedom to shape the book as he saw fit—and had furnished him with a generous, regular advance in order to provide optimum conditions for composition. Dreiser was determined to do it his way or not at all.

By November all was accomplished but the polishing of the final chapters, for which Dreiser hoped to confirm his rendering of the death house scenes by visiting execution row in Sing Sing. He must be certain of his facts, rely as little as possible upon others' eyes, others' words. How many cells in a death block? Arranged in what number of tiers? What were the dimensions of a condemned man's cell? How furnished? What color its walls? How thick a door, and how fashioned? Of what nature the inmates? Details, details, details, and each one, to the writer, of vital import.

Requesting permission to visit the prison and being refused, he appealed to Mencken for help. In this manner Dreiser found possible an arrangement with the New York *World* to enter the death house as a special reporter. Ostensibly he was to interview a certain condemned murderer who was reportedly on the brink of confession.

Hustling home from his visit, his mind packed full as a valise with the details he needed for authentic documentation, Dreiser completed Book Three, in which the death house takes shape almost brick by brick, tier by tier, before the reader's eyes, each sentence inching toward the moment when Clyde Griffiths —accoutred in felt slippers, grey socks, collarless white shirt, and black trousers slit for the metal plate—follows his cellmates through the door of the chair room. In such a sequence Dreiser is at the height of his powers. His mass of detail is no inventory or mere catalog, but an accretion of incident constructing single-mindedly and with heartbreaking inevitability the mirror of reality, typical and unmistakable. It is as genuine as Carrie's desperate search for a job in the brick canyons of 1889 Chicago or the childhood of Jennie Gerhardt or the manipulation of municipal bonds by Frank Cowperwood.

On November 25, 1925, *An American Tragedy* was complete. Dreiser was satisfied to put the final pages of manuscript in the hands of his publisher, while he and Helen began a motor tour of the Eastern coast, heading for Florida and what they hoped might be their long-deserved rest.

## III   *The Tree in Foliage*

What was the nature of the manuscript Horace Liveright received from Dreiser and hurried onto the bookstalls before the year was out? Its massiveness might be its first impact upon a reviewer, sheer weight alone being impressive or depressing, as the case might be. Lengthy volumes were expected from Dreiser, but this was far longer than any single novel he had produced. It amounted to some 840 pages and had to be issued in two volumes, a procedure almost unheard of since the days of the nineteenth-century triple-decker.

This huge new novel's division into three distinct books would remind many of Dreiser's still uncompleted *Trilogy of Desire*. But perhaps from that earlier experience Dreiser had learned the danger of a writer such as himself relinquishing an unfinished story to the press. Without the fate of the *Trilogy* to warn him, he might well have succumbed to the temptation of making a trilogy out of this book too. Supposing, then, any lack of enthusiastic response, he could easily have found himself sidetracked on other ventures. *The Bulwark*, for instance, was still crying to be finished. But for once he chained himself to his desk until the enormous task was done.

The result: a birth-to-death chronicle of an American boy with the same basic aspirations, the same dream of success, as Frank Cowperwood, yet devoid of so much as an ounce of the financier's capacity to succeed. The disparity between Clyde Griffiths and Cowperwood might remind a reader of the contrast between Jennie Gerhardt and Carrie Meeber. Heredity had always figured importantly in shaping Dreiser's characters. Carrie and Cowperwood, Jennie and Clyde are what they are largely because they were born to be either hardy weeds or fragile blossoms. In his single full-length play, *The Hand of the Potter*, in which a sex criminal cries for exoneration with a plaintive "I ain't made right. . . . Can you blame a man when he ain't right?" heredity is blamed almost completely. But environment was significant also. The Chicago into which Carrie was plunged to sink or swim can be credited as much as any single factor with the direction her life takes.

It is so in *An American Tragedy*. Care is taken to make Clyde as much as circumstances permit an "average" American. That is, the extremes of hereditary influence are avoided, leaving the boy neither the mentally crippled deviate of *The Hand of the Potter* nor the squid-devouring lobster of *The Financier*. Clyde stands on middle ground; he is a young man for whom many fates are possible. What happens to Clyde will happen not only because of the drives with which he has been naturally endowed, but because of the influences which mold him and the direction from which the indifferent winds of chance happen to blow.

## IV  *From the Door of Hope to the Green-Davidson*

The first book, which lays the foundation for the structure to follow, Mencken excoriated as "a menagerie of all Dreiser's worst deficiencies."[4] Mencken was a great, good friend of Dreiser's and his most loyal enthusiast; and, though he is more often right than wrong with his criticism, he is not infallible. Prone to overpraise—he ranks *Jennie Gerhardt* far above *Sister Carrie*—Mencken underrates as well. About *An American Tragedy* he seems to have been mistaken from the start.

The sheer weight of detail elaborating Clyde Griffiths' boyhood is precisely what is called for to buttress the actions of books Two and Three, making credible—even predictible— Clyde's actions in the love triangle at the heart of the book. Without the first book and the additions Dreiser later makes to the story of the murder, the central plot would strike us as contrived and pat, whether documented by real life events once or a hundred times over. Fiction demands more than the bare facts baldly presented; the novelist's duty is to relate not what happened, but what probably would happen in a given set of circumstances. The foreshadowing in the first book casts a long shadow, creating such probability that all Clyde's later actions come not as surprise but as a fulfillment.

It is largely this detailing of environmental pressures at all stages of Clyde's story—precisely the method used previously in *The Financier*—that prevents the novel from becoming a mere transcript of the Gillette trial and therefore just another "fictionalized" version of a sordid crime. The first book is invented in its entirety by Dreiser. Although it deals not with the crime at all, and introduces but one of the figures in the love triangle upon which the central story depends, this book's mass of detail establishes Clyde's personality with such precision that we can chart the boy's reactions to later events with slide-rule accuracy. We know Clyde's hopes, dreams, ambitions. We know Clyde's limitations, blindnesses, fears. We have seen how a carrot dangled before Clyde's hungry eyes will stimulate his salivary glands and set him leaping, and we have seen that a crisis will trigger a rush for escape.

Dreiser's hand, in operating this literary camera, never falters, but establishes always the correct focus upon Clyde. Although a plethora of places and the people who inhabit them dominates the story, each locale is graphically sketched, then filled in and populated to furnish for the reader its particular effect upon the boy. The Door of Hope Mission, operated by 'Clyde's ineffectual parents, Asa and Elvira Griffiths, is located in a section of Kansas City some blocks from the heart of the commercial center amid a blighted district which is sliding pell mell into slum. On the ground floor of an old and decrepit wooden structure, a former business establishment now vacant, the mission looks upon the "dreary back yards of equally dreary frame houses" of Bickel Street. The mission's bedraggled walls are papered with homilies attempting to establish, amid this squalor and decay, the image of a paternal, beneficent God. Prominent among the mottoes is the plaintive reminder "How Long Since You Wrote to Mother?" This hand-lettered placard will haunt the perceptive reader throughout the extended mother-son relationship and be reintroduced in the final chapter for its ironic impact.

Essentially pagan in nature, Clyde even at the age of twelve rebels instinctively from the mission environment. His humiliation deepens each time he is dragged through the streets to sing and lecture with the mission group. He is poor as the proverbial churchmouse, yet vain and proud—echoing young Dreiser's refrain "No common man am I"—and finds himself stifling in the fetid atmosphere of Bickel Street: "the whole neighborhood was so dreary and run-down that he hated the thought of living in it." A desperate reluctance to be trapped and the corresponding blind scrambling for escape which characterize his later life are planted in Clyde from this age.

Clyde's parents are of no aid. The father, an amalgam of Dreiser's own father and of the impractical Asa Conklin for whom Dreiser had worked in Chicago while his mother was dying, is "one of those poorly integrated and correlated organisms, the product of an environment and a religious theory, but with no guiding or mental insight of his own, yet sensitive and therefore highly emotional and without any practical sense whatsoever." Asa has dragged his family from town to town on the Midwestern circuit—Grand Rapids, Detroit, Milwaukee, Chicago, Kansas City. The four children, practically unschooled, trail behind like ribbons in the dust.

Elvira Griffiths is another reincarnation of Dreiser's mother, the gentle soul who "would follow love anywhere"; this Dreiser indicates clearly as he describes her: "Mrs. Elvira Griffiths before she had married Asa had been nothing but an ignorant farm girl, brought up without much thought of religion of any kind. But having fallen in love with him, she had become inoculated with the virus of Evangelism and proselytizing which dominated him, and had followed him gladly and enthusiastically in all of his ventures and through all of his vagaries."[5]

What happens to children from such a family, such an environment, when their little mission world collides with the universe beyond its walls? The oldest girl, Esta, reminiscent of Dreiser's sisters, is seduced through "chemic witchery" by an actor and then deserted, pregnant. The episode heightens the contradiction Clyde has already sensed between the God of his parents—the Good Shepherd who cares for His flock—and the matter-of-fact way of the world. Esta, for her transgression, is an outcast from society and nearly so from her family as well. She suffers alone, and her future is black. Clyde himself, as he turns thirteen, fourteen, fifteen, is increasingly magnetized by the attractions of the forbidden streets. A glance in the mirror proves he is not bad looking. Having eyes and using them, he soon discovers what others regard as desirable: money, position, clothes. "If only he had a better coat, a nicer shirt, finer shoes, a good suit, a swell overcoat like some boys had!"

At fifteen, Clyde regards his job as soda-clerk in a third-rate drug store as the ultimate measure of success, but before long he sets his sights on a more glamorous target. In some ways he is brother to Carrie Meeber, reaching forever upward for a new grip on the ladder, engrossed in "the true mirage of the lost and thirsting and seeking victim of the desert." From soda-clerk he graduates to bellboy at the Green-Davidson Hotel. By his standards handsomely uniformed and magnificently paid, he is free for the first time to set his own hours for returning home. He could stay out till midnight if he desired! To what greater glories could a young man aspire? And the hotel itself—that massive tower of brick and green marble whose very sight makes Clyde tremble with excitement and within whose walls he rubs shoulders with wealth and display and also learns the delights and duplicities of sex—is a symbol of the world Clyde's nature starves for. The mission and the hotel—these two structures dominate the first book of the novel and provide Clyde with his ineffectual, misguided education.

## V  *From Thorpe Street to Wykeagy Avenue*

Clyde flees from Kansas City following an automobile accident which kills a pedestrian. By now, flight is established as his characteristic method of meeting a crisis. By coincidence he encounters his wealthy uncle in Chicago. But after then moving to Lycurgus and a position with the Griffiths Collar & Shirt Company, the boy is stalemated once again between two worlds, poor and rich. The polarity between the mission and the hotel is repeated.

Older now, going on twenty-one, Clyde has inched upward in the world somewhat. But Dreiser warns the reader that he has "a soul that was not destined to grow." He will always be a fumbler, a groper, without a mind capable of discerning the direct road to advancement and of striding out confidently upon it. Despite Clyde's hopes of social acceptance his uncle's family rebuffs him because of indifference and of the chance resemblance to his cousin Gilbert who vainly resents having a double. But Lycurgus was also a town of classes: "One had to have castes. One was foolishly interfering with and disrupting necessary and unavoidable social standards when one tried to unduly favor any one—even a relative."[6] Clyde's social world in Lycurgus is bounded by the four walls of Mrs. Cuppy's boarding-house on Thorpe Street.

Being a Griffiths—shirt-tail relationship notwithstanding—Clyde feels superior to his co-workers at the factory and they defer to him, conscious of the ambiguity which places him, while not exactly among the proprietors, certainly beyond the ordinary employee. Yet the Griffiths mansion on "that beautiful Wykeagy Avenue" might as well display a NO ADMITTANCE sign on the gateway for all the notice his relatives take of Clyde. His anomalous position—he is neither fish nor fowl—is truly intolerable. Out of it, with an inevitability of circumstance, grows the tragedy.

Desperate for love and companionship, certain that the wealthy Griffiths mean to exclude him forever from their private lives, yet never quite giving up hope altogether, Clyde drifts into the clandestine affair with Roberta Alden which results in her pregnancy. At the same time, his chance encounter with the society belle Sondra Finchley, her use of him to irritate his cousin Gilbert, Clyde's resultant flurry of popularity with the "set," then his infatuation with Sondra, and finally, incomprehensibly, love—or what passes for love. To possess Sondra! The door to Clyde's dream of success is swinging wide at last.

Upon Sondra's insistence, the Griffiths are goaded into accepting Clyde. His future teems with promise. At the end of the road, perhaps lies marriage into this prominent family, the Finchleys. He sees it all clearly: wealth, luxury, position; himself installed in a mansion on Wykeagy Avenue. On the other hand the picture darkens, the future fades. Roberta herself is trapped and fighting to preserve herself. Clyde finds her petulant, to some extent vengeful. Because of her conventional rearing and Clyde's own promises to her, and above all perhaps because of her desire not to injure her simple family, she insists that Clyde marry her. As Sondra pulls the door to affluence open, inviting entrance, Roberta tugs it shut in his face, bars his way.

Murder is the method Clyde chooses—or is driven to choose?—in order to open the road from Thorpe Street to Wykeagy Avenue. But the novel stands at a far remove from the conventional murder mystery. It has been pointed out by others that Clyde provides the law with every necessary clue to insure his discovery, so that the question is never whether he will be caught, but only when. And it is here that the massive preparation in the first book bears fruit; for Clyde, having determined his *modus operandi*, performs now in precisely the manner one has been led to expect, enhancing the action with an inevitability which neither shocks nor surprises but satisfies a preconceived notion of this new "waif amid forces."

Because Dreiser was bent upon at least explaining and at most exonerating his murderer, Clyde must be understood as acting according to the dictates of his innate capabilities and his environmental drives. A considerable weight of responsibility is lifted from his shoulders by Dreiser's painstaking scrutiny of the various alternatives to killing Roberta. If circumstances permitted, Clyde would flee from this crisis as fast as his sturdy legs would carry him, just as he had run after the automobile accident in Kansas City; and he would not stop running until he holed up in some nook of security far from the scene where he might puzzle over this unfortunate development, absolve himself, and renew his struggle. But too much—his entire dream of success—is at stake to permit flight.

The great point in the *Tragedy* is that, loathing Clyde's motives and his methods, we can still understand and sympathize with the boy in his predicament, as Dreiser slowly, exactingly dramatizes Clyde's bootless fumbling for a solution. He takes Roberta to a physician in hopes of obtaining an abortion, but is refused. He searches out every nostrum and old wives' remedy he can find, ransacking folk medicine in an effort to rid himself of the child. At last he sends Roberta home to Blitz and does his utmost to brainwash himself of the entire experience; if he forgets about her and the baby, perhaps they will vanish like a bad dream.

I. A. Richards has said of tragedy that "suppressions and sublimations alike are devices by which we endeavor to avoid issues which might bewilder us. The essence of tragedy is that it forces us to live for a moment without them." This surely is Clyde's position. Being non-ectoplasmic, the apparition of Roberta obstinately refuses to evaporate. Clyde is forced at last to face the issue squarely. Alternatives were never more clear cut: Either he must marry Roberta voluntarily and discard his dreams of affluence or he must abandon her and see his hopes die when she exposes his duplicity to his rich friends. The former he is constitutionally unable to do. The latter he cannot allow to happen.

If he cannot untangle the Gordian knot, he can sever it— providing he possesses the proper sword. Clyde has ever been the plaything of chance, and once again coincidence provides his answer. He reads in the newspaper the report of an accidental tragedy on a nearby lake. A young couple, enjoying an outing, drown when their boat overturns. Suddenly he knows what must be done, and how. But even having arrived at his decision, Clyde is temperamentally unfit to perpetrate the deed in cold blood. The extended scenes preliminary to the drowning, prolonged by Clyde's vacillation, his nervous bungling, his decision and indecision, are masterful in producing the effect Dreiser was grasping for. In the stalling, the searching for time, time, time, the deciding and reconsidering, they remind one of Eliot's "Prufrock":

> And indeed there will be time
> To wonder, "Do I dare?" and "Do I dare?"
> Time to turn back and descend the stair. . . .
> In a minute there is time
> For decision and revisions which a minute will reverse.[7]

In such a mood Clyde wanders with Roberta from lake to lake, ostensibly searching for the ideal honeymoon spot, but actually seeking the seclusion appropriate to a bloody deed.

For a parallel to the death scene itself, so neatly balanced between guilt and innocence as to provide material for debate in law schools, one must return in thought to Hurstwood bending over the safe in Fitzgerald and Moy's. In their mingling of premeditation and accident at the instant of opportunity, the two scenes tally; but Clyde's dilemma is the more intense, the more crucial, because his stakes are higher. Hurstwood is groping for a route out of what promises to be an unsavory experience; Clyde is fighting for his entire dream of success. To him it is life itself.

Now two young people are at last alone—but for such divergent reasons—on the still waters of Big Bittern. The shore-line is deserted, the wooded inlets are dark with trees, and, so far as one can tell, there are no peering eyes to witness. He hears the harsh, unearthly cry of the weir-weir bird, "Kit, kit, kit, c-a-a-ah!" Roberta prattles innocently about her "Clydie Mydie" and about the new collar factory in Syracuse where he may find employment after they are married. Clyde, tense as a fiddle string, anticipates the perfect moment to kill, yet delays, shrink-ing from the deed. He is paralyzed by the stalemate between a "chemic revulsion" against the very notion of murder and a violent impulse to seize the moment and implement his plan. His nerves are riddled. He squats in a trance, staring at Roberta in a "static between a powerful compulsion to do and yet not to do."

Then, like the accidental click of the safe in Fitzgerald and Moy's which decided Hurstwood's fate, Roberta rises from her seat in the stern of the boat to shatter the counterpoise. Instantaneously the fatal chain of events recommences, precisely as Clyde had originally planned, but not now initiated by him. If any freedom of choice had existed, it now capitulates; and the element of chance takes control. To increase the doubt of guilt, Dreiser arranges not only this happenstance, but puts into Clyde's hand a camera in place of the tennis racket wielded by Chester Gillette. For a camera is a natural accoutrement for a boat ride along the shore of a picturesque lake. But a tennis racket in a canoe? Who can explain it? As Roberta reaches for Clyde's hand, tipping the boat, the boy's bodily reflexes, conditioned now by tension and pressures, cause him to repulse her. She falls, struck accidentally by his camera. The boat tips further. Into the dark deep waters of Big Bittern she plunges, sinks—and at this point Dreiser adds another circumstance to the prototype. The gunwale of the boat, as it capsizes, strikes Roberta on the head, a stunning but non-fatal blow. In this Clyde has no part.

Roberta drowns. Clyde, having failed—out of panic or deliberately?—to answer her one plea for help, crawls dripping up onto the dark shore. In his mind is "the thought that, after all, he had not really killed her."

Or had he? He had meant to, originally. Yet he had not pushed her into the lake. That was her own doing. Nor had he guided the gunwale of that boat to her skull. Yet he had refused to rescue when he might have. But in her frenzy she might have impeded his own survival.

Is he guilty or innocent? Even he does not know for sure.

## VI  *From Big Bittern to Murderers' Row*

The final book of *An American Tragedy* bears toward its conclusion like a boulder roaring downhill, impelled by the momentum of all that has gone before. Dreiser's eye is always on the mark. There is no faltering, no groping for ways and means, no doubt about what he is doing. Yet there is an obvious ease to the writing, an apparent leisure in the telling, as if the author is certain of all the time in the world to tell his story, free of any pressure to cut corners or to oversimplify. The probing examination of each incident, the thorough documentation which lent verisimilitude to the first two books, is not neglected here. But so deftly, rhythmically is it all paced—the trial scenes with their clipped style: "And then . . . and then . . . etc."—so crucially is each segment made to bear upon the total structure that few readers feel length impeding the progress of the story.

One obvious explanation for this may be traced to the subject matter. The capture, the trial, and the execution of Clyde Griffiths are materials of guaranteed interest, nearly sure-fire. From the moment Coroner Fred Heit discovers Roberta's traveling bag at Gun Lodge and from her coat pocket draws the unmailed letter to her mother describing the trip to the lake district as a honeymoon, the search is on for Clifford Golden—or Carl Graham—or whoever may prove to be her mysterious dark, attractive young escort at Grass Lake and Big Bittern with the predilection for the initials C. G.[8]

In no time at all, a bagful of clues is collected which suggests foul play. At first there is only the puzzling failure to locate a second body in the lake. Then come the recollections of inn-keepers at Grass Lake and Gun Lodge regarding the ominous behavior of C. G. Added to these are the inexplicable bruises on Roberta's face and the Coroner's intuitive suspicion of her pregnancy. Through Roberta's unmailed letter her parents are traced, and their remarks result in the search of Clyde's room at Mrs. Peyton's and the discovery there of letters from both Roberta and Sondra, casting light on the triangle. Within four days after the drowning, Clyde is arrested at Shelter Beach on Bear Lake before the astounded eyes of Sondra and her wealthy friends.

The verdict is cut-and-dried before the prolonged trial gets underway. A tonnage of irrefutable circumstantial evidence is introduced. One by one, objects from Clyde's past are entered to confront him. His camera is dredged from the lake, and his tripod is found where he hid it in the woods as he fled in panic from Big Bittern to Twelfth Lake and Sondra. Roberta's clothing is displayed and her pitiful letters are recited aloud in court for the tears they evoke. As a climax, the boat, the identical vessel from which Roberta tumbled into the dark waters, is shown. Supporting these exhibits—each binding Clyde to the victim or to the scene and establishing motive and opportunity—are the testimonies of innkeepers, lawmen, guides, physicians—of one hundred and twenty-seven witnesses in all, including a woman camper who is convinced she heard a desperate scream for help rise from the lake at the exact moment Roberta drowned.

Against these there is little more than the bewilderment and confusion of Clyde, never certain exactly whether he is a murderer or a victim of circumstance, or both. Surprisingly, the predictability of the verdict does not at all diminish the suspense. More important, the story page by page penetrates more deeply into its examination of the American system and the implications to be drawn from it.

A rigorous hewing to the line of Clyde's punishment obscures the complexity of Book Three, which is actually as involved a sequence as Dreiser ever handled. Not only must the cast and action of the first two books be borne forward, but an entirely new group of *dramatis personae* must be added: the district attorney and the coroner and their various assistants; the lawyers and their staffs; judges; newspapermen; wardens; inmates of the death house; and the Reverend McMillan. These not only are introduced but are developed as individuals. Reading the book is like breathlessly observing a master acrobat on a highwire who begins by twirling a hoop about his waist, then juggles half a dozen balls in the air, and, when his agility seems taxed to the utmost, rises on a single toe. The total effect is one of dazzling virtuosity and skill in which individual manipulations lose none of their individuality, yet blend together into one harmonious action.

So many things are to be kept in sight and under control. The *mise en scène,* the wider landscape, must be continued lest the *American* of the title be lost in the particularities of Clyde's trial. What of the wealthy Griffiths, who feel that Clyde has betrayed them, who feel also that they have betrayed themselves and their circle by ever accepting Clyde into their lives? They would like most of all to blockade the doors of their inner sanctum and abandon Clyde to his fate, but social pressure demands that they make at least the gesture of obtaining an attorney for him. They are paradoxically obliged to defend the boy and to cut themselves off from him simultaneously. Gilbert is infuriated at the "little beast" whose defilement of the family name promises to "cost them their position here in Lycurgus society." The father is shaken but forced to admit that his own and his family's actions toward Clyde have been contributory to the horror.

And what of the Finchleys, in whose little vacuum-cleaner empire Clyde dreamed of becoming an executive by marriage? While Clyde and Roberta, being poor, have their lives stripped naked to the public glare, the Finchleys can escape in anonymity to Narragansett; Sondra, through the influence of wealth and power, remains known only as "Miss X"; she is shielded from the newspapers, played down by the trial attorneys. Notwithstanding the distribution of guilt among the many, back of the scenes powerful forces, both economic and political, are at work determining who shall be exposed, who protected—and money and position are the major determinants.

As the trial opens, concessionaires offer popcorn and peanuts to the curious throngs in a carnival atmosphere. Facsimile volumes of Roberta's love letters are hawked on the very steps of the courthouse. But any veneer of levity soon peels away. The grim procedure of juror interrogation begins, and soon a day arrives when twelve hostile men occupy the jury box. In the audience sit the Titus Aldens, their presence raising to a pitch the palpable hatred for the defendant, the pity for his victim.

Courtroom scenes have a way of becoming centers of interest in themselves; and to reduce this danger, to force the trial away from melodrama and toward an intensification of the total complex, Dreiser adds here and there a touch of his own. Men, he had often protested, are neither good nor bad, but mixed. The ambiguity of Clyde's relative guilt or innocence in the drowning had already been strongly and deliberately established. If he is not a conventional villian, then neither must the enforcers of the law be allowed to become conventional heroes. Above all, Dreiser's book must not present good guy versus bad guy; to so oversimplify would be ruinous to its theme.

The idea of the distribution of guilt has been quietly worked into the novel from its first pages, but it rises to the surface every now and then like a fish leaping from still waters to remind one he is there. Doctor Glenn, to cite one instance, whom Roberta consults hopeful of an abortion, piously lectures her on medical ethics. There are, he admits, doctors here and there "who take their professional ethics a little less seriously than I do; but I cannot let myself become one of them." But even as he dismisses Roberta with this sermon, he is conscious of having

a number of times in the recent past performed the same opera-
tion for "young girls of good family who had fallen from grace
and could not otherwise be rescued." *Of good family* is the key
phrase; it means, of course, families of wealth and social status.
Self-interest still rules society, and money speaks in loud, clear
tones of authority.

Mindful of his purpose, Dreiser draws Coroner Fred Heit
as a conniving politician who grimly opposes every move by
Clyde's attorneys for change of venue or delay in order that
the trial may occur in his bailiwick immediately preceding
election day. District Attorney Orville Mason, with his "psychic
sex scar," is portrayed as a foxhound leaping upon its kill. His
assistant, Burton Burleigh, "as sly a person as might have been
found in a score of such backwoods counties as this," considers
legal fraud no obstacle in his determination to convict Clyde.
Not content with the mountain of evidence arrayed against
Clyde and finding no telltale blood in the contents of the boat,
Burleigh visits the Lutz Brothers morgue and ghoulishly snares
a few strands of hair from Roberta's corpse which, deftly
threaded between the door and lens of Clyde's camera, may
be "discovered" as proof the victim was bludgeoned with the
instrument.

As for Clyde's attorneys, the firm of Belknap and Jephson
retained by Samuel Griffiths, they lend patient ears to Clyde's
story, but out of their hard-headed practical experience they
reject it as impossible in terms of legal defense and concoct
in its place a plea of insanity or "brain storm," which they
deem a possibility for saving at least Clyde's life. This in turn
is summarily rejected by the wealthy Griffiths because in its
wider ramifications it threatens to taint their own family line.
Everyone has himself to protect. No one really cares about
Clyde. Of Belknap and Jephson it must be said that they direct
Clyde's defense, hopeless from the start, as well as they can be
expected to; but, the trial once over, their encouragement of
Clyde's mother to launch her public lectures to raise money for
a useless appeal is reprehensibly mercenary.

The reintroduction of Elvira Griffiths in the final section is
a masterful stroke on Dreiser's part. Not only does it signify the
national interest in the trial—the Asa Griffiths are operating
a mission in Denver when they are hunted out by the newspapers and used for headline fodder—but it neatly ties the
end of the story to the beginning and lends a unity to the

novel which, in combination with the epilogue, brings the action full circle. Of course, the mother's struggle to save her son from the electric chair is no more effectual than her struggle to preserve him from the corrupting taint of materialism in the novel's first pages.

> He was alone. He had no one who believed in him. *No one.* He had no one, who, in any of his troubled and tortured actions before that crime saw anything but the darkest guilt apparently. And yet—and yet— . . . he had a feeling in his heart that he was not as guilty as they all seemed to think. After all they had not been tortured as he had by Roberta with her determination that he marry her and thus ruin his whole life. They had not burned with that unquenchable passion for the Sondra of his beautiful dreams as he had. They had not been harassed, tortured, mocked by the ill-fate of his early life and training, forced to sing and pray on the streets as he had in such a degrading way, when his whole heart and soul cried out for better things. How could they judge him, these people, all or any one of them, even his own mother, when they did not know what his own mental, physical and spiritual suffering had been? . . . at times he felt strongly that he was innocent, at others he felt he must be guilty.[9]

The world, having lured Clyde into transgression, now exacts its tribute; and Clyde dies more bewildered than ever.

In the epilogue, it is once again the dusk of a summer night. Amid the tall walls of an American metropolis, the missionaries are again singing to an indifferent and pitying throng "How Firm a Foundation." Another young boy is hauled against his protestations from The Star of Hope Mission to Market Street. Russell, Esta's child, at eight years of age is already fixing his eyes upon the enticements of the world outside, begging for a dime for an ice-cream cone. Once again the polarity of the material and spiritual is brought into focus, the disproportionate battle already lost, the superior strength of "the way society has organized itself" apparent—despite Asa Griffiths' dreamily hopeful "It seemed to me they were a little more attentive than usual," despite the fact that "at least eleven took tracts" (in the novel's beginning parallel scene, twenty-seven took tracts), and despite a single aged gentleman's inquiry as to where the mission is located and when services will be held.

So long as American society persists in organizing itself the way it has, Dreiser appears to be cautioning his reader, the

American tragedies he portrayed in every one of his novels will repeat themselves. The novel ends with young Russell running toward the corner drugstore and with the rest of the missionary group retreating inside the doors of The Star of Hope, on whose window lingers ironically the placard "How Long Since You Wrote to Mother?"

## VII    *"I've Hit the Mark This Time."*

Had the fates granted Dreiser but a single novel in which to dramatize the beliefs and lessons of his lifetime, that volume would of necessity have been *An American Tragedy*. In it, not only are his novelistic shortcomings reduced to their minimum, but the single story blends the author's major attitudes harmoniously. Here, for instance, the reader glimpses again the Dreiser childhood, less detailed, less yoked to reality than in *Jennie Gerhardt*, altered greatly in fact, yet recognizable all the same. Here the world of poverty is squared off once more against the world of wealth, to less extremity than in the *Trilogy* and therefore with wider application and with a greater effect in castigating the idolatry of the dollar, social prestige, and the respectability of façade.

Once again, peering through closed windows into illuminated parlors from which he is excluded, is the lone outsider, by this time a hallmark of Dreiser's novels. Here too are the strife born from extremes of poverty and wealth; the stifling of spiritual qualities by material fascinations which earlier had drawn *Sister Carrie* like a magnet into vacuous mirage; the individual's rage to live pitted against a righteous mass accusing, judging, bent upon casting the transgressor into outer darkness, as in *Jennie* and *The "Genius."* Throughout, as always, the winds of chance whip capriciously, unjustly, disastrously. Sex remains an irresistible force dominating man, submerging him in illusions which lead, in this case, not to mismating alone but to catastrophe.

*An American Tragedy*, actually contains nothing that is new to the Dreiser notion of the formula of life; yet it weaves together every main thread of his philosophy into a single finished fabric. The Gillette-Brown case had proved to be—as Dreiser must have sensed from the start—the "objective correlative" which would spark his most mature and realized piece of fiction.

The ideas which had arisen here and there in his previous work could now be drawn together, to emerge magically in place and in proper proportion:

> I had long brooded upon the story, for it seemed to me not only to include every phase of our national life—politics, society, religion, business, sex—but it was a story so common to every boy reared in the smaller towns of America. It seemed so truly a story of what life does to the individual—and how impotent the individual is against such forces. My purpose was not to moralize—God forbid—but to give, if possible, a background and a psychology of reality which would somehow explain, if not condone, how such murders happen—and they have happened with surprising frequency in America as long as I can remember.[10]

The reception of Dreiser's novel is a valid measure of the changing attitudes toward fiction between 1900 and 1925, changes Dreiser had labored a quarter of a century to influence. If all the points made in the novel had been made previously, Dreiser had been ignored, attacked, suppressed, banned for making them. And how this new book would be received, he did not know. Surely he hoped for the best, but his past experience could scarcely have led him to expect a resounding ovation. After all, the structure of American society itself was attacked; the book's readers would find themselves disclosed as participants in a tragic situation of immense proportions; they would soon discover themselves responsible for a hero who was a murderer. Although in paying the highest penalty for his crime Clyde preserved at least the façade of official justice and morality, Dreiser was calculatedly and openly set on a bold attempt to exonerate the boy, lifting the responsibility off his shoulders and placing it squarely upon the inhabitants of every city and hamlet in the nation.

When the nation proved to be as "ready" for *An American Tragedy* as it had been unprepared for *Sister Carrie,* the irony of the affair could not have helped but strike Dreiser as further corroboration of the inscrutable ways in which life turned. With surprising unanimity the critics spoke out in praise. H. G. Wells termed the book "one of the very greatest novels of this century." Joseph Wood Krutch called it "the great American novel of our generation." Even Stuart P. Sherman, devil's advocate to all Dreiser's previous works—especially the *Trilogy* and *The "Genius,"* and, as such, the logical leader of a storm of opposition—performed a complete about-face and bestowed his highest praise: the book was *moral.* While other writers, remarked George Ade, not excepting himself, had been tacking together chicken coops and bungalows, "Mr. Dreiser has been erecting skyscrapers."[11] The novel was banned in Boston, to be sure, but the power of the vice crusaders had been broken and the movement did not spread. Attacked on the grounds that he had relied so heavily upon materials from the Gillette trial as to produce no more than a plagiarism from life, Dreiser was defended by allusions to Shakespeare, whose plays, it was pointed out, consist primarily of adaptations transformed by the alchemy of genius.

To find himself so defended by the critics was almost as odd as to have his writings bought and read on a wholesale basis. He had produced, for him, a genuine anomaly—a best-seller! In Florida, where he had gone for relaxation and instead had been sucked into the great land boom, joining the rest of *boobus Americanus* in purchasing exorbitantly priced lots which soon would be swept out to sea with the tides, Dreiser remarked to Helen, "Well, it looks as if I've hit the mark this time. I think I'll go back home and collect some of the spoils."[12]

And spoils there were in abundance. Within a year, the *Tragedy* had sold out seven editions and was being read everywhere. Dramatized, it played to packed houses in America and abroad. Soon arrived the ultimate accolade, the genuine symbol of the world's acceptance—a bid from the motion pictures. Less disenchanted with the movies than many writers of the present day profess to be, Dreiser believed that films were even then providing perhaps America's most original contribution to world art. "Ever since the inception of the moving picture technique," he wrote, "I have looked on it as an artistic medium far surpassing for most expressive purposes, writing, painting, and the other arts, and I have hoped that my own work could be satisfactorily transplanted into it."[13]

Now Paramount's Famous Players wanted his book for the screen. How much was he going to ask for the rights? His publisher, with a heavy stake in the prospective sale, was anxious to close the deal. A flat $100,000, said Dreiser. Impossible! $25,000, possibly. At the very top, $35,000. A man must be realistic, after all. Dismayed that the negotiations he had launched might founder upon a request of such astronomical proportions, Liveright made every attempt to dissuade Dreiser from demanding the full amount; but Dreiser, whose business years at Butterick had not been wasted entirely, held firm. This was his chance, and he meant to make the most of it. Taking the deal into his own hands, he met the head of Famous Players, Jesse Lasky, face-to-face in a luncheon conference and emerged with a contract for $90,000.

Overnight Dreiser became, by his standards, a man of wealth. After a quarter of a century and more of labor, he had "arrived" —and the spoils were his. With royalties from the novel and the play and with this lump sum from Famous Players, he was free to indulge himself in luxuries heretofore only dreamed of. And one of his first acts was the leasing of a two-story suite in the Rodin Studios with a living room of cathedral proportions in whose splendor for the next five years the mighty, the talented, the interesting, the offbeat, the exotic and bizarre of New York flocked to his Thursday at-homes.

Known now—a public figure—talked of; in demand as a speaker; and sought after for his views on the American system, on writing, finance, marriage and divorce, capital punishment, he found himself listened to with attentive ears. All at once he was as important as Will Rogers. He too was an American sage; it was the zenith of his career. Visiting Europe again, he was accepted as an authority on anything American; he knew the answers. The Russians, aware of his growing sympathy for the Communist experiment then rounding out its first decade, invited him to tour their nation. He did so, admiring a number of their industrial accomplishments and social reforms. Yet he returned home not fully persuaded that the Soviets had produced the paradise on earth they had boasted of, although he had traveled to observe in a spirit of optimism and receptivity.[14]

His career went well. Stories, articles, and books flowed in an increasing stream. Magazines, which in recent years had shown considerable reluctance to publish his heavy and somber studies, now clamored for anything they might rush into print. Finished pieces, some of which had already circulated fruitlessly, were snapped up by eager editors. From Liveright came *Chains*; a revision of *The Financier*; a first book of poems called *Moods*; *Dreiser Looks at Russia*; *A Gallery of Women*; and in 1931 the initial volume of his autobiography, *Dawn*, which laid bare the childhood already portrayed in his novels. From Random House came a thin volume with his long story "Fine Furniture." Into the Modern Library went *Twelve Men*. No evidence will better illustrate Dreiser's arrival and the changing attitudes toward his work since *Sister Carrie* was suffocated in 1900 than the publication by two scholars of complete bibliographies of his work, the printing of his new volumes in limited editions on handmade paper, the advertising of *A Gallery of Women* for well over a year before its appearance and the 560 copies of the limited edition which contained the writer's autograph.

## VIII   *A Thorn in the Rose*

All this glory was not without its disappointment. The Pulitzer Prize for 1925, which Dreiser surely coveted for *An American Tragedy* and probably deserved, went instead to Sinclair Lewis. Dreiser must have thought it ironic that the apprentice should be honored while the master was neglected, but he remained silent. While he could not have but admired, even applauded, Lewis' audacity in refusing the prize, accompanied as it was by a vituperative attack upon the Prize Committee's methods for selecting winners, his own failure to win this recognition cut deeply into old wounds.

The wounds were reopened in 1930 when the Swedish Academy decided at last to award the Nobel Prize to an American. He and Lewis were the finalists between whom the judges had to decide. When the "gay virtuosity and flashing satire" of Lewis was preferred over "the ponderous and solemn" work of Dreiser, the naturalist, according to Lewis' biographer, Mark Schorer, "sulked in his tent."[15] Since 1911 and *Jennie Gerhardt* days, Dreiser had actively sought this honor; he had written in that year to his friend Mencken:

> Grant Richards, the English publisher who is here says I have a good chance of getting the next Nobel prize for literature following Maeterlinck, if it is worked right. He is going to organize the sentiment in England where he says I am a strong favorite, through Frank Harris, & others and he is going to get the Century Crowd to work for it here. He thought some American Critic of prominence ought to make the suggestion somewhere to which he could call attention & I spoke of you. How about that?[16]

It was not possible, of course, for Mencken to make the nomination, but Dreiser did not know this.

By 1927 he had more substantial reasons for hoping to gain the prize, and he appealed to his personal editor, Louise Campbell, to "write to F.P.A. of N.Y.World—or Broun—and suggest me for the Nobel Prize this year. I might get it."[17] He was mentioned widely for the prize, and efforts were made to obtain it for him, but to no avail. And even though by 1930 Dreiser had understandably become something of a stoic regarding his chances of ever receiving this ultimate recognition for his pioneering efforts in realism, the world-wide accolade showered upon the author of *Babbitt* and *Arrowsmith* hit hard.

Dreiser, the old "pro," was relegated to the sidelines while the fresh young buck was sent in to score the winning touchdown. The defeat was mitigated only by sporadic outcries from disappointed critics who thought that Dreiser of all living Americans should have been honored first and by Lewis' self-effacing remarks in praise of Dreiser in his Stockholm speech. Lewis announced to the staid assemblage:

> I am sure you know by now that the award to me of the Nobel Prize was by no means altogether popular in America, doubtless an experience not altogether new to you.
>
> Suppose you had taken Theodore Dreiser. Now to me, as to many other American writers, Dreiser, more than any other man, is marching alone. Usually unappreciated, often hounded, he has cleared the trail from Victorian Howellsian timidity and gentility in American fiction to honesty, boldness, and passion of life. Without his pioneering I doubt if any of us could, unless we liked to be sent to jail, seek to express life, beauty and terror.[18]

Lewis could hardly have said more, and even this much was atypical of the acid-mouthed satirist. And while the words surely were balm to Dreiser's wound, they could not bring him the prize itself.[19]

On top of these disappointments came the premiere performance of the Famous Players' production of *An American Tragedy* to which Dreiser was invited as the guest of honor and from which he stalked in a violent temper. He condemned the picture as being a complete travesty upon his work, of disemboweling his novel of its basic themes and reducing his tragedy to a cops-and-robbers farce. Charging the movies of a "cheap commercialism" which led them into "toadying to the lowest and most insignificant tastes," he instituted a legal injunction against the film company in hopes of having the picture stopped, but his court action failed. Bitterly disillusioned, Dreiser yet hoped that the motion picture industry would some day mature to the point where his novels might be presented with fidelity. In 1938 he was still writing to Sergei Eisenstein whose productions, including *Ten Days That Shook The World,* he admired, begging the Russian master to consider a remake of the *Tragedy.* It was never done.[20]

Dreiser's years of glory, of public notoriety, were coming to an end; he was slipping back into a period of frustration and turmoil which seemed his natural condition.

## CHAPTER 7

# God and Mammon:
## *The Bulwark*

*"I am (I Think) just One Month off from Finishing* The Bulwark*."*

I

DREISER'S CHRONICLE of Solon Barnes, Quaker, was the last novel he completed during his lifetime and the one which took him longest to finish. Helen Richardson Dreiser believes that her husband conceived the idea sometime around 1910, thirty-six years before its publication. He discussed the project with Edgar Lee Masters in 1912; in 1914 he wrote Mencken that by September he intended making a stab at writing this "dandy story." He made more than a stab; a first draft was completed and sent to Louise Campbell, his typist-editor, in that year. But other affairs intervened, and the manuscript remained in Miss Campbell's apartment till 1942; when she came across the bulky package in a storage closet, she wrote Dreiser apprising him of her discovery, and coincidentally found him at work on a new and different version.[1]

*The Bulwark* gave Dreiser more difficulty than any other single volume. It became a literary stepchild, continually relegated to his desk drawer in favor of manuscripts whose birth proved less difficult. Plays, short stories, and novels were advanced to the "immediate" list while the gestation period of the Quaker novel lengthened by years into decades. *The Titan* and *The "Genius"* were published, raising critical dust storms, and in the commotion surrounding their threatened suppression, his delay on the new story is understandable. Yet in 1916, as the court trial on *The "Genius"* got underway, his declared intention of buckling down seriously to *The Bulwark* gave the

John Lane Company confidence enough to make up a "dummy" of the title page and to circulate it, announcing the publication for 1917 of "the greatest novel that has ever been written."[2]

Changing publishers in 1918, Dreiser was still optimistic about completing the Quaker story. He followed Helen to Hollywood in 1920 and, working in the California sunshine, gained enough momentum to report in August that *"The Bulwark* lags but should be done by Christmas."[3] By November, other plans interfering, he amended "Christmas" to read "spring." When Horace Liveright, his new publishers, wrote him anxiously to determine an explicit deadline, Dreiser could only confess, "All I can say is that some time ago, finding that I was not doing as well with *The Bulwark* as I had hoped I began another, working on *The Bulwark* at spare moments but giving the main line of my attention to this new one."[4] The new book was, of course, *An American Tragedy,* which completely occupied his time for the next four or five years.

Liveright had expected to stimulate Dreiser into hurrying completion of *The Bulwark* by forwarding news of the wide acclaim then greeting the arrival of a flock of new writers such as Floyd Dell, Sherwood Anderson, and Sinclair Lewis. But Dreiser, in his titanic calm, was not to be so easily stirred. "Save your artillery for different game," he advised Liveright. "I always do the very best I can. It is never that I will not but that at times I kinnot. . . . the truth is, as you ought to know by now, that my love is for the work itself and after that I would like to see it sold so that I might get a little something out of it. Beyond that little interests me, not even the arrival of a thousand geniuses."[5]

Hurry or not, the book lodged in his mind, stalled precisely where he had left it. The moment the Clyde Griffiths story went to press, Dreiser sent Louise Campbell another full outline of *The Bulwark;* for he regarded it as his next production. But he shelved it again in 1926 in favor of a revision of *The Financier* and hopes for completion of *A Trilogy of Desire,* already delayed far too long. For the rest of Dreiser's life *The Stoic,* the final volume of the *Trilogy,* and *The Bulwark* competed for time against each other and against other projects which seemed either more pressing or easier to write.

Once again the Quaker novel was announced for publication, this time by G. P. Putnam's Sons, who advertised it for the fall of 1942. But no manuscript arrived. "Quite frankly I am not running a race with any one," Dreiser had scolded Horace Liveright in 1920. Two decades later, this remained his attitude. Praise showered upon younger writers was no spur. The arrival of those "thousand geniuses" (some had both arrived and departed by now) was insufficient reason to force a book that would not be forced. But Dreiser was in a race whether he relished it or not. Time itself was running out, a day approaching when no more work would be possible. Good intentions cannot be printed and put between boards.

He had wanted all along very desperately to finish his last two volumes, initiated so many years before. Failing in health, he rallied with Helen's aid to put forth one last tremendous effort. *The Stoic* would never be wholly completed, but *The Bulwark* was written and sent to Doubleday. Yet who can say how closely it approximated the fruit of the seed first sown in 1910?

## II  *The Inner Light That Failed*

That Theodore Dreiser, fascinated always by the dark power of materialism and repelled by its degrading effects upon human life, should eventually write about the plight of the Quakers in a world where the acquisitive instinct ran riot and men madly erected temples to the bitch goddess, seems no less inevitable than Hawthorne's concern with Puritans or Steinbeck's with migrant Okies. Since Dreiser's childhood days he had felt an attraction to the sect, for he identified it with memories of his dreamy mother. He recalled her meditating in shadowed corners of rented homes in Warsaw and Evansville and dressed in the Spartan black bonnet and dress of the Mennonites, a costume so simple it reminded him of male garb. Moreover her nature was peaceful, and she was unobsessed with property or wealth. Now and again in his stories Quaker references find a use, but usually they furnish events with an ironic twist. We recall Carrie Meeber, clothes-crazy and mad for fame, achieving her first triumph gowned as a modest Quakeress. We remember that the archetype of the financier, for whom the profit motive is all in all, descended from a distinguished line of orthodox Quaker progenitors.

For religion Dreiser generally had little to say in his fiction, preferring to dismiss the subject with a derisive phrase wherever possible. If forced to the issue by events or by the white-heat of an emotional tirade, he might pen scathing pages lambasting the religionists: "Out upon them for a swinish mass! Shut up the churches, knock down the steeples! Harry them until they know the true place of religion—a weak man's shield!"[6]

Yet Dreiser, perhaps paradoxically, admired the Quaker system and had read deeply in basic documents like *The Book of Discipline* and the *Journals* of Fox and Woolman.

So well versed was he in these and secondary volumes written by outstanding Friends that in the 1930's he felt equipped to deliver lectures before audiences in Quaker colleges and to take under consideration the reissuance of Woolman's *Journal*, prefaced by the 1871 introduction by Whittier. This plan did not materialize, but Dreiser did accept an invitation to edit *The Living Thoughts of Thoreau*, for the author of *Walden* appealed to him on the same conspicuously idealistic basis. He envisioned the Quakers as heroic figures who, in the face of overwhelming odds, rejected self-interest, the profit motive, and the status symbols of clothing, property, and wealth—all marks of the American system. In 1938 he wrote Rufus H. Jones, chairman of the American Friends Service Committee: "I am very much interested in the Quaker ideal. Like yourself I rather feel that it is the direct road to—not so much a world religion as a world appreciation of the force that provides us all with this amazing experience called life."[7]

The Quakers were utopians; but, the world being far too much with us, Dreiser could not help believing that Quakerism was doomed to strangulation by the octopus forces controlling society and men's passions. And because this was the fate he saw approaching, *The Bulwark*, with all its compassion, could not avoid becoming one of the darkest stories he had to tell. Another American tragedy, it reads perhaps as Clyde's would had it been written from the point of view of Elvira Griffiths. Dreiser himself suggests this comparison with his great success, for he wrote Louise Campbell in 1945 that the manuscript, at last complete, was "about as long as an American Tragedy and about as tragic." On the first count he was wrong—*The Bulwark* actually comes to 337 pages, his briefest novel. But on the second, he was quite right.

Originally conceived at the time he was engrossed in *Jennie Gerhardt*, *The Bulwark* has more in common, so far as tone and feeling are concerned, with that study than with any other of the novels. The two belong side by side on his shelf; for, if

Jennie is Dreiser's "pet heroine," Solon Barnes is surely his pet hero—the only one, perhaps, that he thoroughly and genuinely admires. Both Jennie and Solon fail, but the compassion with which their failures are reported to us transcends pity.

## III  *Christian in Vanity Fair*

Although *The Bulwark* is far less spectacular a work than *An American Tragedy*, a good case might be made for its more nearly approximating the idea of tragedy. Clyde Griffiths—confused, bewildered, not certain exactly where he wants to go or what he is equipped to do, and without any foundation to steady him—is tragic in the broadest conception only. To many he appears to be no more than a pitiful scrap of humanity, without stature of any sort. But *The Bulwark* centers upon a protagonist more capable of suggesting the stature of the classical tragic hero—a good man, a mature man who fails nevertheless in a lifelong struggle.

The one figure in Dreiser's previous work most closely approximating Solon Barnes is Elvira Griffiths, whom we last saw in the streets of San Francisco, carrying on in the only way she knows how, proselytizing for Christ, and not without irony singing "How Firm a Foundation" to a motley assemblage who, in spite of their distaste for the evangelists, yet perceive her at once to stand apart from and above the rest of the mission group: " 'Well, here is one, who, whatever her defects, probably does what she believes as nearly as possible.' A kind of overruling and watchful and merciful power which she proclaimed was written in her every feature and gesture."8

Solon Barnes is clipped from the same bolt of material. So grounded in his religion that it comes instinctually, life without it incomprehensible, he is epitomized by his author as "a good man—one of the nation's bulwarks." If Solon is as Dreiser describes him, then the nation is in a bad way; for the murky floods of materialism engulf Solon, more subtly, more gradually, but with no less certitude than they drown Clyde.

Solon's tragic flaw is an oversimplified view of life. At an early age he has divided the world arbitrarily into good and bad. In a universe guarded and governed by Divine Providence, the virtuous must ultimately be rewarded, he reasons. Likewise, the bad must be condemned. Quakerism constitutes Solon's firm foundation. By holding himself and his children steadfastly to its tenets, he conceives of his family's road to Paradise as lying ready, broad, and clean-swept. In his life-passage he learns two lessons. He learns that life is far more complex than he has dreamed, good and bad being mingled inseparably in every human affair. And he learns that, in America particularly, no man is an island but part of the continent and that he has no effective tools for walling out the pagan forces that infest the land.

In his introduction to the novel Dreiser defines the predicament in which Solon will act as protagonist. Quakerism, eulogized as the haven of idealism and perfection "in a none too perfect world," has striven to establish a tenable equilibrium between the disparate claims of the world, a coexistence, a balance "without flaw or shadow or error." Because it can be no more than a wonderful dream, the religion of George Fox, like so many other utopian visions, is destined to fall against the onslaught of the everyday world with its vices, deprivations, inequities, its "ordinary routine materiality."

So long as Quakerism is allowed to isolate itself, the illusion of perfection can be maintained. Thus Rufus and Hannah Barnes, Solon's parents, face no real challenge so long as they remain on their isolated acres in a remote corner of Maine, northernmost of the States and relatively untouched by the main current of society. But upon the death of Hannah's brother-in-law, the family moves to New Jersey; and, although their new home is in a community of Friends, it is a community too intimately spliced with the non-Quaker to survive the taint of the money ideal. Even Phoebe Kimber, as dedicated a Quaker as one might hope to find, proposes the move to Rufus on the basis of the area's prosperity and the "advantages" that nearby Philadelphia schools offer over those of Maine.

What Solon must learn, but can learn only to his sorrow, is simply this: so corrosive a despoiler is the world that no compromise between materialism and idealism is possible. For Quakers, coexistence with the way society has organized itself is a delusion. When the veil is rent, the insidious triumph of materialism will be apparent.

In *The Bulwark* this conflict is symbolized first by the family's residence at Thornbrough, a pretentious ante-bellum mansion now owned by Phoebe. Even in disrepair, the house retains "an echo of ease and comfort . . . a kind of social grandeur" such as the family has never known. Surrounded by its ornate iron fence, the Thornbrough property is cut by curving driveways leading to carved oak doors, inside of which Rufus comes "face to face with the form, if not actually the present substance, of luxury." An elaborate reception hall forested with pillars, clearly intended for glittering social gatherings; crystal-prismed chandeliers designed to gleam upon jewels and silks; a handsome staircase of carved and polished walnut down which impressive entrances may be possible—every detail of the house implies not only waste and show but "greed, drunkenness, immorality, and the other sins of living which George Fox and the faith he proclaimed had so valiantly sought to put aside forever."

The house at Thornbrough, in short, is no place for solid, staid Quakers. Rufus stands before it open-mouthed, timorous as a skater who has already tied on his blades when he spies the DANGER—THIN ICE sign on the river. The only proper action —and Rufus' first impulse—is to retreat. He should sell the house as soon as possible to some poor soul who sets store by display. It is the only way to sidestep this devilish temptation.

But the house is not Rufus' to sell. It belongs to Phoebe, and she has invited him to live in it—only temporarily, of course. He will repair, paint, landscape, and make the property marketable, for it cannot be advantageously disposed of until it has been rendered suitable for use as a country home. Then some wealthy Philadelphian will buy it. So Rufus makes his first dangerous compromise with materialism. The needed restorations involve a state of luxurious living incompatible with his religious beliefs; yet, as steward of the widowed Phoebe's property, he feels obligated to render the house salable: "between the two horns of this dilemma—simplicity for himself and reasonable luxury for a possible buyer—he was fairly caught."[9]

He attempts to save himself by restoring the house in as simple a manner as he can manage and by living in as small and unpretentious a portion of it as possible. But what seems a solution is but the first step into quicksand, for Phoebe in gratitude refuses to deed the house to anyone but Rufus or his children. Rufus considers this proposal. The family is comfortably established, and without apparent detriment to their Quakerism. Rufus concludes it is far easier to remain than to risk offending Phoebe. This first concession, prophetic as it is of the course events will take, suggests Alexander Pope's lines on vice:

> Yet seen too oft, familiar with her face,
> We first endure, then pity, then embrace.

While Rufus himself strays no further than toleration—and the same might be said, though with less conviction, for his son—the embracing awaits only the passage of time.

## IV   *God's Gold*

Solon Barnes at the age of ten comes to live at Thornbrough. Solidly under his parents' influence, he is not visibly infected by the estate's luxury. Yet, growing up accustomed to the spaciousness, the fine woodwork, and the craftsmanship which everywhere delights the senses, he lacks the full recognition of the disparity, which disturbed his father, between this house and his religious tenets. Are not its walls covered with homely Quaker mottos and truisms? Has not his family life remained plain, even amid this grandeur?

Solon's first awakening to "the problem of wealth as opposed to simplicity" comes with his youthful attachment to Benecia Wallin, later his wife. Justus Wallin, shrewd in his stewardship of the properties Providence has granted him and consequently an even more prosperous Quaker than Rufus Barnes, notes the affection between Solon and Benecia. Impressed with Solon's business acumen, Wallin invites the Barnes family to his home on Philadelphia's Girard Avenue—the same prestigious location which readers of *The Financier* will recognize as Frank Cowperwood's choice for his first showplace. The visit is a revelation to Solon: "There were carved mahogany tables and chairs, parqueted floors strewn with rugs and animal skins, and large ornate vases filled with flowers and grasses. Soon after they entered the living room a servant appeared, offering silver plates containing tall glasses of fruit juice—a procedure which astonished and somewhat disconcerted the entire Barnes family."[10] Solon has gained his first insight into the encroachments made by the materialistic spirit upon the Quaker community. More revelations follow.

He becomes aware of Quakers in disturbing numbers compromising their ideals or abandoning them altogether to the claims of wealth and display. He notes his cousin, Rhoda Kimber, sprung from the same stock as he, yet "consciously out to go somewhere in this world, and not . . . at all interested in the Quaker idea of plainness." Rhoda escapes Quakerism through marriage, becoming rich and socially prominent. Rhoda is of an age with Solon, but in her family the acids of materialism have had an extra generation during which to etch their evils. Were Solon perceptive enough to project the image of Rhoda upon his own children, he might foresee the troubles to come.

But Solon is a poor judge of men. In the black-white world he constructs for himself, he is continually misestimating others. All Quakers he expects and presumes to be good. The rest, while they may chance to be good, are very likely evil. "He did not know life. Rather, to him, all those who had sinned were thoroughly bad, their souls irredeemable."[11]

As a young clerk in the Traders and Builders Bank, Solon witnesses a street scuffle and, intervening, apprehends the victim while the thief makes off with the stolen wallet. This duplicity of appearances, superimposed upon his simple view of life, hampers Solon. At the bank a young boy, Walter Briscoe, trusted by Solon because he is a Quaker, embezzles money. Discovery of the theft shakes Solon "to the very core of his moral being." When the Quaker father begs another chance for his son, Solon refuses; but Walter is no sooner sentenced to the penitentiary than Solon recognizes his moral error, even if in the world's eyes justice has prevailed. Recalling his *Book of Discipline*—"If a man be overtaken in a fault, ye which are spiritual, restore such an one in the spirit of meekness, convincing thyself, lest thee also be tempted"[12]—Solon acknowledges a serious offense against his religious principles.

Troubling as such episodes prove, Solon is convinced that his feet tread the path of righteousness. Active participation in the financial world might be expected to dismay a Quaker, but so confident in his faith is Solon that life as a banker gives him little direct anguish. He strides rapidly toward wealth, a state which youth at Thornbrough has well prepared him to rationalize. "We surely have been favored by Providence; that is, if it intends that we should enjoy or display so many luxuries,"[13] he remarks to Benecia after they are settled in the new home presented to them by Justus and furnished lavishly with Sheraton, Chippendale, Hepplewhite, fine linens and crystal, and a small fortune in silver, china brass and copper ware. With his marriage settlement of forty thousand dollars and with an auspicious career underway at the Traders and Builders, Solon realizes "the dream of his schooldays come true: a good position, a handsome home, a beautiful young wife, powerful friends and relatives, health and strength."[14]

The America in which Solon Barnes prospers is the same America in which Frank Cowperwood schemed his way to the top, the same America in which young Dreiser wandered from city to city observing with wonder and dismay the massive accumulation of wealth. "A lust for wealth and power was in the air," yet Solon manages, he feels, to keep his own hands clean. Desirous of success, but not at the expense of his principles, he avoids such monopolistic dealings as young Cowperwood gloried in; he prefers instead "simpler realms where profits were comparatively small and the troubled face of ethics was not so plainly visible."[15] Under the philosophy that God, holding His earth in the palm of His hand, is in supreme control, Solon sees "everything in terms of divine order." No matter how darkly obscured, the vicissitudes of life are a part of this perfect order and run according to divine will, for an ultimate good. Any concentration of wealth, therefore, must in its way be also a part of the divine pattern. And there is always the *Book of Discipline* to guide the individual: "When any become possessed of ample means, they should remember that they are duly stewards who must render an account for the right use of the things committed to their care."[16] Solon's wealth is a sacred trust for him to guard and guide, a reflection extremely satisfying to the Quaker despite irksome occurrences that would attempt a breach in the wall of his faith.

An old man, desperate for cash, sells Solon his chicken farm at a fraction of its market value. Is this right? It is good business, surely, but is it in accord with Quaker dictates of justice? Solon wonders about this. Then at public auction he purchases a block of houses for seventeen thousand dollars, having already in mind a prospective buyer who will take them for twenty-seven thousand, exactly the type of transaction to whet a young Cowperwood's appetite and to spur him to even more profitable manipulations. But it troubles Solon. Where is the dividing line? How does one determine in any given case the border between good stewardship and greed, "between the desire for power and wealth and a due regard for Quaker precepts?"[17]

Solon's business associates give him even more pause. At the beginning, the Traders and Builders is a staid concern, conservative and ethical. But as time passes, new directors enter. There is Skidmore, a Quaker and director of the bank, but possessed of "a most pretentious house in Rittenhouse Square." There are Wilkerson, Seay, Baker, "exactly of the temperament which organizes, suborns, controls," men devoid of morals in financial matters. Discovering that his fellow directors are taking legal but unethical advantage of a law by allowing banks to invest depositors' funds and then investing these funds in shaky concerns controlled by themselves, Solon is deeply grieved.

Affairs soon have drifted beyond his power to rationalize or excuse. A clean break with the bank seems the only honorable solution. He informs the government and resigns his position. Financially, Solon is little affected, being well along in years by now and solidly taken care of in his own right. What is important is his implicit admission that the system dominating the nation cannot be bucked by men like himself; it can only be seceded from—presupposing one is fortunate enough to possess a secure, currency-lined shell into which to retreat. If his career is ended, at least his religious principles—and these to Solon are always of the first import—appear to survive.

### V   "In Much Love to the Rising Generation"

Had Solon remained childless, his striking a balance between the material and the ideal would have been relatively painless. As it is, Dreiser employs the world's corruption of the rising generation to demonstrate the craftiness with which the worm has bored its way to the apple's heart. Solon and Benecia produce five offspring. From their tenderest years Solon hopes to inculcate these five with his own vigorous Quakerism. He will provide a perfect home atmosphere and protect his children from the corrosive influences that have touched but not, he persists in believing, tainted his own life. Growing up in such an environment, how could the new generation avoid blossoming into "perfect examples of well-brought-up children: earnest, truthful, just and kind"?

Isobel, Orville, Dorothea, Etta, Stewart—one by one the children are born; and one by one they bewilder Solon as their disparate natures confound his plans for their futures. The oversimplified world he has created to accommodate his theories begins to crumble before the children are out of their cradles,

as he watches the emerging personalities take their own directions, irrespective of his surveillance. As the twig is bent so
grows the tree, this is his axiom. Yet his children follow paths
not of his choosing, but of Nature's. "They are born so."

Isobel, born without physical attractiveness but with a highly
sensitive, perceptive nature, early realizes the "sharp distinction"
between herself and the pretty girls at school. By degrees she is
forced back into a shell of introspection. She is passive, lacks the
mysterious magnetism that sparks friendship or love. Aware of
the trap of spinsterhood, she yearns for marriage, but no suitors
appear, and her own timidity prevents her from seeking them
out. She drifts into loneliness—the personification of Sherwood
Anderson's protest against a world which stimulates us to desire
love but offers no plan for providing our lovers.

Isobel's sisters are as singular as she. Dorothea, beautiful and
sensual by inclination, spends her youth "dreaming of her
eventual escape from quiet Thornbrough" to the world of society
with its wealth and display of jewels and gowns. In contrast,
Etta, the youngest of the girls, is born dreamy and romantic,
of an artistic bent. Etta exists in a world of her own ideals, the
type of girl who, chancing to see a young couple kissing, thinks
*this is love*; who, reading *La Dame aux Camelias*, feels a new
world of "romance and reality" opening for her.

The natures of the two brothers are no less different. Orville
is a born conservative, "a saver of pennies" destined to worship
that idol, reputation; Stewart from his earliest years is "a
veritable firebrand" in pursuit of pleasure. As the boys mature,
their natures only assert themselves more forcefully. Orville is
drawn to the wealthier relatives, whose handsome homes,
servants, gardens, horses and carriages he admires. Stewart,
while taking for granted his material ease, is attracted by the
excitements of "color, motion, beauty, the more vivid forms of
life." He is a born rebel, dominated by sensuality, preoccupied
with sex.

Five children, sprung from the same parents, nurtured in the
same Edenic environment, yet what disparate paths they take!
The true substance and import of the novel lies in the tracing of
their careers from birth, without which Dreiser's story would be
no more than a pale and relatively pointless shadow of his
philosophy. Through the children, Dreiser tells us two things of
consequence. First, that the dominant influences upon a human
being are the inborn "chemisms" which combine with whatever

social and economic forces rule society to produce the eventual adult. Second, that the influence of home environment is comparatively trivial. If *An American Tragedy* left a residual implication that a different, less restricted childhood might have altered Clyde Griffiths—and in that novel this seems to be Elvira's belief as she determines to be more liberal with young Russell—*The Bulwark* pretty well demolishes the theory. Clyde would have been Clyde irrespective of his rearing, just as Solon Barnes's children, like photographic prints emerging slowly in a chemical bath, become more and more distinguishably themselves as the years pass. The influence of home environment is revealed as an illusion; Nature in the end asserts its control.

## VI  *"Life Was Very Strange."*

The emergence of his children into young adulthood poses Solon's real problem; it confronts him with the enigma of life, reveals to him his error in oversimplifying the world's organizing principles, and bewilders him with religious conflicts. How mistaken to imagine his children carbon copies of himself, instilled with his own principles and strong enough, with the guidance of a religious home training, to find a satisfactory balance between God and Mammon! "Solon did not quite realize that while he might be able thus to control their outward conduct, it was not possible to control the minds of his children."[18]

Orville, whom Solon considers most like himself and therefore most successful, is in reality an insufferable snob. Orville looks like Solon, acts like Solon, succeeds even more brilliantly than Solon, but he possesses no more substance than a meringue. His religion is a mere badge of respectable conformity. He marries a wealthy girl, Althea Stoddard, to whom the precepts of Quakerism are important, not religiously, but socially. "But with such a marriage he would be rich, secure, comfortable, respected, and admired, and he wanted no more than that in this world."[19] Dorothea and Orville become very close, and rightly so, for they are stamped from the same die. With the help of her Aunt Rhoda, Dorothea marries the son of a street-railway magnate in a ceremony designed for maximum social impact, for which the guest lists are checked against the Social Register. Orville and Dorothea are lost irrevocably to Mammon, and Solon is unable to see it.

What he is able to see is the manner in which his other children fall short of Orville's and Dorothea's achievement. Matriculated at Llewellyn College, Isobel finds life miserable, since the college provides only the most watered-down Quaker atmosphere. It has dwindled into a factory for transforming commonplace girls into snobs. The more the social cliques exclude her, the more Isobel retreats to her room and her studies; she is convinced that there is "nothing in store for one so poorly equipped physically as she."

Unable to help Isobel in her despair, Solon questions life. Believing all things to be ruled by Divine Providence, contrived for the ultimate good of earth's children, he must believe in the possibility that some blessing is intended here, but what it may be escapes him. Clearly, he must help the girl develop what charms and abilities she has been granted. But how? And to what end? Hold as Solon will to his beliefs, the seeds of doubt are sown: "It was another of those illuminating truths about life which Solon was being compelled to learn, but very slowly, namely, that in spite of a divinely ordered scheme of things and a willingness on the part of anyone to ally himself with the manifested plan, as far as one could determine it, still these things would occur."[20]

Isobel remains a worry to her father, but since she is outwardly placid, a quiet, dutiful girl, she provokes no crisis; instead she silently succumbs to her own misery.

It takes Etta and Stewart to smash through the respectable façade by which—without being fully conscious of it—Solon sets so much store. They create problems affecting their father with more immediacy. Etta is allowed to enter Oakwold College, where she comes under the influence of Volida La Porte, who introduces the girl to books such as Daudet's *Sappho* and leads her toward new horizons of intellectual and artistic discovery. Under an ultimatum to abandon Volida, Etta pawns her mother's jewels to join her friend at the University of Wisconsin. She has made her break and will not return home. The two girls travel to New York, where Etta becomes the mistress of a Greenwich Village artist. Orville, stumbling upon knowledge of the affair, panics for fear of notoriety which might damage his social reputation and confronts her with a demand that the relationship cease at once. Etta refuses, recognizing that "the hateful reproaches of Orville emanated from a small mind, full of greed and ambition for worldly success, and she was glad that she was no longer a part of such a world." Significantly, Solon, when dealing with a transgressor, was at least conscious of Quaker teachings; but Orville gives no thought whatsoever to helping Etta. From now on, she is no sister of his.

Etta is allowed to cause minimum distress to her parents. Redemption of the jewels enables Solon to hide the theft from Benecia, and the other children contrive to keep Solon unapprised of Etta's love affair. But in Stewart's case notoriety is not so easily quashed; it provides the fuse to detonate Solon's crumbling world.

Stewart's sensual nature drives him into companionship with rich college friends, devotees of fast cars and girls; and when, for financial reasons, he finds himself unable to keep pace with his cohorts, he looks for ways and means of obtaining money. One immediate resource is his Aunt Rhoda, who determines to cultivate her good-looking nephew as she had Dorothea. Thus, ironically, one Quaker corrupts another. But even Rhoda's generosity has a limit, and Stewart steals, first with timidity, then brazenly, from his mother's purse, from Orville's wallet, from his roommate's desk.

Stewart's dissolute life, tame as it has been until now, flares into catastrophe on a wild automobile ride. One of the boys, determined to overcome his girl's scruples, slips into her drink a nerve remedy pilfered from his mother's medicine chest. Ordinarily the drops, which are a sort of tranquilizer, produce no more than a mood of assent; but, unbeknown to the boys, the girl has a heart weakness upon which the drops react fatally. Instead of securing a physician, the panicky youths dump her by a lonely roadside. At dawn she is found dead; and the boys, having made it "practically impossible for the police not to track them down," are soon behind bars.

Now the winds of scandal are loosed; the fire which has smoldered so long breaks into flames engulfing the family. Stewart commits suicide in jail. Benecia, so protected from any inkling of family trouble that she is incapable of enduring the shock, dies of heartbreak. Solon is dazed. What has so dimmed the Inner Light which was to cast such radiance on all their lives? "Had he not done all in his power to obviate any such deadly consequence in connection with his family?" How and where had his stewardship gone so awry?

## VII  *The Mare of the World*

When Solon was a child his mother had been terrorized by a dream concerning him. She saw her son leap astride a handsome black mare, stoutly thwarting the animal's attempts to throw him off. The mare snorted and pawed the earth, reared on its hind legs, swung to left and right, but was incapable of unseating its rider. Then, when it most appeared Solon might break the mare to his will, the horse rushed a fence, tore the rider from his seat, and threw him. At the sight of her son unconscious on the ground, Hannah Barnes awoke, cold with perspiration at the possible significance of the dream:

> . . . that beautiful mare, its friendly actions and then its subsequent erratic, murderous conduct. And Solon, all the while, up to the moment he was in the saddle, seemingly so confident of the mare's friendly and obedient spirit.
>
> What could it mean? . . . there was the feeling that in some way or other it might be connected with . . . the sudden shift in their material and social status.[21]

And so it is. Apparently the dream foreshadows Solon's struggle to tame the materialistic forces rampant in the world, to subordinate them and sensuality to the religious will. But the mare of the world at last throws him, and disastrously.

The world has defeated Solon, broken his hopes, laid waste his plans. Incomprehensibly, his endeavor to tread unscathed the perilous line between God and Mammon, in which until now he had been so buoyed with assurance, has failed. His state of mind, stunned as from a blow of a tremendous hammer, causes us to imagine a self-possessed traveler riding through a plague-ridden town and—believing it safe enough to direct his mount down the center of the street, not touching shoe to stone or flesh to flesh—is dumbfounded to reach the exit gate and discover the air itself polluted, the first fatal boils already firing his skin.

## VIII  *"I Am Crying for Life"*

In the closing chapters of *The Bulwark*, Solon Barnes meditates the fate of his house, stricken like Job's for reasons he cannot fathom. Then by slow degrees, he finds his faith in God revitalized by a rediscovery of the creative force that lies behind all life, including its tragedies, and by recourse to the

*Journal* of John Woolman. And it becomes apparent that Dreiser is, with his last book, offering a final estimate of his own father.

In his autobiography he had described John Paul Dreiser as "wandering distrait and forlorn amid a storm of difficulties: age, the death of his wife, the flight of his children, doubt as to their salvation, poverty, a declining health."[22] The catalog, barring poverty, accurately depicts Solon in his last days. Both men are strongly religious fathers who attempt to raise their families according to the codes they have accepted for themselves. Both see their sons and daughters seduced into a world which, being irreligious, can only be evil. The Barnes children, like the young Dreisers, "could not help being confronted by the marked contrast between the spirit of the . . . home and that of the world at large. In spite of the many admirable qualities of the home, these were distinctly at variance with the rush and swing and spirit of the time itself, and this fact could scarcely fail to impress even the least impressionable minds."[23]

If Solon Barnes is intended as a portrait of the elder Dreiser, and Helen Dreiser insists that this is the case, then Theodore's oft reiterated antipathy for his father and his Church must be squared with this compassionate portrayal of the Quaker. The answer lies in time, with its merciful tendency to leach the bitterness from early memories. Dreiser, says Helen, after his father's death "recalled traits in him, too, that he admired: his honesty, his austere Germanic way of living—and there grew in his mind the desire to build a story around him."[24]

Because Dreiser's antagonism toward Catholicism had not waned, even though he grew less caustic in his attitude toward religion generally, in the interests of objectivity he altered the religion of his protagonist. Some memories had cut too deeply, and he desired his novel to point toward encomium, not indictment. He at last was prepared to forgive. Life was life, after all. He had always insisted that in life there was no black and no white; there were only victims. Why, then, search for scapegoats?

Dreiser had pointed toward such a portrait of his father for a good many years. It may be true that his long delay in completing *The Bulwark* can be attributed to the psychological block against portraying his father in any light of radiance. It was a block only time could sweep away, but even a hasty survey of his fiction reveals a steady softening of hostile lines, as bit by bit his own maturity, combined with his steady observation of life, aided him to put aside old quarrels. The autobiographies are marked initially by attacks on the parent that can only be termed savage—venomous portraits into which the redeeming milk of human kindness seeps drop by drop as the years pass. First there is only the most grudging admission that there may be more than one side to the father, then comes pity, then understanding, and finally sympathy. By 1940 Dreiser could declare by letter that his father had been "a truthful man and a devout Catholic."[25] But since he still insisted "If I have a battle cry, it is this: Destroy the Catholic Church in every land on the face of the earth." To distinguish the father from the institution was essential.[26]

One recalls this pattern having long since been inaugurated. In *Jennie Gerhardt,* which contains his father's first sympathetic portrait, Lutheranism was consciously substituted for Catholicism. Edward Butler in *The Financier* reminds one of John Dreiser, but Butler remains a Catholic and the portrait is not flattering. The father in *The Hand of The Potter* becomes Jewish and is compassionately drawn. The most ingenious solution to the parentage dilemma occurs in *An American Tragedy.* Dreiser's inclination, when relying upon his family for source material, was to follow the archetype composed of the ineffectual but stringently religious father and the loving, admirable mother who follows the father's lead. In the *Tragedy* this is altered sufficiently to combine both parents in one. Elvira Griffiths possesses not only the commendable traits of Dreiser's mother, but also the religious drive of the father; as a result, Asa Griffiths hovers in the background, a ghost.

When at last Dreiser felt psychologically prepared to focus upon the father as father, the solution evident in *The Bulwark* suggested itself to him. It was a long time dawning and was completed only in the nick of time. Dreiser returned the galley proofs to Doubleday at the end of August, 1945, to be readied for February or March publication. On December 28, after suffering an acute kidney attack, he died.

Dreiser, this "foggy giant" who solitarily from his tragic peak viewed life as confused, unjust, and without light for earthlings, left no children. But had he been survived, his sons and daughters might easily have echoed the words Dreiser himself gave to Etta Barnes as she emerged from the funeral service for her father: "Oh, I am not crying for myself, or for Father—I am crying for *life.*"

## CHAPTER 8

# "The World's Worst Great Writer": Dreiser's Artistry

> *"It is by now an established part of our folklore that Theodore Dreiser lacks everything except genius"*
> ——Alfred Kazin

CLOSE TO TWO DECADES have now passed since Dreiser's death. His work, disengaged from his personality, must stand or fall upon its own merits. For a writer, the second glance can spell oblivion or immortality. More authors than not are sent to the junkheaps by the indifference of generations immediately following them. But in Dreiser's case the passage of time has resulted only in a steady accretion of reputation and in a niche in American literature which seems ever more clearly defined, more permanent, more secure. In 1930 the critical camps might have raised howls of anguish at the possibility of Dreiser's selection by the Nobel jury to represent America; but in the 1960's those howls have been silenced by the endurance of the man's work, and scarcely a murmur of dissention will be heard against awarding him the label of "great."

## I  *Truth and Power*

Now that the idiosyncracies of the man no longer clutter the scene and block our view of the writer, certain facts stand out for emphasis. First, Dreiser's range. Of a major writer, one expects scope. And although he is known primarily—and rightly so—as a novelist, Dreiser labored with some distinction in every major genre of modern literature. His short stories are cut from the same fabric as his novels and share the same merits, the same defects. For a time he thought of himself as a poet, and surely there was a touch of the poet, at least of the mystic, in him; but it was heavy-handed and unlyrical. His *Moods* sacrifice image to philosophy, are overwhelmed by thought instead of feeling. His ideas found a more proper outlet in the essay form to which he turned increasingly. The enormous manuscript which was to have elucidated his final and complete vision of life, finishing what *Hey, Rub-A-Dub-Dub!* had begun a quarter of a century before, is indicative of his natural feeling for the prose form. Even so, the ideas in his essays seemed more vital and were projected with more impact when dramatized in his novels.

The same is also true of his books of sketches, such as those included in *The Color of a Great City.* "Sketches" is a good term for them, for while they are interesting in themselves, and some are semi-poetic, they are but groundwork for stories and become of significance only when incorporated in fiction. Between 1915 and 1920 Dreiser thought of himself as a playwright, and while some of his dramas were produced, the stage was not his métier. Outside of the novel form, it was as a writer of autobiography that Dreiser realized his greatest triumphs. His *Dawn* and *Newspaper Days* have been called unsurpassed. They read like novels, and perhaps that is the secret of their success. Reading them, we can only grieve that the man never completed his *A History of Myself,* of which these represent the first two volumes.

Second, Dreiser's unabashed honesty. In *An American Tragedy* Dreiser represents a spectator watching Clyde Griffiths' mother sing hymns on the street and thinking as he watches: "Well, here is one who, whatever her defects, probably does what she believes as nearly as possible." It is precisely this reaction which has been instrumental in keeping Dreiser's books alive in the general readership for the past half-century. Life, unillusioned, unromanticized, runs through them like a stream of clear water. The reader is quite willing to overlook the minor imperfections which were so harped upon in his own day, the failures in artistic structure, the supposed indignities of diction which seem less gauche as our language moves toward informality and idiomatic expression. After reading the novels, we simply feel: This is the way life was, *and is.*

Dreiser was the first American to portray with truth and power our modern world of commerce and mechanization, the first to portray the dismal depersonalization of the individual which results from urbanization and intensifying societal pressure to conform, the first to draw us frankly and grimly as a nation of status-seekers. The measure of his success is marked by the persistent validity of his novels. And tame as his "erotic episodes" now read to a generation accustomed to stronger fare, he led the way in openly and honestly treating sex as a major force. Henry Adams, pondering over American literature, questioned "whether he knew of any American artist who had ever insisted on the power of sex, as every classic had ever done." He could think only of Walt Whitman—with whom, interestingly, Dreiser is most often compared today. "American art," concluded Adams, "like the American language and American education, was as far as possible sexless." Adams was writing of the year 1900; even then, Dreiser, by publishing *Sister Carrie*, was about to change all that.

Third, Dreiser's explicit view of life. Disappointingly few writers impress one as possessing a coherent philosophy. Hemingway had this quality, and perhaps to a lesser extent, Faulkner. They, like the nineteenth-century giants—Melville, Hawthorne, Whitman, Twain—saw life clearly and distinctly, if by necessity from limited vantage points. They seemed to examine life as through binoculars which allowed them to penetrate and yet at the same time restricted their fields of vision. We must be able to count on a great author not only to describe life but to interpret it. Dreiser, of all twentieth-century writers, belongs in this illustrious company. His works—poems, essays, dramas, as well as novels—are monolithic. In them life is everywhere seen through the same binoculars; it is a colorful, kaleidoscopic, unpredictable riddle, at bottom tragic. *Sister Carrie* of 1900 and *The Bulwark* of forty-five years later, aside from particulars, tell the same story about America. Man is a mechanism, his pitiful existence determined by factors of biology and social environment which Dreiser, for want of a better term, labels "chemisms." The cosmos operating in his stories is uncaring, unfeeling; at bottom it is an unfair universe, controlled by gods who disdain involvement in their creation. We can nod in agreement with the writer or cavil at the darkness of his pessimism, but we are forced above all to stop, to consider, to think.

Fourth, Dreiser's magnificent compassion. Probably because of his philosophy—we are all companions in the same sinking ship— Dreiser feels keenly the plight of each individual human soul at the mercy of chance and of forces beyond his control. It is significant that, though failures abound in his novels, there are no villains, only human beings who are more or less fortunate than their neighbors. In the Dreiser world, each life is necessarily a tragedy. One by one, from high to low, the objects of his pity are exposed to our view, trailing their stars of illusion into oblivion: Carrie, Hurstwood, Jennie, Cowperwood, Witla, Clyde, Solon Barnes. Man is a tool of the universe, at the mercy of hypnotic, incomprehensible drives for sexual conquest, for esteem, fame, power, money. Each life is a shooting star; and, as it burns itself out in the cold, unfriendly atmosphere, Dreiser's sympathy is with it.

## II  *"Barbarity"*

The furor over Dreiser's subject matter, his handling of sexual matters in particular, has dropped below the level of a whisper; but the critical dispute concerning his other values as a novelist rolls merrily along. The river of Dreiser criticism runs, like the Mississippi, in an ever fluctuating channel, but it breaks clearly on the rock of fictional artistry and pours into distinct forks.[1]

This is nothing new, but it has continued for well over half a century. The word we hear most often from those who lament his influence is "barbarity." And hearing it, we are reminded— without intending so much as a hint of the sacrilegious—that Shakespeare himself once was represented, to an age which prided itself upon its taste, as a Great Barbarian. Actually, a good case can be made for Dreiser's abilities as an artist, to demonstrate at the very least that the novels did not spew from his pen in an explosion of uncontrolled emotion. For there is much more to his work than the barbaric yawp which apparently has stymied the sensibilities of many critics.

The style in which a major author writes is a matter of natural concern to his readers and critics, and Dreiser's became a subject for heated controversy from the time of *Sister Carrie*. His disparagers found in it a flaw to cavil at; his admirers, a weakness to excuse. On more than one occasion it has been seriously questioned whether Drieser has a style at all. But this is more like asking whether a man has eyes to see with. It also avoids the issue, for every writer has a style of some sort.

Those who would render Dreiser styleless are angry principally because he fails to write in the manner they prefer. John Cowper

Powys has offered the most obvious refutation of their charge: "One would recognize a page of Dreiser's writings as infallibly as one would recognize a page of Hardy's. The former *relaxes* his medium to the extreme limit and the latter *tightens* his; but they both have their 'manner.' A paragraph written by Dreiser would never be mistaken for anyone else's."[2]

The only relevant point is the degree to which Dreiser's style is meritorious, an issue over which readers have long been in dispute. When *Sister Carrie* was published, for instance, the reviewer for the Newark *Sunday News*—after admitting the "very real" nature of the characters but lamenting the absence of any true "lady or gentleman" among them—takes the book to task for its "utter lack . . . of a literary manner of diction. . . . The style is in many ways excellent, at times even nervous. . . . But one does not wish to have a writer express himself in the same way as do his somewhat uncultivated characters. . . . If only Carrie could be more like Trilby!" Yet Agnes Repplier, reviewing the novel for the Philadelphia *Ledger*, praises Dreiser for "the faculty of picturing his scenes so vividly in clear-cut English that they compel instant and abiding interest."[3]

These two contemporaneous reviews strike at the issues which have remained basic for the past half-century: one camp criticizes Dreiser for being Dreiser and not Du Maurier—or Henry James or Ernest Hemingway; the other recognizes the style as an effective, if admittedly blunt, tool for communicating vital experiences. The controversy exhibits no signs of being resolved. Instead it splits further and more definitely into two camps. One is highly attuned to the uses or misuses of individual words, the syntax of sentences. In vain, it scans pages in search of poetic qualities, sensitivity to diction, compression and stripping away of nonessentials. The other admits candidly it is quite willing to overlook particular sins of language and to find value instead in the total impact of scene.

The memory is teased by a statement concerning the methods of Emily Dickinson. Made during a somewhat analogous controversy, it spoke to the effect that, when a thought takes the breath away, the lesson in grammar is impertinent. Even so, it is safest to admit at once that Dreiser is not what E. B. White would call a "word man"—a writer willing to revise and reshape with infinite pains until he has refined the essence of his statement so that each sentence accomplishes its task as well as it can, with words chosen discriminately for exact shades of meaning and connotation. But status as a word man is not the sole legitimate ambition of the writer, and besides, as *Esquire* comments, such writers are more often born than made:

> There are, and have been, writers who could not be classed as word men. Dreiser, for instance, wasn't one, and Scott Fitzgerald, equally for instance, was. Mencken and Nathan both were, but Sinclair Lewis wasn't and Upton Sinclair isn't. And, as with gourmets, not everybody is who says he is. Because a word man must be not only skilled, but in love, with words—in and of themselves, and for their own sake. Many writers are so headlong in their rush after ideas that they are inclined to let the words fall, like chips, where they may. For the words themselves, such writers care very little. In contrast, the word men among writers are like misers with their treasures; they take them out and look at them, fondle them, and almost gloat over the rare ones.[4]

Not completely insensitive to stylistic perfection, Dreiser was aware of his own limitations and trespasses—he could hardly avoid being, considering the critics' strident protests over his "butchery" of the language; and many times he professed a desire and intention of revising all his novels with style in mind. Only *The Financier* received this treatment, and then not entirely to its benefit; for if awkwardnesses and repetitions were deleted, so were a number of valuable commentaries. The fact is that, over and above his not being by nature a "word man," Dreiser forever had too many projects in the works, too many statements to be made and books to be written to spare the necessary time for such revision. He had a choice to make, and he made it instinctively.

As a result, Dreiser produces a rough-hewn but solid and serviceable plank full of knots which, while not diminishing the plank's utility, add nothing to its beauty. In reading *Sister Carrie,* one stubs his toe upon the roughness of statements such as this: "The, to Carrie, very important theatrical performance was to take place at the Avery on conditions which were to make it more noteworthy than was at first anticipated."[5] Or more grievous yet is: "They had young men of the kind whom she, since her experience with Drouet, felt above, who took them out."[6] Yet one can set beside these blunders, to prove them not the rule, well-turned sentences like: "Amid the tinsel and shine or her state walked Carrie, unhappy,"[7] or "Her mind delighted itself with scenes of luxury and refinement, situations in which she was the cynosure of all eyes, the arbiter of all fates."[8]

*An American Tragedy* contains sentences so muddied in progression and so awkwardly qualified as to assume almost the shape of a whirlpool:

> One day, not so long after Clyde's discovery of his sister Esta, Hortense, walking along Baltimore Street near its junction with Fifteenth—the smartest portion of the shopping section of the city—at the noon hour—with Doris Trine, another shop girl in her department store, saw in the window of one of the smaller and less exclusive fur stores of the city, a fur jacket of beaver that to her, viewed from the eye-point of her own particular build, coloring and temperament, was exactly what she needed to strengthen mightily her very limited personal wardrobe.[9]

But the novel also contains passages whose narrative function is clear, whose dramatic sense is unimpaired, and whose direction is straightforward rather than spiral.

One salient fact remains incontrovertible, however: the gaucheries are present and no amount of polishing in neighboring regions will remove them. There is, besides, an irritating playing of words to death, no doubt subconscious upon the writer's part. In *An American Tragedy*, for instance, Dreiser plays upon *chic* in the manner of a sophomore who, having just discovered the term, is determined to wrest a place for it in the unlikeliest situations. In the *Trilogy of Desire* it is *trig* which is ridden till it can no longer stand, and in *The "Genius"* the word *subtle* eventually cracks beneath a burden it should never be forced to bear—explaining every dark, mysterious force and act for which Dreiser cannot logically account. Also, he betrays an unfortunate tendency toward grandiloquence, and passages where this tendency gains control, sound as if another—and much less mature—writer has taken over. Alexander Kern has commented tellingly upon this weakness: "Like Whitman, Dreiser, in compensating for a lack of education and culture, strove painfully for an elaborate vocabulary, and like Whitman, is at his worst when his style is least natural."[10] Such flaws marred Dreiser's writing until the end, despite a perceptible effort toward fluidity and grace.

H. L. Mencken once reported in exasperation, "I spent the better part of forty years trying to induce him to reform and electrify his manner of writing, but so far as I am aware with no more effect than if I had sought to persuade him to take up golf or abandon his belief in non-Euclidian arcana."[11] We have eventually to face the fact that Dreiser was Dreiser, immovable and ponderous. "Take me as I am or take me not at all," was Dreiser's attitude. His eye was trained first on the lives presented in his tragic books; at best, the words were secondary. If the desire to present the one truthfully and with force caused the other to suffer, that was regrettable but hardly a matter that could induce him to rend his garments and strew ashes on his head. "To sit up and criticize me for saying 'vest' instead of 'waistcoat'; to talk about my splitting the infinitive and using vulgar commonplaces here and there, when the tragedy of a man's life is being displayed, is silly," he protested impatiently. "More, it is ridiculous. It makes me feel that American criticism is the joke that English authorities maintain it to be."[12]

## III  *Historian to an Era*

Dreiser produces not the "novel *démeublé*" of Willa Cather, but a highly furnished, perhaps even overcrowded, room with a view of all outdoors. Such a method not only lends itself to but is based upon the piling up of background trivia. Often this appears to be done indiscriminately. Yet details which in many instances by themselves seem of no import do in the mass create the world of his stories. It is as if he were insisting that— in this place, at this time, under these precise circumstances—his people lived and acted, and in no other place or time or environment of forces could the same events have led to the same end.

So we read what are not always brief dissertations upon the origin of department stores, or descriptions of trolley systems and urban architecture, or the furnishings of rooms, rooms, rooms. The influence of Balzac and Zola is at once apparent. His discovery of Balzac, made at the Carnegie Library in Pittsburgh, was likened by Dreiser to a new and inviting door to life suddenly thrown open: "It was for me a literary revolution." Linking this discovery with earlier advice offered by H. B. Wandell in St. Louis, Dreiser had found his method. For Wandell had suggested: "Remember Zola and Balzac, my boy, remember Zola and Balzac. Bare facts are what are needed in cases like this, with lots of color as to the scenery or atmosphere, the room, the other people, the street, and all that." "All that," we now recognize rather clearly, is what in the larger sense enabled the naturalistic movement to make its substantial contribution to our literature.

And it is in the larger sense that these detailed treatises of actuality must be judged, just as all of Dreiser's works must be judged as totalities. "It is impossible," he wrote Evelyn Scott, "to produce any novel or painting or whatever which does not have some social background which is presented favorably or unfavorably either by implication or directly, because the material and the artist himself are products of the same."[13] Inevitably the portrayal of the social background emerges as one of Dreiser's major values as a writer. Like Sinclair Lewis, he is historian to an era.

On occasion, of course, given his proclivity to write overmuch and indiscriminately, he goes too far. The lengthy description of the prison in which Cowperwood awaits parole comes to mind at once. Although the building plays the most minor of roles in the story, we are handed it brick by brick, cell by cell:

> The corridors, forty-two feet wide from outer wall to outer wall, were one hundred and eighty feet in length, and in four instances two stories high, and extended in their long reach in every direction. There were no windows in the corridors, only narrow slits of skylights, three and one-half feet long by perhaps eight inches wide, let in the roof; and the ground-floor cells were accompanied in some instances by a small yard ten by sixteen—the same size as the cells proper—which was surrounded by a high brick wall in every instance.[14]

This architectural catalog and the data accompanying it, such as the information that the prison dated from 1822, authentic as such detail may be, can scarcely affect the story Dreiser has to tell. Such trivia has a way of cluttering the vital action, as it does in *The Titan* when, after a violent quarrel over her husband's mistress, Aileen Cowperwood attempts suicide. Even at the climactic moment, Dreiser cannot resist the temptation to pause for background data—and never was it more irrelevant:

> To Cowperwood it seemed unreal, bravado, a momentary rage intended to frighten him. She turned and walked up the grand staircase, which was near—a splendid piece of marble and bronze

fifteen feet wide, with marble nereids for newel-posts, and dancing figures worked into the stone. She went into her room quite calmly and took up a steel paper-cutter of dagger design— a knife with a handle of bronze and a point of great sharpness. Coming out and going along the balcony over the court of orchids, where Cowperwood still was seated, she entered the sunrise room with its pool of water, its birds, its benches, its vines. Locking the door, she sat down and then, suddenly baring an arm, jabbed a vein.[15]

Dreiser is on the wrong track here. He is seeing—or trying to— with separate eyes, each focused upon a different object; one upon Aileen, the other upon the richness of the décor. In writing, the two mix poorly.

Perhaps this simultaneous focus is impossible for a writer. It anticipates another medium, for in the hands of a sensitive and expert cameraman, the motion picture can achieve precisely what Dreiser was attempting in language. Orson Welles, in *Citizen Kane*, did in fact reproduce essentially the same scene: Kane and his wife are amid the extravagant wealth of their Xanadu; she is contemplating suicide. Welles's camera was able to focus upon the action and simultaneously—and with magnificent subtlety—to mirror the implications of that environment of massive rooms, their riches of statuary ransacked from the world, the emptiness of a friendless mansion. But in *The Titan* it fails to come off.

More important, the accumulation of detail is more successful than not. The death house in which Clyde Griffiths awaits execution is developed in the same manner and at greater length than the Philadelphia prison of *The Financier*, but it plays a more integral part in the story. A fuller treatment is warranted; and, even though Dreiser perhaps oversteps the bounds in cataloging detail, the effect is relevant and of considerable power.

If we are willing to overlook Dreiser's occasional lapses and excesses, we soon realize that it is precisely from their load of minutiae that the novels derive a good share of their remarkable sense of life. Enough detail of the right sort will eventually assume the shape of a mountain, and this is the image to which Dreiser's novels are most often compared—mountainous, craggy, rugged and ungainly perhaps, but solid and formidable. The proof of the method is found in those novels where its absence is conspicuous. *The Bulwark* and *The Stoic*—written out of a sense of obligation and necessity, long after the original stimuli and data upon which they were based had passed from the mind—seem sketches for novels to come, first drafts or outlines to be fleshed out later. They are bare trees upon whose limbs the leaf-buds have yet to burst.

At one point in his life, Dreiser could write of his Chicago or New York without recourse to notes, simply by opening the cocks of memory and allowing the physical setting, replete with detail, to gush forth. But in finishing *The Bulwark* on the West Coast, far from the story's locale, he found himself needing to write Louise Campbell for information on Etta's Greenwich Village adventure: "Give me the names of a few downtown residence streets running between Broad and the Delaware River—to the north of Market," he requested. "I want to place a character in a decent furnished room there."[16] Time was when he would have had the neighborhood with every street corner and a dozen appropriate rooms all well in mind. Without the full social background of its companion books, *The Stoic* provides a limp ending to the Cowperwood saga, while *The Bulwark* splits into a panel of separate incidents.

## IV  *Narrative Devices*

In shaping his novels, Dreiser prefers the method of straight chronology. He begins most characteristically with the birth of his protagonist and drives forward slowly, steadily until death or a more critical termination is reached. We feel impelled to comment upon the superiority—for Dreiser's type of story—of this method in supplying the fullness so woefully lacking in much of today's fiction. The infinite probing of a moment for every bit of light it can cast upon a sensitive personality has its very positive values and is not to be made light of. But Dreiser's themes of slow growth, of gradual personal disintegration, of life's inevitable reversals, require a different approach. The crucial events of his stories are the result of the passage of time and occur as the consequence of innumerable prior experiences. Being the result of time, Dreiser's most memorable denouements—Clyde's execution, Hurstwood's suicide, Frank Cowperwood's estate picked bare by legal vultures—can be arrived at effectively only by the presentation of extensive periods of time.

Only once, in *The Bulwark,* does he experiment with beginning a novel *in medias res* and then flashing back to the beginning. And every novel starting with youth pushes ahead, through that indispensable learning process, toward adulthood. But not for Dreiser is the modern story with its child or adolescent hero. The child lives in his own world, after all, a restricted and personal sphere. While this world may be of momentous significance to the child at its center, it of necessity puts limitations upon the broad social landscape whose depiction is one of the glories of Dreiser's achievement. Knowing that the child is but father to the man, Dreiser paints these formative years for their own sake, but always with the future in mind. His adults act in consistency with early experiences. So Carrie's life is conditioned by her schooling in Chicago's concrete jungle; Clyde's, by the tension between poverty and wealth; Frank's, by his observation and acute analysis of life's basic struggle; and Solon's, by his isolated and rigid Quaker upbringing. Looking from the last day, we can peer far back down the road to the inception of a particular life's journey; and the route is clear. These lives form patterns, are all of a piece, and, as such, achieve meaning.

The modern preoccupation with rigidly controlled point of view has given us a number of masterpieces, but we must admit that it has resulted as often in obscurity. It has its dangers: limitation of scope and fragmentation of experience are two of these. It results in mere novelty as often as it achieves enlightenment. Even though Dreiser keeps his eye, for the most part, upon his central actor, he reserves his right to omniscient authorship, so that he may if he wishes—and he often does wish—make a leap in time and space or enter the story to comment and interpret the action, particularly in its philosophical or sociological aspects.

Omniscience provides also for one of his most effective narrative devices—the portrayal of simultaneous action, generally for ironical counterpoint. We feel the effect of it in all his novels. One outstanding example is the continued tension set up in us between the rise of Carrie and the collapse of Hurstwood. That long series of chapters which deal alternately with these two principals culminates in a fourfold presentation. We observe Carrie rich but unhappy; Hurstwood turning on the gas; Drouet unchanged; Mrs. Hurstwood and Jessica aboard a luxury train. Four routes of life having been portrayed, the destinations are now made clear, can be compared, contrasted, understood in terms of both personality and social milieu. The larger picture of "the way life has organized itself"—which we now see as Dreiser's real intention in the novel—is clarified. The device works brilliantly throughout *An American Tragedy*—for instance, in the flight of Clyde while the posse is dogging his trail, and even more effectively in the trial sequence. The advantage gained is in completeness of scene. A reader senses that he is dealing with a broad canvas of life rather than with the miniature of an isolated individual. He feels that nothing essential is being withheld, the machinery of society is stripped bare. And, while Dreiser avowedly cared only for the individual and nothing for the mass, there exists no individual except as a member of the crowd, formed by the crowd, pitted against the crowd.

## V  *Imagery, Settings*

Dreiser deals with a wealth of imagery and figure, but this artistry is often obscured by the mountain of realistic detail. The use of the rocking chair in *Sister Carrie* to indicate indecision, contemplation, stagnation, and restiveness is but one example. In the same book, water images are used consistently to portray the forces which sweep men forward, out of control; Carrie is described variously as "getting into deep water. She was letting her few supports float away from her" and as "an anchorless, storm-beaten little craft which could do absolutely nothing but drift."

Imagery from the animal world abounds, linking Dreiser with literary Darwinism; the jungle of nature overshadows human society. We think first of obvious instances, such as the lobster-squid duel in *The Financier* which sets young Cowperwood's notions firmly in the groove they are to follow until his death. In the same book the coda "Concerning Mycteroperca Bonaci," obtrusive as it undeniably is, furnishes a valuable analogy for the understanding of the *Trilogy's* protagonist. Cowperwood is generally portrayed through the figures of lions, tigers, and leopards, or other predators: "Like a wolf prowling under glittering, bitter stars in the night, he was looking down into the humble folds of simple men and seeing what their ignorance and their unsophistication would cost them."[17] These images furnish a consistent counterpoise to Dreiser's obvious admiration of the man's force and self-reliance. Cowperwood, magnificent human adventurer though he is, remains a lion raging in the streets of society; and, as such he must be overthrown.

A pattern of symbolism buttresses Dreiser's concepts; clothes and dwellings are the most prominent. Both serve to dramatize human beings trapped in illusory materialism—exterior symbols of show and display which furnish ultimately no nourishment for the soul. Without clothes as an emblem of status and achievement and worth, *Sister Carrie* would be hard pressed to convey the pointed comments it does upon American society. It is in this novel that clothes symbolism is sharpest. But the device carries over. Through her contrasting indifference to silks and ribbons we are enabled to perceive the more solid values of Jennie Gerhardt. And Clyde Griffiths places as much premium upon appearance as Carrie does; his delight in his bellhop's uniform tells us this at once. The episode in which that insufferable gold-digger, Hortense Briggs, calculatedly suggests that Clyde may enjoy her favors only if and when he advances money to buy the sleazy coat she so admires, is crucial in that it causes a number of Clyde's life-attitudes to jell.

Dreiser is also fond of emphasizing human dwellings in order to heighten the impact of his stories. Any reader of the novels can at once call to mind a dozen or more localities which have lingered in his consciousness. From *Sister Carrie* we recall scenes which also represent the rise and fall of the characters: the shabby little flat on West Van Buren Street in which Carrie Meeber's sister is imprisoned; Drouet's apartment in Ogden Place with its green plush couch, pier-glass mirror, and Brussels carpet "rich in dull red and lemon shades, and representing large jardinières filled with gorgeous, impossible flowers." From these scenes we move upward until we reach the splendid hotels in which Carrie, without charge because of the publicity her presence lends the establishments, is furnished with every modern comfort except happiness and contentment. At the same time we slide downward with Hurstwood from home to flat to flophouse, to his narrow coffin-sized cubicle where he stuffs the cracks with his ragged clothes and turns on the gas jets.

The story "Fine Furniture," published as a separate volume by Random House in 1930, is Dreiser's most pointed treatment of the furniture theme. So thesis-ridden as to deserve the subtitle "Craig's Wife in a Logging Camp," it concerns the efforts of Opal Broderson to compete for status with Mrs. Saxtrom, dictator of the microscopic social sphere in Red Ledge camp: "Mrs. Saxtrom wanted it generally known that hers was the best furnished cottage in the camp as well as hers the best furnished table and she best dressed—quite the richest, at least—for didn't her husband, the superintendent, get the biggest salary?"[18]

Determined to outdo Mrs. Saxtrom's red plush and heavy walnut, Opal spends her husband's $3,000 savings on a vanload of tables, rugs, chairs, and lamps.

> When it came to furniture. ... . Halt, mortal! Consider! There, indeed, should be her triumph! So eventually, to Red Ledge, came furniture such as the camp, to say nothing of Clem himself, had never seen here or elsewhere. Hearken! Behold! Item: one fumed walnut living-room or parlor set, consisting of davenport, table, parlor lamp, two overstuffed chairs, a rug (of a delicate yellow and orange), a footstool, and a victrola. (After these were all properly placed in the sixteen-by-twelve front room, there was just space enough between them to make one's way if one did it carefully.) Item: one ivory-finished bedroom set, decorated with moulded pink and blue floral motifs—bed, dresser, chest of drawers, two chairs, a wall mirror, and curtains of old gold to harmonize. Item: one oval rag rug of mingled greys and blue to be laid under all this.[19]

Needless to say, it is unthinkable that Clem Broderson, with his spiked logging boots, his grimy, sooty camp clothes, should be allowed to desecrate this temple. The new furniture brings a new order not only to the home but to the camp, where it upsets the established status. Mrs. Saxtrom waits for her revenge until a move is made to a new logging site; then, by a rearrangement of the shake and clapboard shacks, Clem and Opal are moved from the main line facing the tracks to the third line of buildings. In the logging camp this constitutes a social disaster without parallel: "The main thing to regret or avoid was not being in the first line facing the track, since to be behind the first line or across the tracks was somehow déclassé."[20]

Clem, protesting this affront to his wife, loses his job with the company. But he is determined to begin afresh and to locate a position where Opal may display her finery in suitable circumstances. The furniture has trapped him as well as her. He will never be the same carefree logger again. Having joined the army of men Thoreau speaks of, he is a poor immortal soul "well-nigh crushed and smothered under its load, creeping down the road of life, pushing before it a barn seventy-five feet by forty."

Or we might turn to the *Trilogy,* which of all Dreiser's works most depends upon house symbolism, and find here the pleasure domes of Frank Cowperwood, each one more extravagant than the last, more crammed with buccaneer's loot—and yet emptier. If any book rivals the *Trilogy* in emphasizing places, it is *An American Tragedy.* The book could almost be said to be structured in terms of dwellings: the Door of Hope Mission and the Green-Davidson Hotel; Mrs. Cuppy's rooming house and the Griffiths mansion on Wykeagy Avenue; Roberta's room and the death house. Dorothy Dudley says that *An American Tragedy* is a massive structure "composed of a number of structures, now poor, now rich, now private, now public, doors leading to doors. . . . Between the doors of the mission house in Kansas City and the death room in Sing Sing what trivial front doors and momentous back doors and secret front doors are imagined by this mystical realist."[21]

Dreiser's *dramatis personae* exist in a material world, and by their material preferences we know them. We never forget the elaborate office which Eugene Witla occupies at the United Magazines Corporation. Its white, blue, and gold décor, ornate vases loaded with roses and sweet peas, and massive plate-glassed rosewood desk represent the richness of material with which Eugene attempts self-seduction into an enduring alliance with business while his art is deserted. But the grandeur of the office points, for him, only toward a wasteland of mental anguish and eventual breakdown. And we cannot escape the piercing irony of the gracious home at Thornbrough in which Solon Barnes's family falls from Quaker grace. All of these dwellings, even more than they reflect the tastes of their inhabitants, shape the fears and joys, the frustrations and triumphs of those who live in them. They are little worlds over which they can rule, from which they can escape, or to which they will succumb.


## VI   *Foreshadowings*

Judicious foreshadowing again reveals the artist in control of his material. Carrie Meeber's success on the stage may astonish her, but it has been long prepared for. When it occurs, we remember her earlier triumph in Chicago in the Custer Lodge of the Order of Elks' production of "Under the Gaslight" when, almost single-handedly, she rescued that amateur theatrical from disaster. And Hurstwood's plunge into beggary is intimated not only by all of Carrie's earlier experiences in Chicago streets but explicitly by the brief scene at the end of Chapter XIV. A panhandler has just accosted the trio of Carrie, Drouet, and Hurstwood on their way home after a theater party:

> "Say, mister," said a voice at Hurstwood's side, "would you mind giving me the price of a bed?"
> Hurstwood was interestedly remarking to Carrie.
> "Honest to God, mister, I'm without a place to sleep."
> The plea was that of a gaunt-faced man of about thirty, who looked the picture of privation and wretchedness. Drouet was the first to see. He handed over a dime with an upwelling feeling of pity in his heart. Hurstwood scarcely noticed the incident. Carrie quickly forgot.[22]

At times the shadows of future events are prepared for rather clumsily. The codas of the books in the *Trilogy* are cases where we feel the author pointing his finger perhaps a trifle too explicitly; yet the desire to cast the mind ahead to indicate the eventual working out of the "the equation inevitable" and the fall of the mighty is clear:

> At the ultimate remove, God or the life force, if anything, is an equation, and at its nearest expression for man—the contract social—it is that also. Its method of expression appears to be that of generating the individual, in all his glittering variety and scope, and through him progressing to the mass with its problems. In the end a balance is invariably struck wherein the mass subdues the individual or the individual the mass—for the time being. For, behold, the sea is ever dancing or raging.[23]

In later works, where Dreiser picks up the method and terminology of the psychoanalysts—when he first begins employing terms like "repressions" and "subconscious," "psychic sex scar" and "Freudianism"—we are also compelled to notice foreshadowing as it occurs. The dream sequence in *The Bulwark* is representative. Solon's mother sees her son thrown to the ground by a mare after he has struggled to dominate the beast. Not only does she attempt to interpret her dream, but we, seeing no other plausible explanation for the dream's presence in the story, are caused to wonder at its possible implications for the future.

The later events of *An American Tragedy* are prepared for by the most extensive and artistically successful foreshadowing Dreiser was capable of. The preparation for Clyde's reaction to frustration, his characteristic panic in stress situations, has already been treated in Chapter 6. But much more is involved. Roberta's plight is seen in clear perspective when we recall the care with which Esta's shame—her elopement, pregnancy, and consequent abandonment—is described in Book One. Clyde's infatuation with Hortense Briggs—his naïve susceptibility to a pretty face and his eagerness to sacrifice all to gain it for his own—prepares the way for the Sondra-Roberta chapters which lie ahead. And when young Russell is introduced in the epilogue, we have the entire novel as a foreshadowing of his doom. Here the artist has clearly superseded the reporter.

## VII  *"Crag of Basalt"*

The precise nature and degree of Dreiser's artistry will remain always a matter for sharp disagreement. His critics have cried down and his defenders shored up his reputation ever since 1900. Sidney Lanier once said of the Good Gray Poet: "Whitman is poetry's butcher. Huge raw collops slashed from the rump of poetry, and never mind gristle—is what Whitman feeds our souls with." When we substitute for Whitman, Dreiser and for poetry, fiction, the resulting paraphrase serves to summarize all that Dreiser's detractors agree upon.

Against this we must set the positive values of this man's work. What has made his novels endure is, in the end, not the presence or absence of delicately balanced sentences or fine and precise diction. It is rather the tragic and real sense of life pulsing through their pages that causes his books to be read and reread. We feel that, whatever else is meritorious or crude, Dreiser's are portraits drawn straight from the varying strata of human existence; he is more Daumier or Goya than Raphael. Contributing to this effect is the effort expended on development of the *mise en scène,* the social panorama which ever reminds us of precisely what America was like while the action of any particular novel was unfolding.

Contributing even more grandly is the Dreiserian view of human existence. The artist becomes, not a camera obscura, but an interpreter. What is missing in lesser writers—the impression of life witnessed from a definite and stated viewpoint—becomes more and more with passing years a virtue that sets Dreiser above and apart. Whatever image we select to express the man's stand—whether it be the grim picture of life as a jungle with human beasts raging and clawing for survival, or of life as a maelstrom blindly, indifferently hurling human souls through the years on winds of chance—we recognize commitment to a philosophy.

And whether we join in that commitment or find it dismaying, there is pleasure and satisfaction in witnessing it, in having it elucidated, in having at least one window on life opened wide and clear so that we may all look, see, and judge for ourselves. More and more, the judgment of readers has exonerated Dreiser of the charges made against him in his early career. More and more, that judgment places him securely in the front rank of American fictionists; he becomes more solidly than ever what Mencken called him, "a crag of basalt." Whatever its beauty or grimness, the crag unmistakably marks our native landscape.

# Notes and References

## Chapter One

1. For factual information up to *Newspaper Days*, I have relied heavily upon Dreiser's autobiography *Dawn*, which documents these early years extensively, though not with invariable reliability.

2. Hamlin Garland, *Crumbling Idols* (Chicago, 1894), pp. 57-79.

3. Shortened later to Snepp; as such, referred to in Dreiser's autobiographical writings.

4. For a more complete exposition of the process by which Dreiser's father entered his fiction, see Chapter 7.

5. Whether Dreiser was as much of a ladies' man as he intimates is open to debate. It is reasonably certain that he was a participant in a number of love affairs; but, for the most part, we must depend upon his own testimony, and the suspicion grows that the man protests too much.

6. Theodore Dreiser, *Dawn* (New York, 1931), p. 200.

7. *Ibid.*, p. 370.

8. Dreiser in *Dawn* refers to this man as Levitt, but he confides that he has employed a number of pseudonyms in his autobiographies. I have relied for the name of Yakey upon Dreiser's biographer, Robert H. Elias.

9. For material from this point to the end of the chapter, I have relied heavily upon Dreiser's autobiography *A Book About Myself* (later editions appear under the title *Newspaper Days*).

10. Theodore Dreiser, *A Book About Myself* (New York, 1922), p. 36.

11. Dreiser in *A Book About Myself* refers to this young lady as Alice Kane; again, I have relied upon Elias for the name Lois Zahn.

12. This story appears in *Free, and Other Stories*. Told from the girl's viewpoint, it retains the essential facts of the relationship. The girl had a middle-aged sweetheart whom she was content to marry until Dreiser entered her life. When he deserted her, she was forced to return to a man she no longer cared for. In the fictional version, Dreiser paints himself in darker tones than are perhaps necessary.

13. Dreiser, *A Book About Myself*, pp. 132-33.

14. *Ibid.*, p. 406.

15. *Ibid.*, p. 240.

16. C. T. Yerkes was used later as the prototype for Frank Cowperwood in *The Financier.*

17. Dreiser, *A Book About Myself*, p. 265.

18. *Ibid.*, p. 260.

19. This story appears in *Free, and Other Stories* under the title "McEwen of the Shining Slave Makers."

20. These stories appear in *Free, and Other Stories*, the first under the title "Old Roagum and His Theresa."

21. Incredible as it may seem, Dreiser insisted that this was the process by which the novel came to be written—title first and story later. It seems probable, however, that his own sisters' experience had long been in his mind as potential literary material.

## Chapter Two

1. The voluminous manuscript of this projected volume may be found in the Dreiser Collection at the University of Pennsylvania Library, together with the reading notes used by the author. A comprehensive account of the manuscript's content and arrangement may be found in Mrs. Neda Westlake's "Theodore Dreiser's *Notes on Life.*"

2. Theodore Dreiser, *A Hoosier Holiday* (New York, 1916), p. 285.

3. *Ibid.*

4. Theodore Dreiser, *Sister Carrie* (New York, 1900), p. 83.

5. *Ibid.*, p. 107.

6. *Ibid.*, pp. 121-22.

7. *Ibid.*, pp. 127-28.

8. *Ibid.*, p. 321.

9. *Ibid.*, p. 484.

10. *Ibid.*, p. 488.

11. *Ibid.*, p. 554.

12. Theodore Dreiser, *The Color of a Great City* (New York, 1923), p. 99.

13. Dreiser, *Sister Carrie*, p. 342.

14. With minor alterations, Dreiser reports this same story in *A Book About Myself*, p. 438.

15. Dreiser, *Sister Carrie,* pp. 4-5.

16. The report of Clark's decline is told in detail in *A Book About Myself* (pp. 223-25).

17. Theodore Dreiser, "Curious Shifts of the Poor," *Demorest's Family Magazine,* XXXVI (November, 1899), 26.

18. Dreiser, *A Book About Myself,* pp. 463-64.

19. Robert H. Elias, ed., *Letters of Theodore Dreiser* (Philadelphia, 1959), III, 980.

20. One is struck by the recurrence of this key phrase, evidently of great importance to Dreiser in demonstrating the unfair retribution meted out to those who break society's arbitrary codes. The phrase is used in *A Hoosier Holiday; Jennie Gerhardt* had *The Transgressor* for a working title; and in Chapter XXXII of *An American Tragedy* it is used again to sum up the doom of Clyde Griffiths. In one sense, all of Dreiser's novels center around the harsh treatment accorded the transgressor.

21. In *A Book About Myself* (p. 64) Dreiser writes: "I was now quite alone in the world and free to go anywhere and do as I pleased. I found a front room in Ogden Place overlooking Union Park (in which area I afterwards placed one of my heroines)."

22. Dreiser, *Sister Carrie,* p. 557.

23. Dreiser, *A Hoosier Holiday,* p. 253.

## Chapter Three

1. William Dean Howells, *Criticism and Fiction* (New York, 1959), p. 70. Many will consider my treatment of Howells unnecessarily harsh, and surely he deserves the praise he has been given for furthering the cause of realism in American fiction. Yet his was but a first step and, once having taken it, he stopped cold. His refusal to lend his immense prestige to the defense of Dreiser's *The "Genius"* is indicative of his later position.

2. Frank Luther Mott's *Golden Multitudes* reports the best-sellers of the era including the Reverend Wright's *Shepherd of the Hills* (1907) and *The Winning of Barbara Worth* (1911) and Mrs. Porter's *Freckles* (1903) and *The Girl of the Limberlost* (1909).

3. Elias, *Letters,* II, 417-21.

4. Dreiser, *A Hoosier Holiday,* p. 456.

5. This period in Dreiser's life is reflected in "Culhane, the Solid Man," one of the portraits in *Twelve Men* (New York, 1919).

6. Elias, *Letters,* I, 95.

7. Dreiser, *Dawn*, p. 147.

8. Theodore Dreiser, *Jennie Gerhardt* (New York, 1911), p. 10.

9. Dreiser, *Dawn*, p. 13.

10. Dreiser, *Jennie Gerhardt*, p. 112.

11. *Ibid.*, p. 173.

12. *Ibid.*, p. 238.

13. *Ibid.*, p. 430.

14. Dreiser refers to Jennie as "my pet heroine" in *A Hoosier Holiday* (p. 190) when commenting on the similarity of Erie, Pennsylvania, to Jennie's native city of Columbus, Ohio, a city Dreiser had never visited at the time he used it as the setting for his novel. The author's affection for Jennie is evident at once in practically every reference he makes to her or to the novel; it was an affection which was contagious, Mencken being among those who were swept up by Jennie's story.

## Chapter Four

1. Stuart P. Sherman, "The Barbaric Naturalism of Mr. Dreiser," in *The Stature of Theodore Dreiser*, ed. by Alfred Kazin and Charles Shapiro (Bloomington, 1955), p. 78.

2. Dreiser, *A Hoosier Holiday*, p. 58.

3. This information and most of that explaining "genus financier" is to be found in "The American Financier," one of the essays in *Hey, Rub-A-Dub-Dub!* (New York, 1920). The essay is of inestimable value in understanding the ideas which underlie Dreiser's *Trilogy*.

4. This information is to be found in "Equation Inevitable," another of the essays in *Hey, Rub-A-Dub-Dub!*, and is, with "The American Financier," an indispensable companion piece to the Cowperwood saga. The importance Dreiser attached to the essay is attested to by his intention to include it in the final arrangement of *The Mechanism Called Man*.

5. Dreiser, "Equation Inevitable," pp. 167-80.

6. Dreiser, *Hey, Rub-A-Dub-Dub!*, p. 8.

7. Theodore Dreiser, *The Financier* (New York, 1912), p. 47.

8. Dreiser, *A Book About Myself*, p. 108.

9. New York *Tribune* (Jan. 4, 1906), p. 11.

10. Emelie Grigsby was Yerkes' mistress and the prototype of Berenice. The newspaper headline here reproduced refers to her "loss" of Yerkes to his wife when the body was brought to the home

to lie in state and the funeral arrangements put into Mrs. Yerkes' hands.

11. Chicago *Tribune* (Jan. 3, 1906), p. 2.

12. Chicago *Sunday Tribune* (Dec. 31, 1905), p. 1.

13. New York *Tribune* (Jan. 2, 1906), p. 9.

14. New York *Tribune* (Jan. 3, 1906), p. 1.

15. Edwin Lefevre, "What Availeth It?" *Everybody's Magazine,* XXIV (June, 1911), 836-48.

16. Charles E. Russell, "Where Did You Get It, Gentlemen?" *Everybody's Magazine,* XVII (September, 1907), 348-60.

17. Ida M. Tarbell, "Commercial Machiavellianism," *McClure's Magazine,* XXVI (March, 1906), 458-59.

18. Theodore Dreiser, *The Titan* (New York, 1914), p. 125.

19. Tarbell, "Commercial Machiavellianism," p. 455.

20. Dreiser, *The Financier*, p. 244.

21. Dreiser, *The Titan*, p. 372.

22. Lewis Mumford, *The Golden Day* (New York, 1926), p. 239.

23. The best and most available article describing the Yerkes home is Lefevre's "What Availeth It?"

24. Frederick Lewis Allen, *The Lords of Creation* (New York, 1935), p. 108.

25. Dreiser, *The Titan*, p. 71.

26. Dreiser, *The Financier*, p. 39.

27. Sherman, "The Barbaric Naturalism of Mr. Dreiser," an article well worth reading in its entirety as an example of the extreme right-wing reaction to Dreiser's novels.

28. Dreiser, *The Titan*, p. 246.

29. Waldo R. Brown, *Altgeld in Illinois* (New York, 1924), pp. 235-41.

30. "C. T. YERKES DEAD," New York *Daily Tribune* (December 30, 1905).

31. Dreiser, *The Titan*, p. 433.

32. Dreiser, *The Financier,* p. 780.

33. Theodore Dreiser, *The Stoic* (New York, 1947), p. 283.

34. Lefevre, "What Availeth It?", p. 845.

35. *Ibid.,* p. 836.

36. Elias, *Letters,* III, 1035.

37. Dreiser, *The Stoic,* p. 306.

38. Robert H. Elias, *Theodore Dreiser, Apostle of Nature* (New York, 1949), p. 160.

## Chapter Five

1. Helen Dreiser, *My Life with Dreiser* (Cleveland, 1951), p. 81.

2. Theodore Dreiser, *The "Genius"* (New York, 1915), p. 12.

3. *Ibid.*, p. 37.

4. This section of the manuscript appears as an entity in *Free, and Other Stories*. The names are changed from those used in *The "Genius"* and the hero appears as a musician, but the situation is immediately recognizable.

5. Dreiser, *The "Genius,"* p. 99.

6. *Ibid.*, p. 150.

7. *Ibid.*, p. 222.

8. The description of this painting tallies precisely with the elements in Alfred Stieglitz's 1893 photograph: *Winter, Fifth Avenue*. It is an example of Dreiser's easy matter-of-factness in utilizing source materials. He admired Stieglitz's work immensely, as well as that of the veritist painters, and he felt that in his novels he was attempting to convey the same impressions as they.

9. Dreiser, *The "Genius,"* p. 250.

10. Dorothy Dudley, *Forgotten Frontiers: Dreiser and the Land of the Free* (New York, 1932).

11. In the *Letters* (Vol. I), Suzanne Dale is revealed to be Thelma Cudlipp, and Dreiser's infatuation is manifest, even downright embarrassing, as he addresses her as "Flower Face," "Honeypot," and gushes "Do ju lub me? Had you sweet doe eyes? Or are dey dough eyes? (Oooh what a slam) And will jus always love me?" Reading these, we are no longer puzzled as to the inspiration for Sondra's letters to Clyde in *An American Tragedy;* they are originals.

12. Dreiser, *The "Genius,"* p. 274.

13. Dorothy Dudley, *Forgotten Frontiers*, pp. 335-36. The most complete account of the suppression of *The "Genius"* and the resulting trial is contained in Miss Dudley's volume. She was given access to H. L. Mencken's considerable collection of materials concerning the affair, and I have relied upon her account.

14. Elias, *Letters*, I, 221.

## Chapter Six

1. Dorothy Dudley, *Forgotten Frontiers,* pp. 409-10.

2. My account of the writing of *An American Tragedy* is based upon Helen Dreiser's recollections in *My Life with Dreiser.*

3. Helen Dreiser, *My Life with Dreiser,* p. 110.

4. H. L. Mencken, Introduction to *An American Tragedy* (Cleveland, 1948), p. 7.

5. Theodore Dreiser, *An American Tragedy* (New York, 1925), I, 13.

6. *Ibid.,* p. 181.

7. T. S. Eliot, "The Love Song of J. Alfred Prufrock," *Modern Verse in English 1900-1950,* ed. by Cecil and Tate (New York, 1958), p. 316.

8. It is of interest regarding Dreiser's methods that in adapting the actual murder for his novel, he retains the initials of the murderer for Clyde Griffiths and, in turn, has Clyde use his own initials for each pseudonym he uses in the lake district.

9. Dreiser, *An American Tragedy,* II, 392.

10. Elias, *Letters,* II, 458.

11. Dudley, *Forgotten Frontiers,* p. 461.

12. Helen Dreiser, *My Life with Dreiser,* p. 120.

13. Elias, *Letters,* III, 789.

14. For a full account of the Russian visit, see *Dreiser Looks at Russia.*

15. Mark Schorer, *Sinclair Lewis: An American Life* (New York, 1961), pp. 546-47.

16. Elias, *Letters,* I, 127.

17. Louise Campbell, *Letters to Louise* (Philadelphia, 1959), p. 43.

18. Sinclair Lewis, "Our Formula for Fiction," in *The Stature of Theodore Dreiser,* pp. 111-12.

19. Interestingly enough, Lewis was instrumental in seeing that the 1944 gold medal award of the National Institute of Arts and Letters was given to Dreiser. Lewis, with his reputation for irascibility, and in view of his many disputes with Dreiser, comes off very well in the affair. He wished it kept secret that he had been instrumental in urging the award, being afraid that, should Dreiser discover this, he might reject the medal.

20. However, in 1950, after Dreiser's death, the movies had another go at *An American Tragedy.* With a new title, *A Place in the Sun,* considerable updating of the *mise en scène,* and remarkable

fidelity to Dreiser's intent, the picture—which starred Elizabeth Taylor, Shelley Winters, and Montgomery Clift—emerged as one of the year's best. The picture won a number of awards; and, although a series of film productions of Dreiser's stories have been issued through the years, it remains outstanding.

## Chapter Seven

1. Louise Campbell, *Letters to Louise*, pp. 106-7.

2. A facsimile of the title page and a description of the intent to publish may be examined in Vrest Orton's *Dreiserana* (New York, 1929), pp. 40-41.

3. Elias, *Letters*, I, 271.

4. *Ibid.*, p. 309.

5. *Ibid.*

6. A reader of Dreiser's autobiographies, non-fiction works, and letters soon becomes acclimated to these outbursts which are likely as not to come unheralded, whirling at one like desert dust-devils in an otherwise serene landscape. The curious thing is that the more often they recur, the more one is convinced of Dreiser's basically religious nature. The violence of his protestations might call to mind Quentin Compson's "I *don't* hate the south!" in *The Sound and the Fury*. Dreiser's suggestion that the word "organized" preface the Marxist slogan "Religion is the opium of the people" may reveal more exactly the nature of his complaint.

7. Elias, *Letters*, III, 822.

8. Dreiser, *An American Tragedy*, I, 5.

9. Theodore Dreiser, *The Bulwark* (New York, 1946), p. 12.

10. *Ibid.*, p. 51.

11. *Ibid.*, p. 35.

12. *Ibid.*, pp. 119-20.

13. *Ibid.*, p. 103.

14. *Ibid.*, p. 104.

15. *Ibid.*, p. 112.

16. *Ibid.*, p. 38.

17. *Ibid.*, p. 113.

18. *Ibid.*, pp. 168-69.

19. *Ibid.*, p. 149.

20. *Ibid.*, p. 127.

21. *Ibid.*, pp. 61-62.

22. The best descriptions concerning the change in Dreiser's attitude toward his father are found in *A Book About Myself,* particularly in Chapter XXXIX. Dreiser had been away from Chicago for a year and now, visiting the World's Fair, he was able to see his father with some degree of objectivity. In *A Hoosier Holiday* (p. 284) the mixture of attitudes is obvious as he speaks of: "my dogmatic father, who was a Catholic and a bigot. I never knew a narrower, more hidebound religionist, nor one more tender and loving in his narrow way. He was a crank, a tenth rate Saint Simon or Francis of Assisi, and yet a charming person if it had been possible to get his mind off the subject of religion for more than three seconds at a time. He worked, ate, played, slept and dreamed religion."

23. Dreiser, *The Bulwark,* p. 138.

24. Helen Dreiser, *My Life with Dreiser,* p. 290.

25. Elias, Letters, III, 887.

26. *Ibid.,* II, 705.

## Chapter Eight

1. A valuable cross-section of Dreiser criticism is available in Kazin and Shapiro's *The Stature of Theodore Dreiser.*

2. John Cowper Powys, "The Writer And His Writings," in *Theodore Dreiser, America's Foremost Novelist* (New York, *ca.* 1917), pp. 19-21.

3. These and other comments from the time of *Sister Carrie's* first publication are conveniently gathered in *The Stature of Theodore Dreiser,* pp. 53-68.

4. "Publisher's Page," *Esquire,* LVI (December, 1961), 6.

5. Dreiser, *Sister Carrie,* p. 178.

6. *Ibid.,* p. 62.

7. *Ibid.,* p. 556.

8. *Ibid.,* p. 174.

9. Dreiser, *An American Tragedy,* I, 102-3.

10. Alexander Kern, "Dreiser's Difficult Beauty," *The Stature of Theodore Dreiser,* p. 162.

11. H. L. Mencken, Introduction to *An American Tragedy,* p. 8.

12. Dudley, *Forgotten Frontiers,* p. 217.

13. Elias, *Letters,* III, 799-800.

14. Dreiser, *The Financier,* p. 678.

15. Dreiser, *The Titan*, pp. 508-9.
16. Campbell, *Letters to Louise*, p. 109.
17. Dreiser, *The Financier*, p. 770.
18. Theodore Dreiser, *Fine Furniture* (New York, 1930), p. 9.
19. *Ibid.*, pp. 11-13.
20. *Ibid.*, p. 28.
21. Dudley, *Forgotten Frontiers*, pp. 445-46.
22. Dreiser, *Sister Carrie*, p. 153.
23. Dreiser, *The Titan*, pp. 550-51.

# Selected Bibliography

## PRIMARY SOURCES

### 1. Original Manuscripts

The majority of Dreiser's manuscripts reside in the Dreiser Collection of the University of Pennsylvania Library, Philadelphia. Dreiser personally deposited many of his papers there, and they were added to after his death by Helen Dreiser. Included are manuscripts of the majority of his books; galley and page proofs; first, subsequent, and foreign editions of the novels; correspondence; notes and worksheets; clipping files; portraits and busts by various artists.

The manuscript of *Sister Carrie*, presented to H. L. Mencken, resides in the New York Public Library. The manuscript of *Dawn* resides in the Library of Indiana University, Bloomington.

### 2. Novels (Arranged in order of publication)

*Sister Carrie.* New York: Doubleday, Page, 1900.
*Jennie Gerhardt.* New York: Harper, 1911.
*The Financier.* New York: Harper, 1912. Completely revised edition; New York: Boni & Liveright, 1927.
*The Titan.* New York: John Lane Company, 1914.
*The "Genius."* New York: John Lane Company, 1915.
*An American Tragedy.* New York: Boni & Liveright, 1925.
*The Bulwark.* Garden City: Doubleday, 1946.
*The Stoic.* Garden City: Doubleday, 1947.

### 3. Stories and Collections (Arranged in order of publication)

*Free, and Other Stories.* New York: Boni & Liveright, 1918.
*Chains.* New York: Boni & Liveright, 1927.
*Fine Furniture.* New York: Random House, 1930.
*The Best Short Stories of Theodore Dreiser,* ed. by Howard Fast. Cleveland: World, 1947.
*The Best Short Stories of Theodore Dreiser,* ed. by James T. Farrell. Cleveland: World, 1956.

### 4. Drama (Arranged in order of publication)

*Plays of the Natural and the Supernatural.* New York: John Lane Company, 1916.
*The Hand of the Potter.* New York: Boni & Liveright, 1918.

5. *Poetry (Arranged in order of publication)*

*Moods, Cadenced and Declaimed.* New York: Boni & Liveright, 1928. Revised edition. New York: Simon & Schuster, 1935.
*The Aspirant.* New York: Random House, 1929.
*Epitaph: a poem.* New York: Heron Press, 1929.

6. *Autobiography (Arranged in order to provide the best chronological sequence of Dreiser's life)*

*Dawn.* New York: Liveright, 1931.
*A Book About Myself.* New York: Boni & Liveright, 1922 (editions beyond the seventh appear as *Newspaper Days*).
*A Traveler at Forty.* New York: Century, 1913.
*A Hoosier Holiday.* New York: John Lane Company, 1916.

7. *Letters*

*Letters of Theodore Dreiser,* ed. by Robert H. Elias. Philadelphia: University of Pennsylvania Press, 1959.

8. *Non-fiction (Arranged in order of publication)*

"Life, Art and America," reprinted from *The Seven Arts,* February, 1917.
*Twelve Men.* New York: Boni & Liveright, 1919.
*Hey, Rub-A-Dub-Dub!* New York: Boni & Liveright, 1920.
*The Color of a Great City.* New York: Boni & Liveright, 1923.
*Dreiser Looks at Russia.* New York: Liveright, 1928.
*A Gallery of Women.* New York: Liveright, 1929.
*My City.* New York: Liveright, 1929.
"What I Believe," *Forum* (November, 1929), 279-81. Dreiser's own statement of his mechanistic philosophy. As he puts it, "My intention is solely to present my reactions to a world that is as yet completely immersed in mystery."
*Tragic America.* New York: Liveright, 1931.
"Presenting Thoreau," Introduction to *The Living Thoughts of Thoreau.* New York: Longmans, Green & Company, 1939, pp. 1-32.
*America Is Worth Saving.* New York: Modern Age Books, 1941.
*To The Writer's League of America.* Hollywood, May 13, 1941.

## SECONDARY SOURCES

1. *Bibliography*

McDONALD, EDWARD D. *A Bibliography of the Writings of Theodore Dreiser.* Philadelphia: The Centaur Book Shop, 1928.

Selected Bibliography

MILLER, RALPH N. *A Preliminary Checklist of Books and Articles on Theodore Dreiser.* Kalamazoo: Western Michigan College Library, 1947.

ORTON, VREST. *Dreiserana: A Book About His Books.* New York: The Chocurua Bibliographies, 1929.

2. *Biography, books*

AARON, DANIEL. *Writers on the Left.* New York: Harcourt, Brace and World, 1961. Contains numerous references to Dreiser's part in the Marxist movement, including Dreiser's reports on the Harlan County coal strikes and his trip to Russia. Aaron attributes a good deal of Dreiser's sympathy with communism to the writer's anti-Catholicism.

ANDERSON, SHERWOOD. "Dreiser's Party." *Sherwood Anderson's Memoirs.* New York: Harcourt, Brace, 1942. An account of Anderson's first meeting with Dreiser; valuable for its detailed portrait.

BOYD, ERNEST. "Theodore Dreiser." *Portraits: Real and Imaginary.* New York: George H. Doran, 1924. A first-hand account of an interview with Dreiser while the novelist was living in Greenwich Village with Helen. "Dreiser is a primitive" is one of Boyd's conclusions.

CAMPBELL, LOUISE. *Letters to Louise.* Philadelphia: University of Pennsylvania Press, 1959. A valuable series of Dreiser letters from 1917 to 1945, with a running commentary by Louise Campbell, his typist-editor.

DREISER, HELEN. *My Life with Dreiser.* Cleveland: World, 1951. One of the indispensable items. Mrs. Dreiser chronicles her twenty-five years of life with the author with amazing candor.

DUDLEY, DOROTHY. *Forgotten Frontiers: Dreiser and the Land of the Free.* New York: Harrison Smith & Robert Haas, 1932. The first sizable Dreiser biography, by a woman holding strong prejudices in favor of the novelist. Contains material not treated elsewhere.

ELIAS, ROBERT H. *Theodore Dreiser: Apostle of Nature.* Philadelphia: University of Pennsylvania Press, 1949. The first scholarly biography, written with Dreiser's cooperation. A basic source and, to date, the best single book about Dreiser.

HOFFMAN, FREDERICK J. *The Twenties.* New York: Viking, 1955. Equates Dreiser with his times. Valuable for its picture of the era in which Dreiser produced *An American Tragedy.*

MATTHIESSEN, F. O. *Theodore Dreiser*. New York: William Sloane Associates, 1951. An excellent critical-biography for the general reader.

PATTEE, F. L. "Theodore Dreiser." *The New American Literature, 1890-1930*. New York: Century, 1930. Presents a thumbnail biography and an analysis of the influences which produced Dreiser.

RASCOE, BURTON. *We Were Interrupted*. Garden City: Doubleday, 1947. First-hand accounts of Dreiser's life during the early 1920's.

SCULLY, FRANK. "Dreiser." *Rogues' Gallery*. Hollywood: Murray & Gee, 1943. An account of Dreiser in Hollywood following publication of *An American Tragedy*. Notable for its penetrating scrutiny of Dreiser's anti-Catholic bias.

Various Authors. *Theodore Dreiser, America's Foremost Novelist*. New York: John Lane Company (*ca.* 1917). Writers such as Edgar Lee Masters, Merton Lyon, and John Cowper Powys discuss Dreiser as person and novelist.

## 3. *Biography, periodicals and pamphlets*

DREISER, HELEN. *Talk by Mrs. Theodore Dreiser given at the presentation program at the Los Angeles Public Library*. Mrs. Dreiser presents *Mss* of "Nigger Jeff" and "The Blue Sphere" to the library and reads correspondence from Farrell, Mencken, and Masters.

HALEY, CARMEL O'NEILL. "The Dreisers," *Commonweal* (July 7, 1933), pp. 265-67. Accounts of Paul and Theodore Dreiser and of Dreiser, Sr., by a friend of Mary Dreiser.

HUTH, J. F., JR. "Theodore Dreiser: 'The Prophet,'" *American Literature* (May, 1937), pp. 208-17. Concerns Dreiser's tenure as editor of *Ev'ry Month*, 1895-97.

VAN GELDER, ROBERT. "Interview With Theodore Dreiser," New York *Times* (March 16, 1941), pp. 2, 16. Dreiser speaks of the difficult years after *Sister Carrie* was published and suppressed.

## 4. *Criticism, books*

ADAMS, J. DONALD. "The Heavy Hand of Dreiser." *The Shape of Books to Come*. New York: Viking, 1944. A general analysis of Dreiser's qualities and defects as important influences upon writers of his time.

## Selected Bibliography

ANDERSON, SHERWOOD. Introduction to *Free, and Other Stories*. New York: Boni & Liveright, 1925. A brief survey of Dreiser's contributions to American literature.

————. "Dreiser." Introduction to *Horses and Men*. New York: B. W. Huebsch, 1923, pp. *xi-xii*. A brief but important appreciation of Dreiser by one of his contemporary authors.

ANGOFF, ALLAN, ed. "An American Tragedy." *American Writing Today*. New York: New York University Press, 1957. This book, a printing of a special edition of *Times Literary Supplement*, contains many references to Dreiser and his influence; also, a contemporary British review of *An American Tragedy*.

BROOKS, VAN WYCK. "Theodore Dreiser." *The Confident Years: 1885-1915*. New York: E. P. Dutton, 1952. Presents Dreiser as the product of his environment and upbringing, as a man whose ability to convey actuality in his novels triumphed over his literary weaknesses.

COWLEY, MALCOLM. "Naturalism in American Literature." *Evolutionary Thought in America*. Ed. by Stow Persons. New Haven: Brazziler, Inc., 1956. Cowley presents a comprehensive survey of the naturalistic tradition in literature, with which he identifies Dreiser and in which he places all Dreiser's novels except *The Bulwark*.

————. "Naturalism: No Teacup Tragedies." *The Literary Situation*. New York: Viking, 1954. Explores Dreiser's continuing influence upon writers who followed him.

DRUMMOND, EDWARD J., S.J. "Theodore Dreiser: Shifting Naturalism." *Fifty Years of the American Novel*. Ed. by Harold C. Gardiner. New York: Scribner's, 1951. A Catholic appraisal, noteworthy for its presentation of the complexities and paradoxes in Dreiser's thinking and for its tracing of the gradual changes in Dreiser's philosophy of life from *Sister Carrie* to *The Bulwark*.

EDGAR, PELHAM. "American Realism, Sex, and Theodore Dreiser." *The Art of the Novel*. New York: Macmillan, 1933. A British appreciation of Dreiser as the leader of the break with the English tradition of novel writing. In some detail, Edgar compares Dreiser with Zola.

ELVEBACK, HELEN B. "The Novels of Theodore Dreiser with an Analysis of His Other Writings." Unpublished Ph.D. dissertation, University of Minnesota, 1946.

FARRELL, JAMES T. "Dreiser's *Sister Carrie.*" *The League of Frightened Philistines.* New York: Vanguard, 1945. Farrell explains why *Sister Carrie* retains its position as an "American classic."

————. Introduction to *The Best Short Stories of Theodore Dreiser.* Cleveland: World, 1955. An appreciation of Dreiser as an author of short stories.

FAST, HOWARD. Introduction to *The Best Short Stories of Theodore Dreiser.* Cleveland: World, 1947. An appreciation, perhaps overenthusiastic. "I know of no better example in American story telling than Theodore Dreiser," says Fast.

GELFANT, BLANCHE HOUSMAN. "Theodore Dreiser: The Portrait Novel." *The American City Novel.* Norman, Oklahoma: University of Oklahoma Press, 1954. Draws heavily upon Dreiser's novels and autobiographies to establish Dreiser as "a key figure in American city fiction."

GEISMAR, MAXWELL. "Theodore Dreiser: The Double Soul." *Rebels and Ancestors: The American Novel, 1890-1915.* Boston: Houghton Mifflin, 1953. A lengthy, detailed analysis of Dreiser's novels, stories, and autobiographies. Valuable for its insight into the novelist's methods and intentions.

HARTWICK, HARRY. "Hindenburg of the Novel." *The Foreground of American Fiction.* New York: American Book Company, 1934. Discusses the slow creation of an audience for Dreiser's books and the influence of Shakespeare, Machiavelli, and Darwin upon his ideas and literary methods.

HATCHER, HARLAN. "Theodore Dreiser." *Creating the Modern American Novel.* New York: Farrar & Rinehart, 1935. Reviews Dreiser's novels through *An American Tragedy;* presents Dreiser as a novelist with a "nearly perfect" background to become "chief spokesman for the realistic novel" in America.

HICKS, GRANVILLE. *The Great Tradition.* New York: Macmillan, 1933. A brief analysis of the purpose and effect of Dreiser's novels.

HOFFMAN, FREDERICK J. "Prewar Naturalism, 1900-1915." *The Modern Novel in America.* Chicago: Regnery, 1951. Assesses Dreiser's achievement as "an ideal test case in the history of naturalistic fiction."

HOWELL, EILEEN. "Theodore Dreiser's Development as a Naturalist." Unpublished M.A. thesis, New York University, 1950.

KAZIN, ALFRED. *On Native Grounds.* New York: Reynal & Hitchcock, 1942. Kazin anatomizes the environment from which Dreiser emerged and the unique contribution he was able to make to American naturalism.

KAZIN, ALFRED, and CHARLES SHAPIRO, eds. *The Stature of Theodore Dreiser*. Bloomington: Indiana University Press, 1955. A basic document for Dreiser study, it contains a generous selection of the best, most representative criticism appearing between 1900 and 1955.

LERNER, MAX. "On Dreiser." *Actions and Passions*. New York: Simon & Schuster, 1949. An elegiac essay supporting Lerner's judgment of Dreiser as "the greatest American writer we have had in this twentieth century."

LYNN, KENNETH S. "Theodore Dreiser: The Man of Ice." *The Dream of Success*. Boston: Little, Brown, 1955. An excellent analysis of Dreiser's novels as demonstrations of the novelist's conviction that the chief values of American society concern "pecuniary and sexual success."

MENCKEN, H. L. "The American Novel." *Prejudices: Fourth Series*. New York: Alfred A. Knopf, 1924. Strong presentation of Dreiser's influence in freeing American writing and in making the novel "true."

————. "Theodore Dreiser." *A Book of Prefaces*. New York: Alfred A. Knopf, 1917. An early, intense apologia by Dreiser's greatest admirer. Mencken presents his ideas on what Dreiser is attempting. Contains an attack on those who would suppress *The "Genius"* and on censorship generally.

*Letters of H. L. Mencken*. Ed. by GUY J. FORGUE. New York: Alfred A. Knopf, 1961. Contains a remarkable series of letters written over an extensive period of time. Invaluable biographically and critically, for its first-hand reactions to Dreiser's work, for its personal advice offered to Dreiser, and for its private opinions of Dreiser and his writing (not invariably in accord with opinions appearing in public print).

MUMFORD, LEWIS. "The Shadow of the Muck-rake." *The Golden Day*. New York: W. W. Norton, 1926. Relates Dreiser to the muck-raking writers of the early 1900's.

PARRINGTON, VERNON. "Theodore Dreiser: Chief of American Naturalists." *Main Currents of American Thought*. Vol. III. New York: Harcourt, Brace, 1930. A sympathetic analysis of the literary philosophy and method which produced the most "frank and detached projection of reality" since Whitman.

Rascoe, Burton. *Theodore Dreiser.* New York: Robert McBride & Company, 1926. Among the earliest substantial studies of Dreiser and the first appearing as a separate volume. Defends Dreiser against Stuart P. Sherman's attack.

Rubin, Louis D., Jr., and John Rees Moore, eds. *The Idea of an American Novel.* New York: Crowell, 1961. Contains evaluations by Mencken, Benchley, Trilling, and Farrell, balanced pro and con.

Shapiro, Charles. "Dreiser and the American Dream." Unpublished M.A. thesis, Indiana School of Letters, Indiana University, 1953.

Snell, George. "Theodore Dreiser: Philosopher." *The Shapers of American Fiction, 1798-1947.* New York: E. P. Dutton, 1947. Places Dreiser in "the company of the great tragic writers," explains his predominant view of the human dilemma, and records the changes which become apparent in *The Bulwark.*

Spiller, Robert E., *et al.* "Theodore Dreiser," *Literary History of The United States.* New York: Macmillan, 1948. A most useful and comprehensive summary of Dreiser's life, works, ideas, and methods.

Stepanchev, Stephen. "Dreiser Among the Critics." Unpublished Ph.D. dissertation, New York University, 1950.

Stovall, Floyd. "From Realism to Naturalism." *American Idealism.* Norman, Oklahoma: University of Oklahoma Press, 1943. Emphasizes Dreiser's role in the decline from literary idealism beginning with Garland, Crane, Norris, and London.

Thorp, Willard. "The Persistence of Naturalism in the Novel." *American Writing in the Twentieth Century.* Cambridge: Harvard University Press, 1960. Excellent, recent treatment of Dreiser in his relation to other naturalists, to his themes, and to later writers.

Van Doren, Carl. "Theodore Dreiser." *The American Novel.* New York: Macmillan, 1940. Discusses Dreiser's work in order to establish the reasons for his achieving a "permanent place in American fiction" despite much public and critical disapproval.

Wagenknecht, Edward. "Theodore Dreiser, the Mystic Naturalist." *Cavalcade of the American Novel.* New York: Holt, 1952. Attempts to correct the "oversimplification of the Dreiser problem" by demonstrating that the writer worked in a wider scope and range of ideas than the purely naturalistic.

Walcutt, Charles Child. "Theodore Dreiser: The Wonder and Terror of Life." *American Literary Naturalism, A Divided Stream.*

Minneapolis: University of Minnesota Press, 1956, Traces the changes and contradictions in Dreiser's ideas, explaining how "his mixture of despair and idealism, of wonder and fear, of pity and guilt, of chemistry and intuition has given us the most moving and powerful novels of the naturalistic tradition."

## 5. Criticism, periodicals and pamphlets

ANDERSON, SHERWOOD. "An Apology for Crudity," *The Dial* (November 8, 1917), pp. 437-38. Granting Dreiser's crudity in expression, Anderson defends him against the opposite extreme of slickness and mechanical plotting.

Anonymous. "Dreiser's Novels as a Revelation of the American Soul," *Current Opinion* (September, 1917), p. 191. An estimate of Dreiser's achievement to 1917, praising him for bringing "a new American quality" to our literature.

Anonymous. "Shall It Be Dreiser?" *Commonweal* (October 22, 1930), p. 626. Typifies the outburst of disapproval of Dreiser's work as late as 1930, in connection with the possibility of his being awarded the Nobel prize.

ASSELINEAU, ROGER. *Theodore Dreiser's Transcendentalism*, reprinted in 1961 from pp. 233-43 *English Studies Today*, Second Series, ed. by G. A. Bonnard. Studies the "dark hemisphere" of Dreiser's world, presenting him as "a poet and in several respects a belated transcendentalist in his naturalistic novels as well as his poems."

BERNARD, KENNETH. "The Flight of Theodore Dreiser," *University of Kansas City Review* (June, 1960), pp. 251-59. Emphasizes Dreiser's life before and after the period of the writing of his novels, the years Bernard considers Dreiser's "flight" from life.

BOURNE, RANDOLPH S. "Theodore Dreiser," *New Republic* (April 17, 1915), supplement 7-8. Presents Dreiser as one of the few writers one can read "without shame and embarrassment" because of his truthful portrayal of life and his repudiation of the popular theme of moral redemption.

CHESTERTON, G. K. "The Skeptic as a Critic," *Forum* (February, 1929), pp. 65-69. A prominent British literary figure takes issue with H. L. Mencken's defense of Dreiser and with Dreiser's basic philosophy of life.

FADIMAN, CLIFTON. "Dreiser and the American Dream," *The Nation* (October 19, 1932), pp. 364-65. A brief comprehensive survey of Dreiser and his achievement, pointing out reasons why Dreiser's victims are more impressive than his successes.

FLANAGAN, JOHN T. "Theodore Dreiser in Retrospect," *Southwest Review* (Autumn, 1946), pp. 408-11. A defense of the novelist, cataloging his literary virtues while not denying his faults.

FLINT, R. W. "Dreiser: The Press of Life," *Nation* (April 27, 1957), pp. 371-73. An estimate of Dreiser as "*the* great American novelist of his time and place."

HICKS, GRANVILLE. "Theodore Dreiser," *American Mercury* (June, 1946), pp. 751-56. A review of *The Bulwark*, presenting that novel as a "remarkably appropriate climax" to Dreiser's career and suggesting further that the book sounds "the death knell of literary naturalism."

————. "The Twenties in American Literature," *The Nation* (February 12, 1930), pp. 183-85. "A survey of the twenties is rather sad business," says Hicks. "The writers of the twenties did not develop . . . whatever the explanation, the tragedy of the twenties is apparent."

JONES, HOWARD MUMFORD. "Dreiser Reconsidered," *Atlantic Monthly* (May, 1946), pp. 162-70. A review of *The Bulwark* which in its course catalogs Dreiser's strengths and weaknesses as a writer.

KWIAT, JOSEPH J. "Dreiser's *The "Genius"* and Everett Shinn, The Ashcan Painter," *PMLA* (March, 1952), pp. 15-31. Presents Shinn as the original of Eugene Witla. Contains photographs of Shinn's works which correspond to descriptions of Witla's paintings in the novel.

MENCKEN, H. L. "The Creed of a Novelist," *Smart Set* (October, 1916). An early defense of Dreiser by his foremost critical supporter.

ROSS, WOODBURN O. "Concerning Dreiser's Mind," *American Literature* (November, 1946), pp. 233-43. Attacks the position held by Mencken and others that Dreiser is not a thoroughgoing mechanist, that "one-half of the man's brain, so to speak, wars with the other half."

SPILLER, ROBERT E. "Dreiser as Master Craftsman," *Saturday Review of Literature* (March 23, 1946), p. 23. Review of *The Bulwark*, praising it as a major novel and "unique" in its clearly defined moral issue.

STEWART, RANDALL. "Dreiser and the Naturalistic Heresy," *Virginia Quarterly Review* (Winter, 1958), pp. 100-16. Attacks the naturalistic school as holding an untenable philosophy of life.

Dreiser and his *An American Tragedy* are used as principal examples.

WALCUTT, CHARLES CHILD. "Naturalism in 1946: Dreiser and Farrell," *Accent* (Summer, 1946), pp. 263-68. Review of *The Bulwark* used as an occasion to define the naturalistic movement and Dreiser's place in it.

WESTLAKE, NEDA. "Theodore Dreiser's *Notes on Life*," *University of Pennsylvania Library Chronicle* (Summer, 1954), pp. 69-75. A fine description of the lengthy manuscript "of what Dreiser hoped would be an explanation of his personal philosophy," by the custodian of the Dreiser Collection at the University of Pennsylvania where the manuscript has been deposited.

WILLEN, GERALD. "Dreiser's Moral Seriousness," *University of Kansas City Review* (March, 1957), pp. 181-87. Examines the personal responsibility allotted Dreiser's characters in reference to the ethics of the society in which they move.

# Index

# Index

*Index*